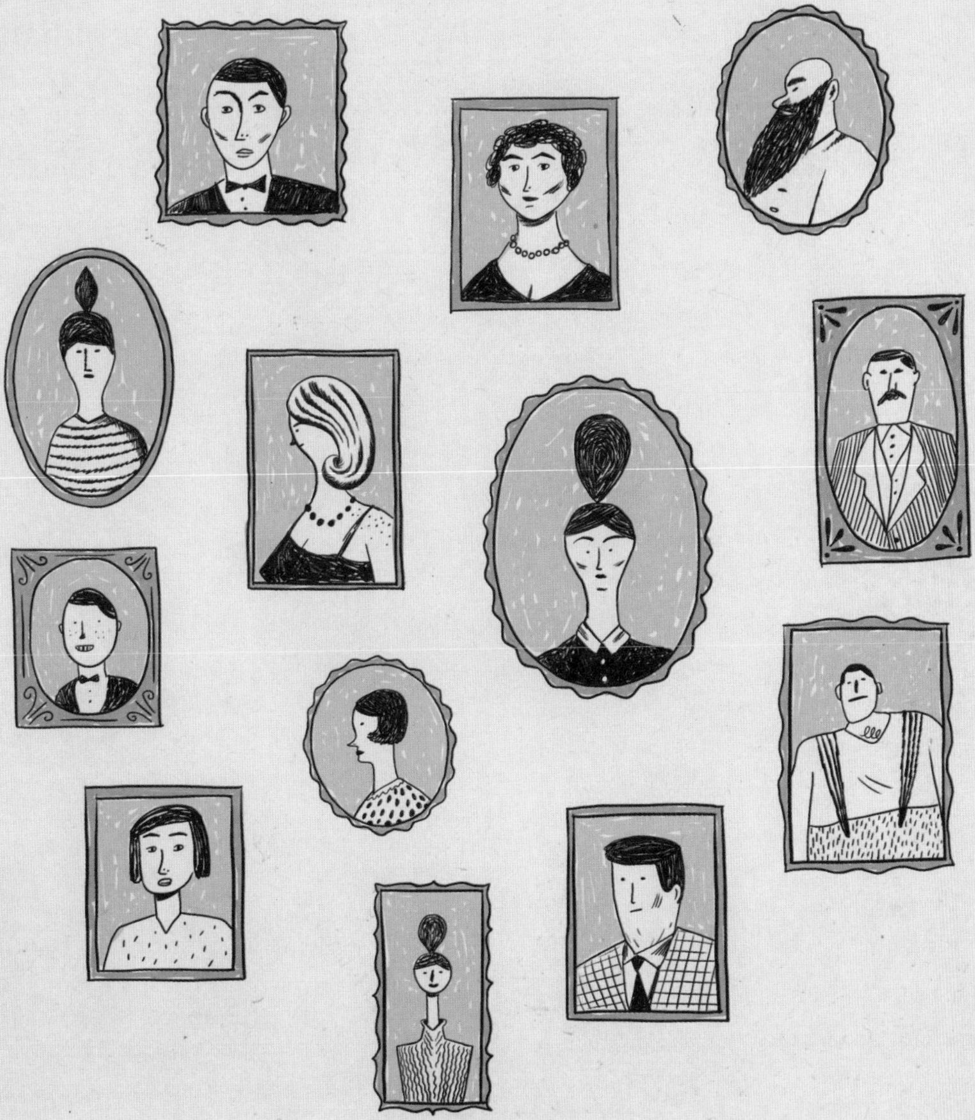

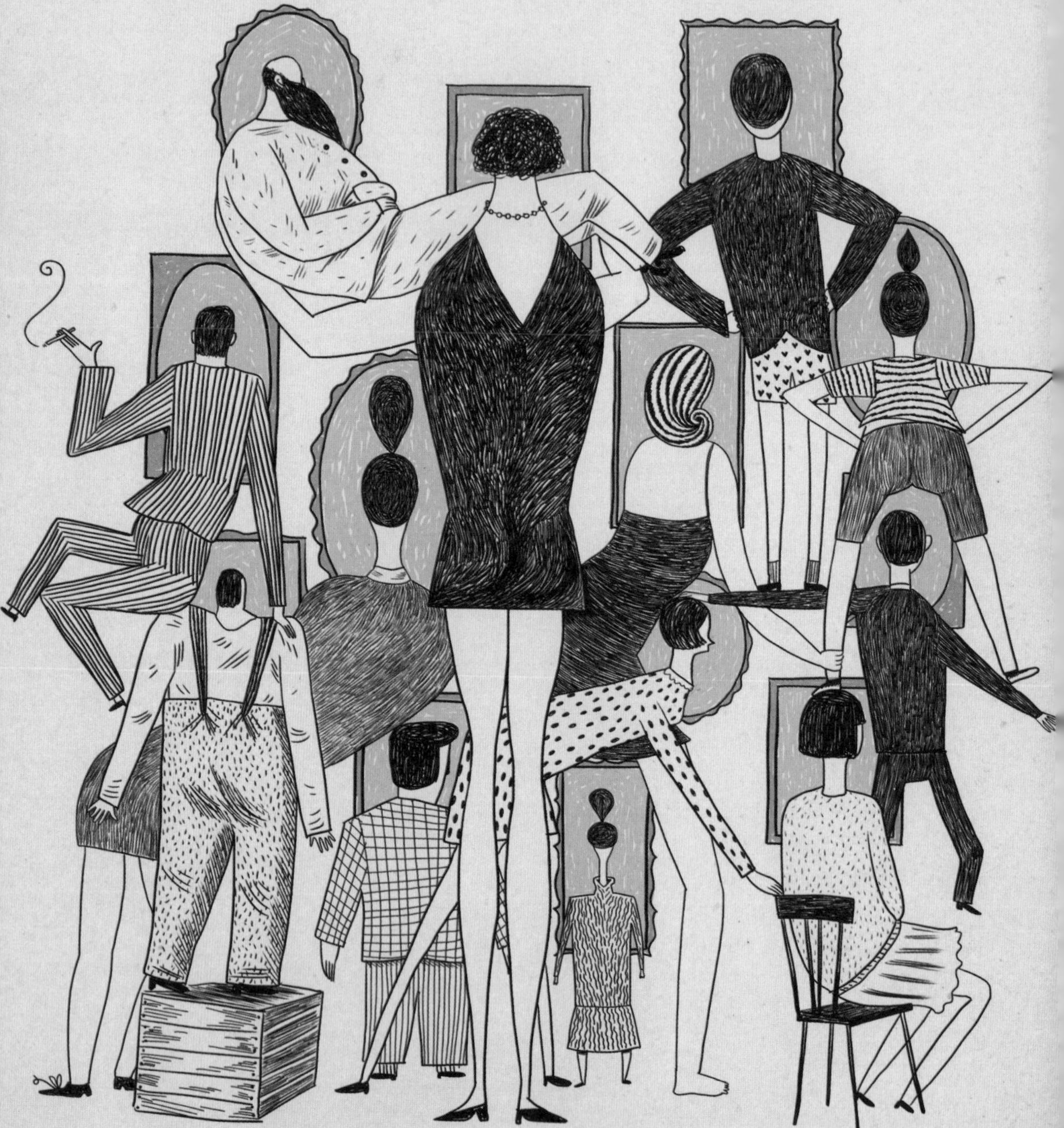

HEADS

Oꓤ

TAILꙄ

LiLLi CARRÉ

Heads or Tails by Lilli Carré

Editor and Associate Publisher: Eric Reynolds
Designed by Lilli Carré
Production by Paul Baresh
Published by Gary Groth and Kim Thompson

Fantagraphics Books, Inc.
7563 Lake City Way NE
Seattle WA 98115 USA
fantagraphics.com

Distributed in the U.S. by W.W. Norton and Company, Inc. (800-233-4830)
Distributed in Canada by Canadian Manda Group (410-560-7100 x843)
Distributed in the U.K. by Turnaround Distribution (44 020 8829-3002)
Distributed to comic book specialty stores by
Diamond Comics Distributors (800-452-6642 x215)

First printing: September 2012

ISBN 978-1-60699-597-6

Printed in Thailand

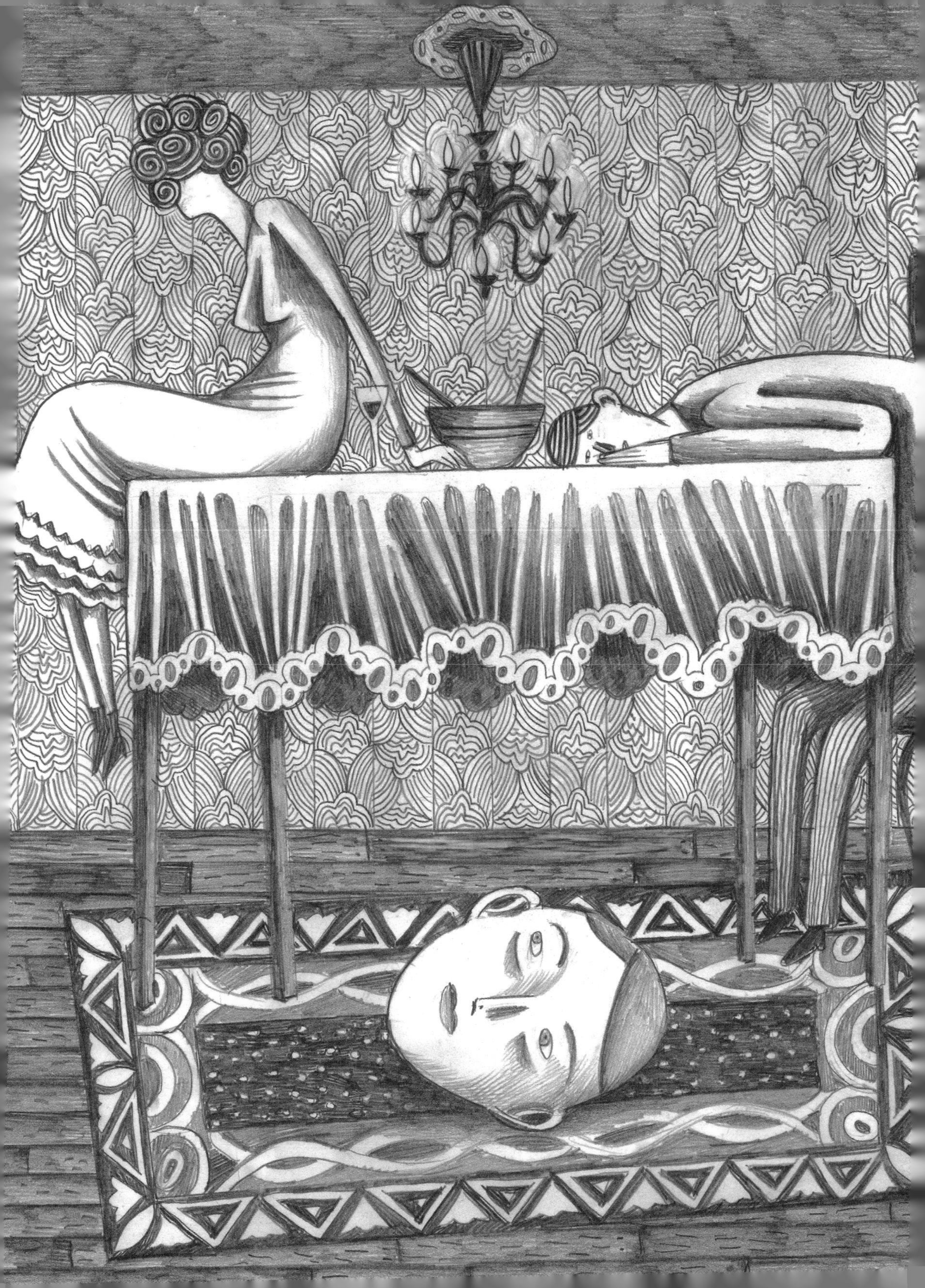

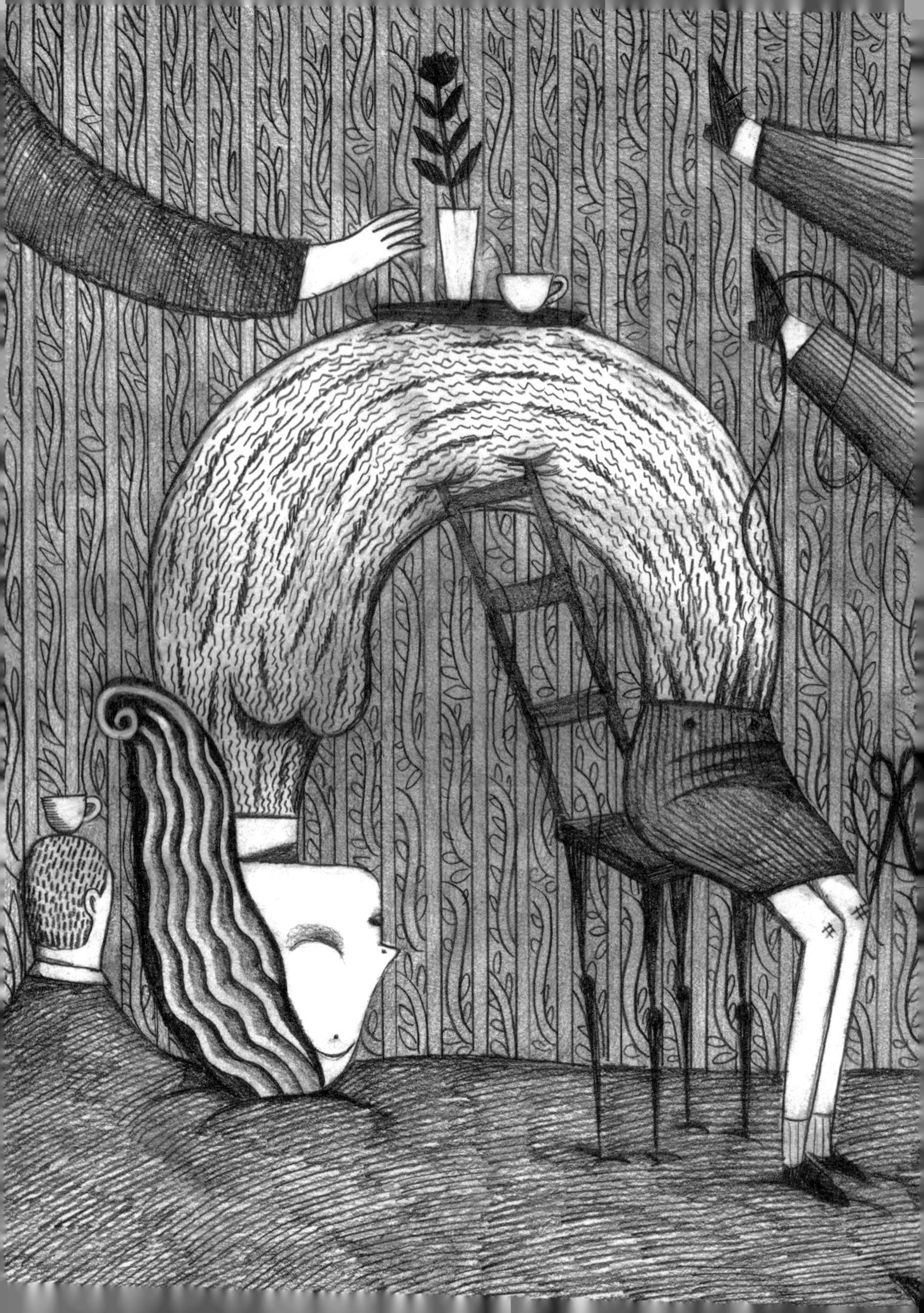

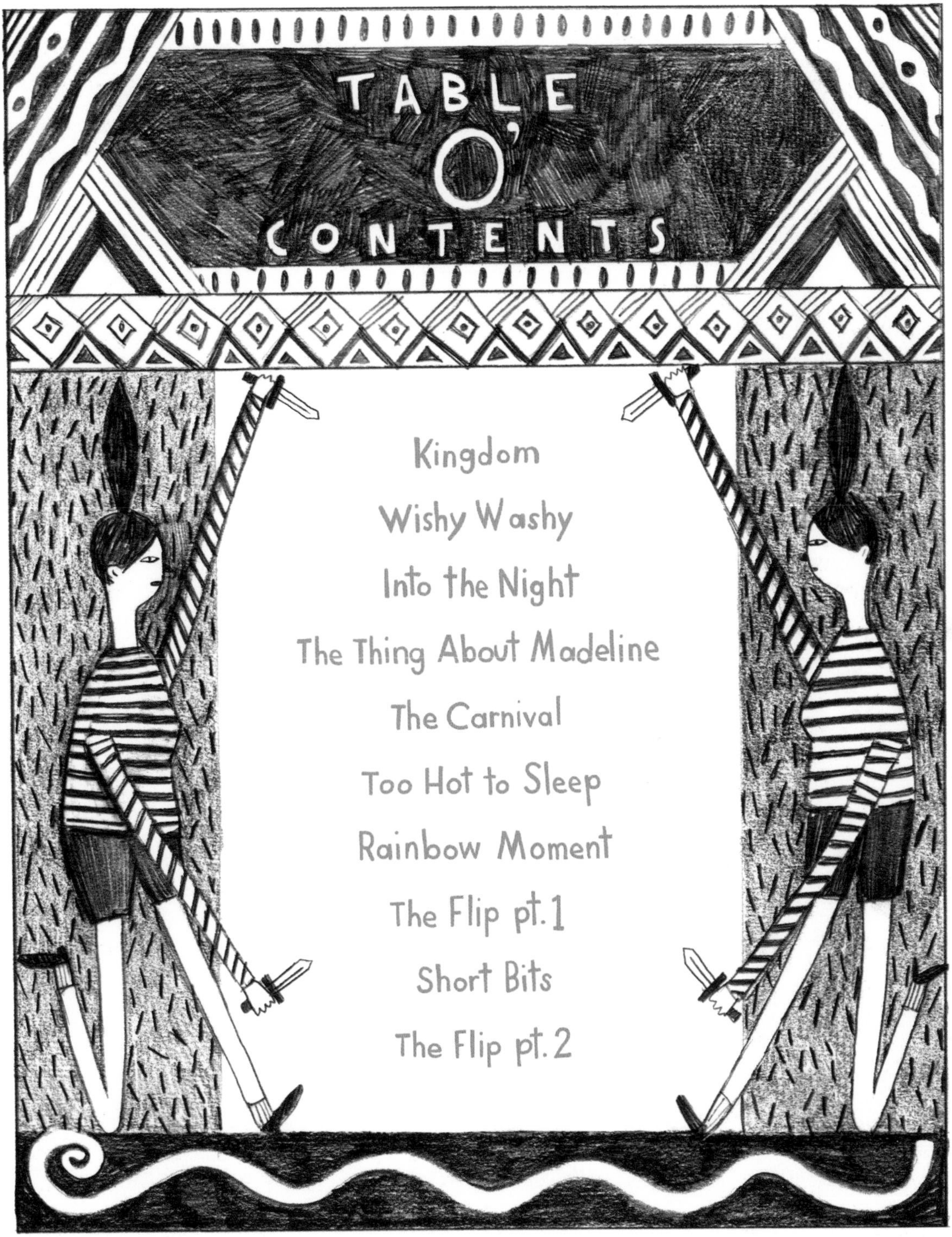

TABLE O' CONTENTS

WELCOME

TO MY

KINGDOM

IT IS

WILD

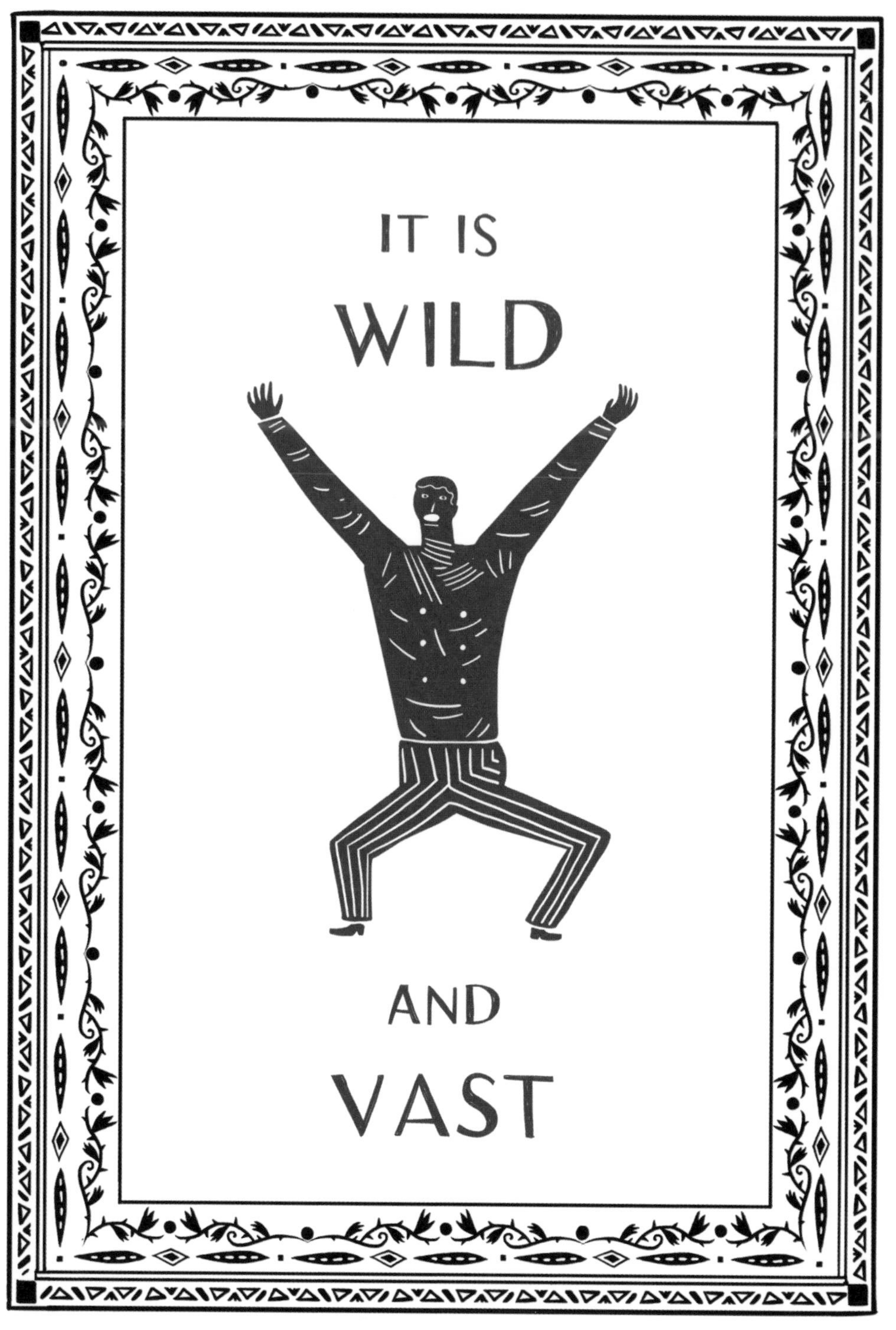

AND

VAST

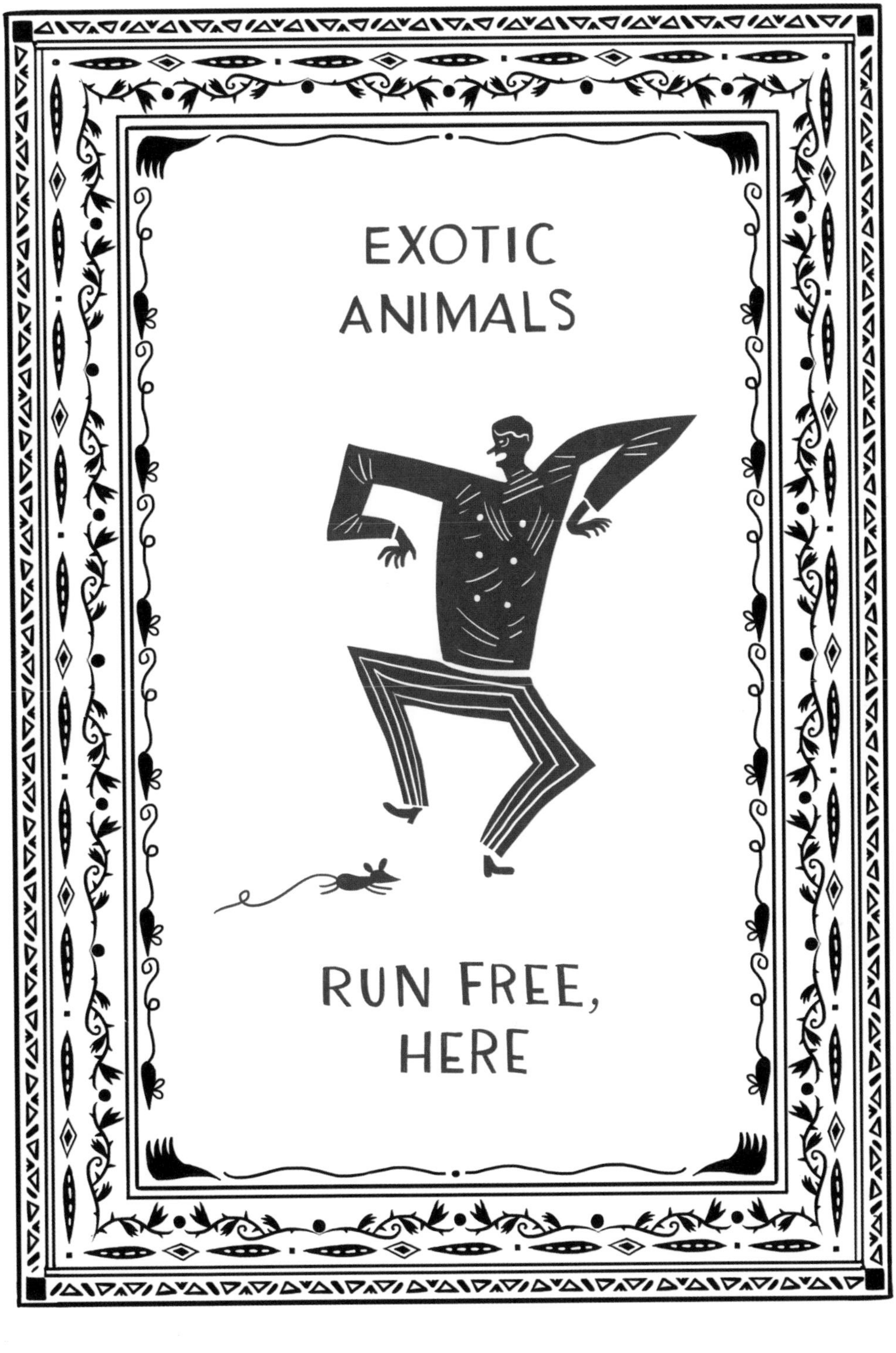
EXOTIC ANIMALS
RUN FREE, HERE

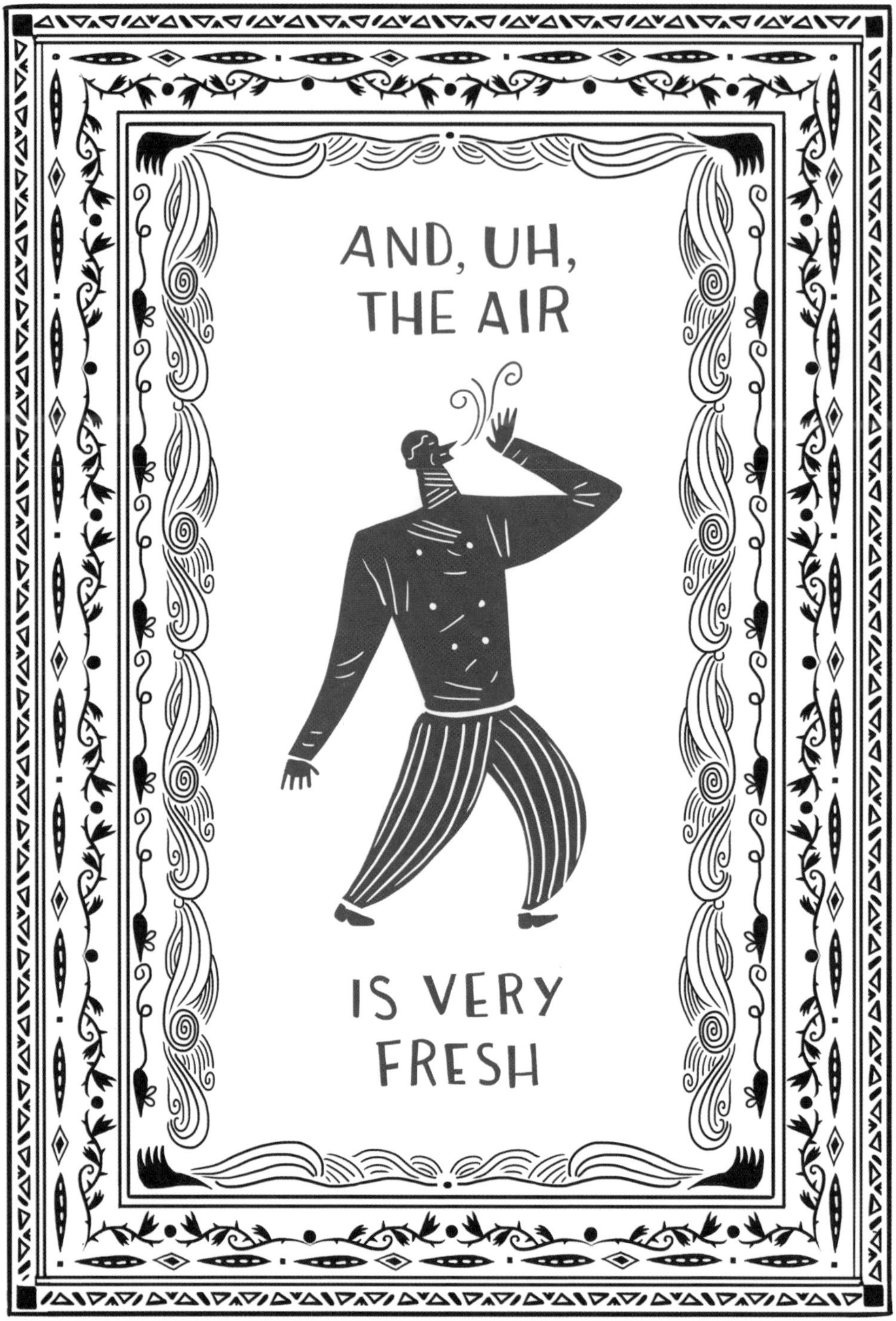
AND, UH, THE AIR
IS VERY FRESH

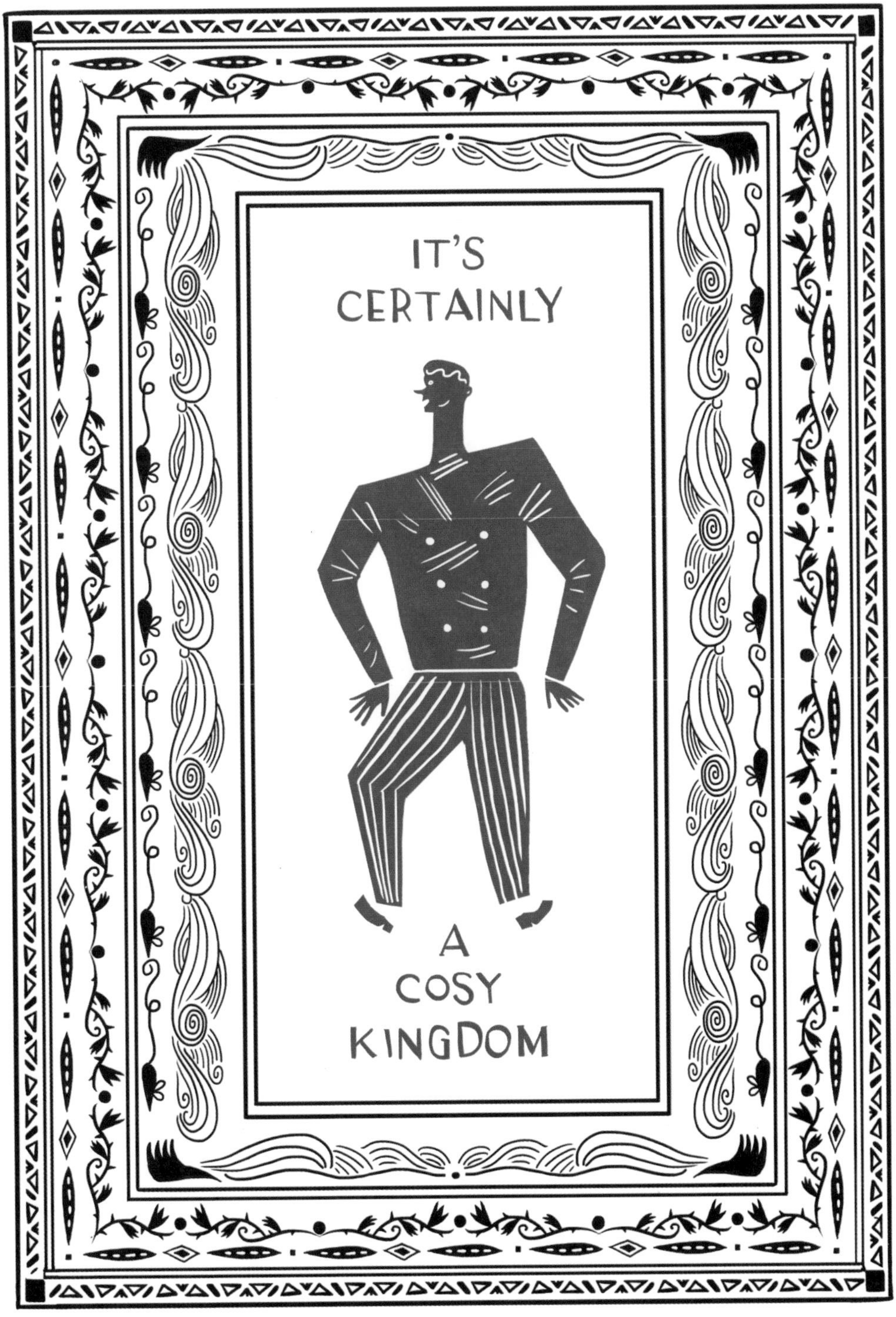
IT'S
CERTAINLY
A
COSY
KINGDOM

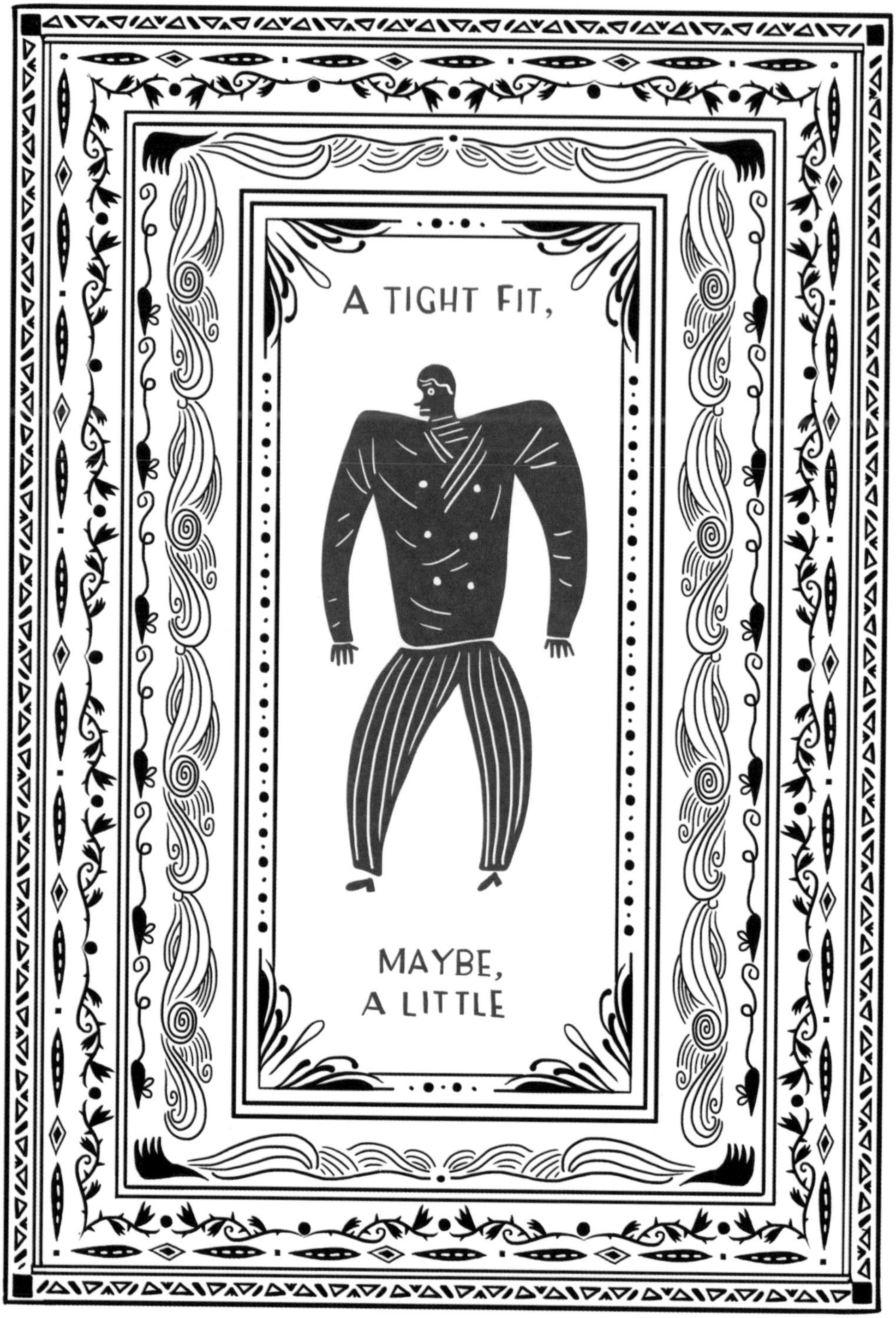
A TIGHT FIT,
MAYBE,
A LITTLE

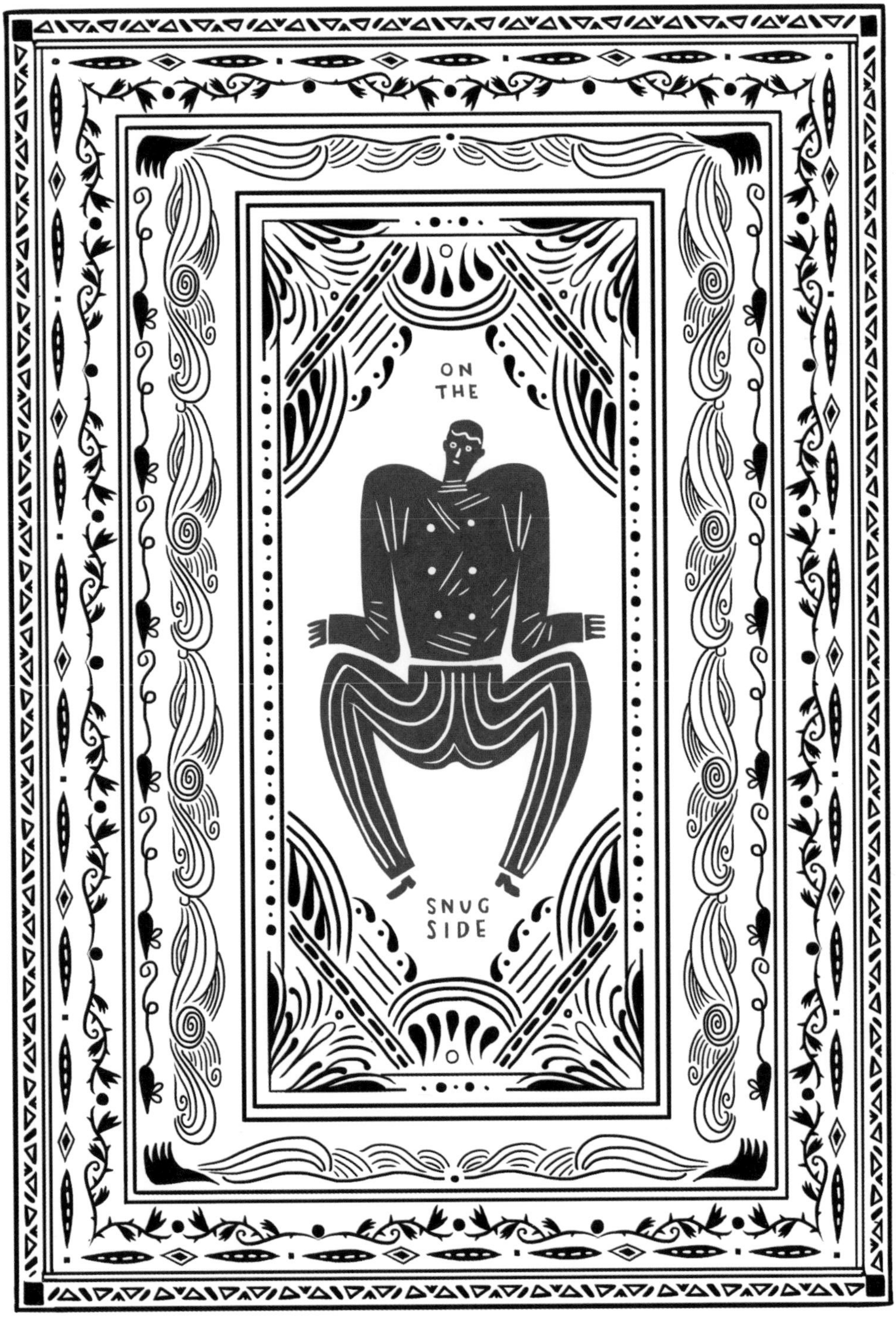
ON
THE
SNUG
SIDE

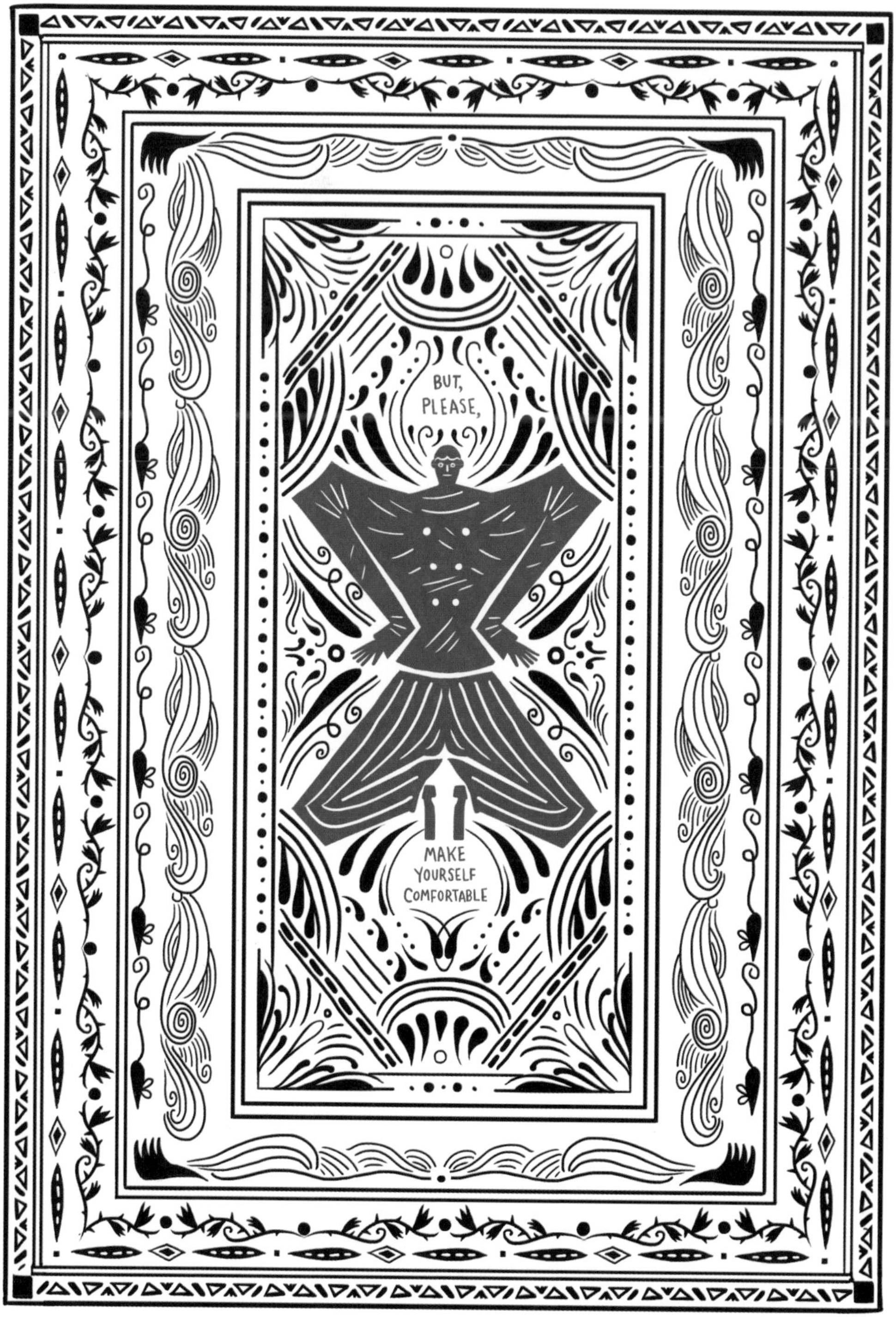
BUT, PLEASE,
MAKE YOURSELF COMFORTABLE

Wishy Washy

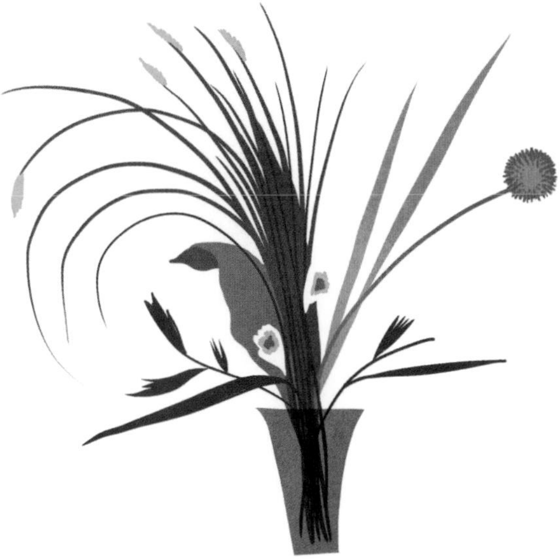

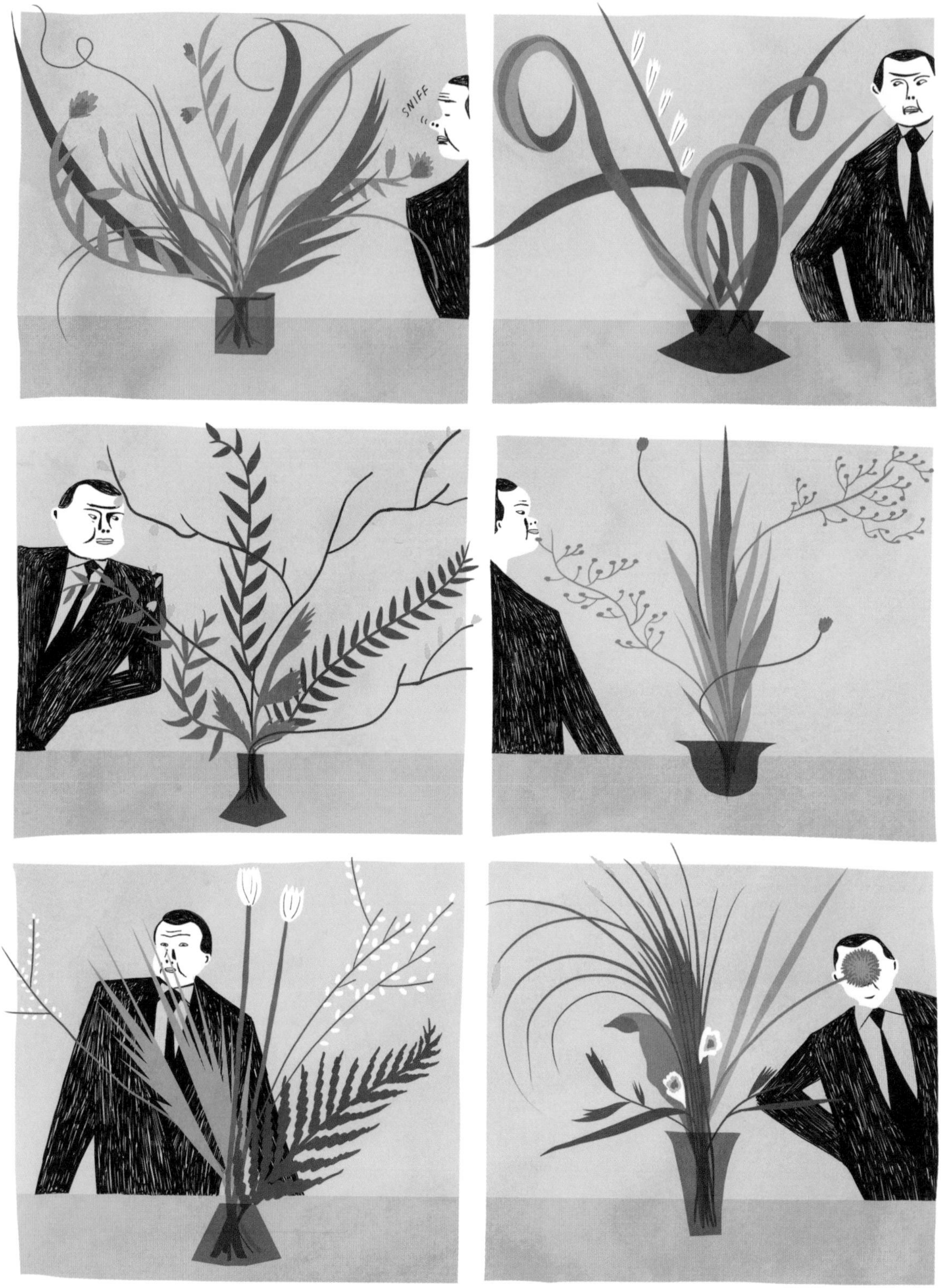
SNIFF

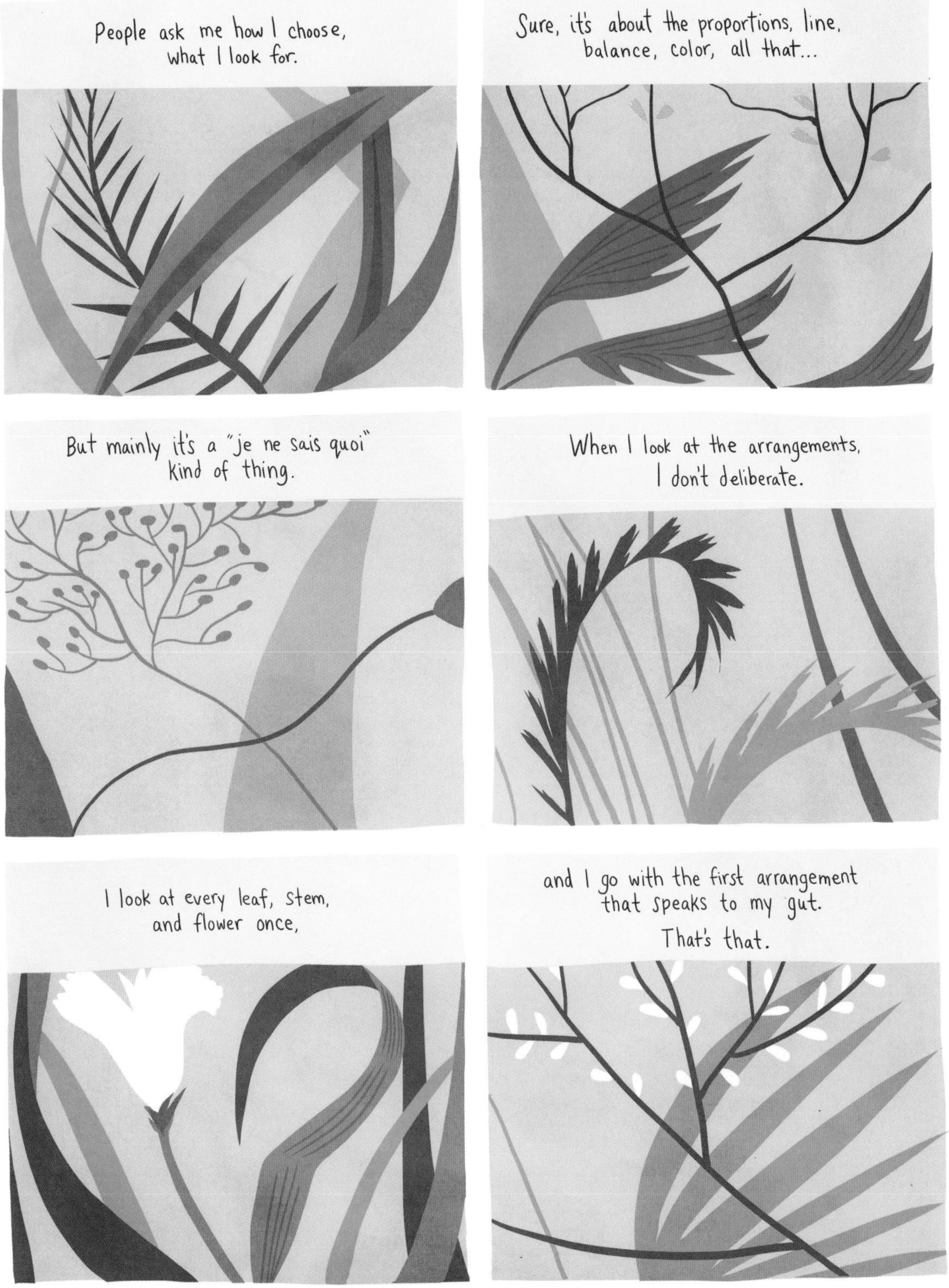
People ask me how I choose, what I look for.
Sure, it's about the proportions, line, balance, color, all that...
But mainly it's a "je ne sais quoi" kind of thing.
When I look at the arrangements, I don't deliberate.
I look at every leaf, stem, and flower once,
and I go with the first arrangement that speaks to my gut.
That's that.

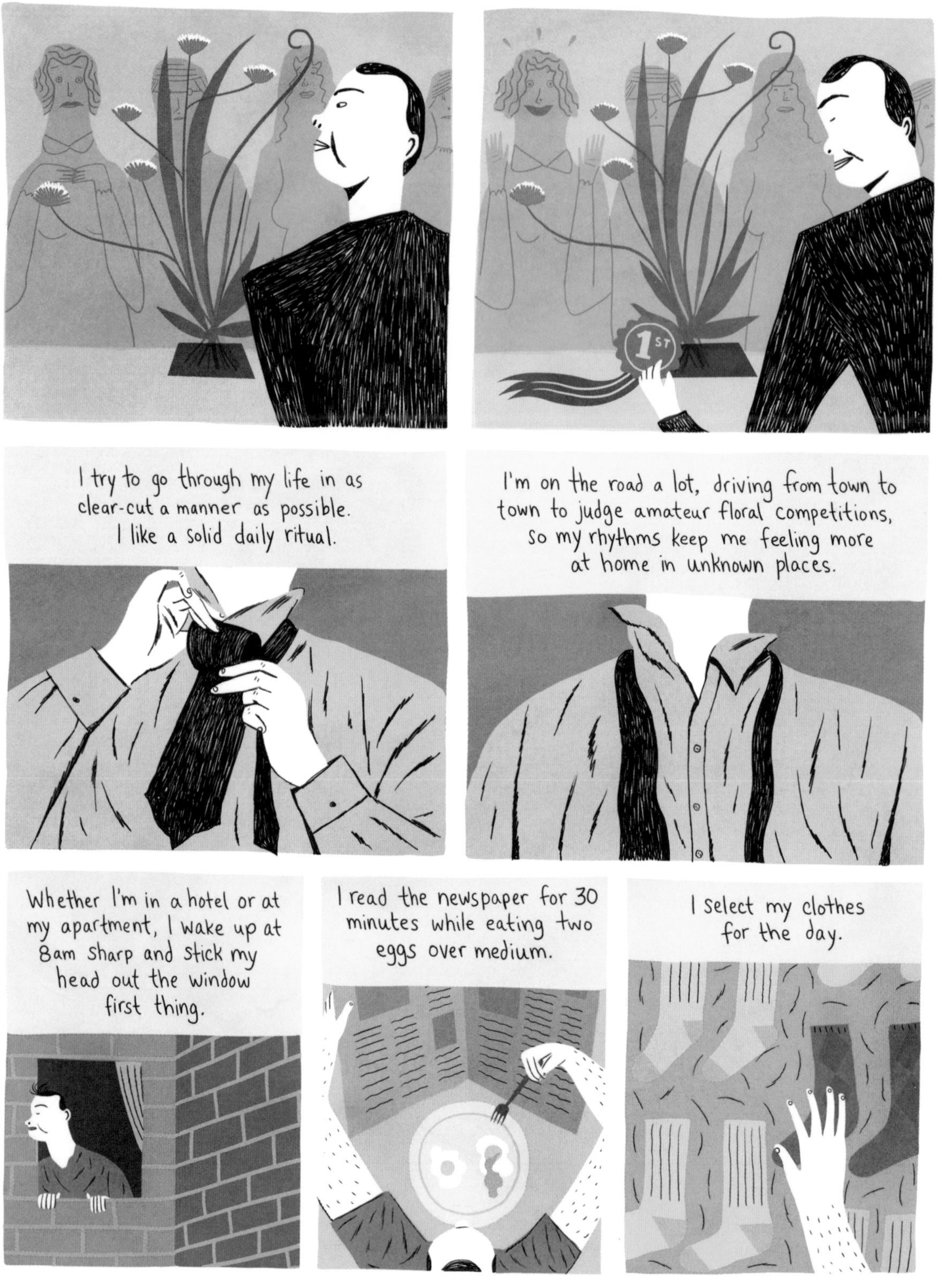
1ST
I try to go through my life in as clear-cut a manner as possible. I like a solid daily ritual.
I'm on the road a lot, driving from town to town to judge amateur floral competitions, so my rhythms keep me feeling more at home in unknown places.
Whether I'm in a hotel or at my apartment, I wake up at 8am sharp and stick my head out the window first thing.
I read the newspaper for 30 minutes while eating two eggs over medium.
I select my clothes for the day.

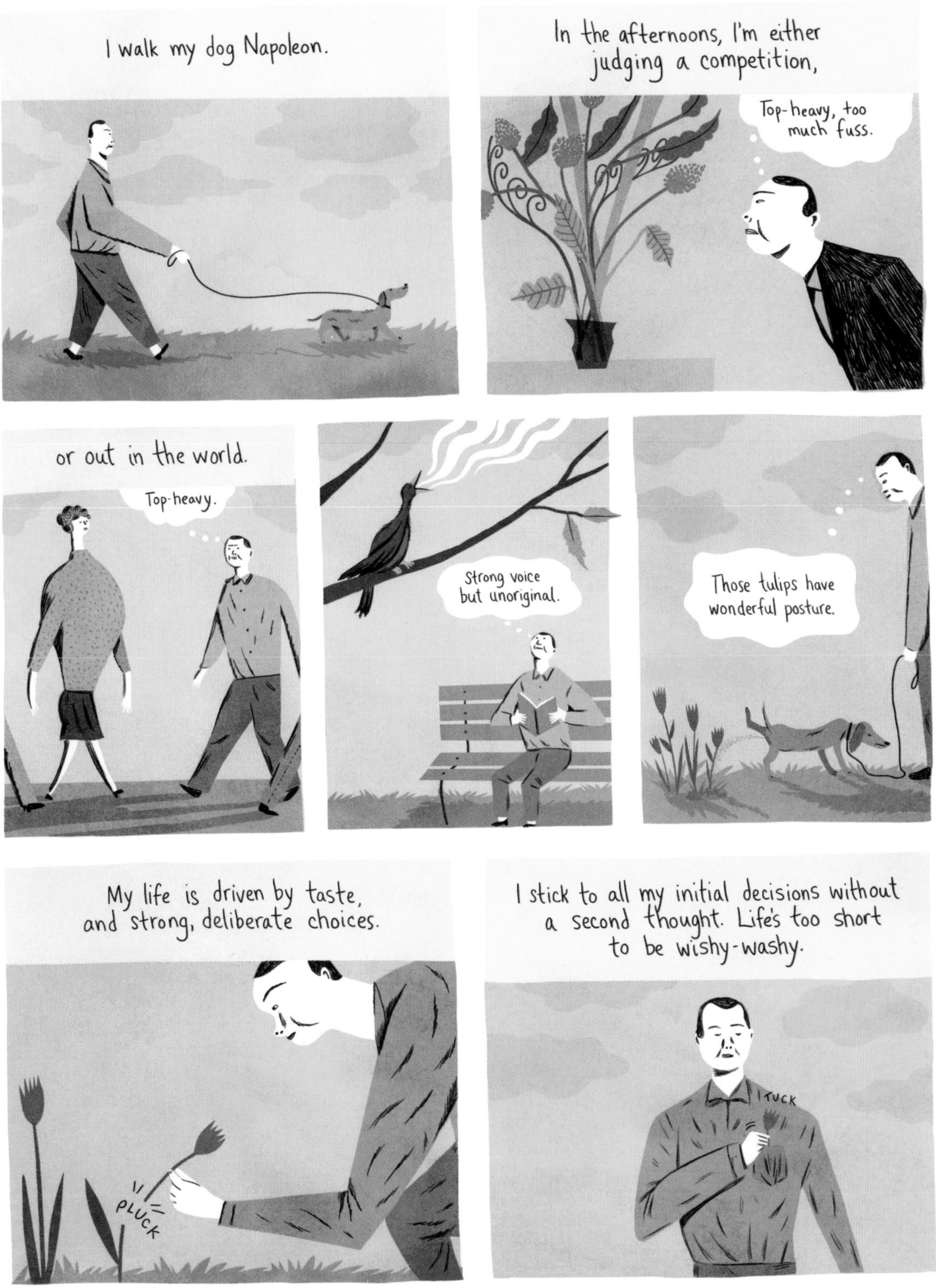
I walk my dog Napoleon.
In the afternoons, I'm either judging a competition,
Top-heavy, too much fuss.
or out in the world.
Top-heavy.
Strong voice but unoriginal.
Those tulips have wonderful posture.
My life is driven by taste, and strong, deliberate choices.
PLUCK
I stick to all my initial decisions without a second thought. Life's too short to be wishy-washy.
TUCK

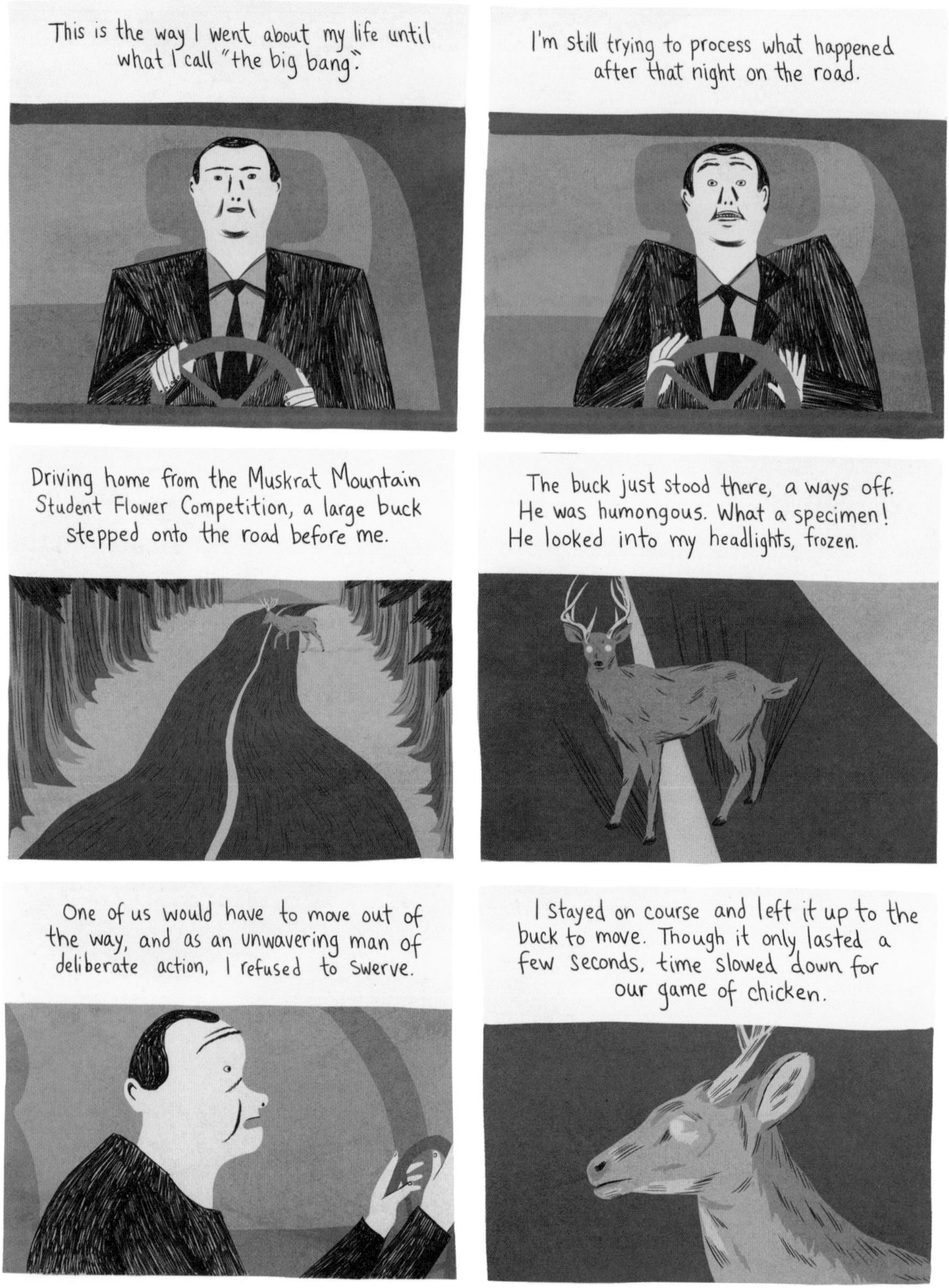
This is the way I went about my life until what I call "the big bang."
I'm still trying to process what happened after that night on the road.
Driving home from the Muskrat Mountain Student Flower Competition, a large buck stepped onto the road before me.
The buck just stood there, a ways off. He was humongous. What a specimen! He looked into my headlights, frozen.
One of us would have to move out of the way, and as an unwavering man of deliberate action, I refused to swerve.
I stayed on course and left it up to the buck to move. Though it only lasted a few seconds, time slowed down for our game of chicken.

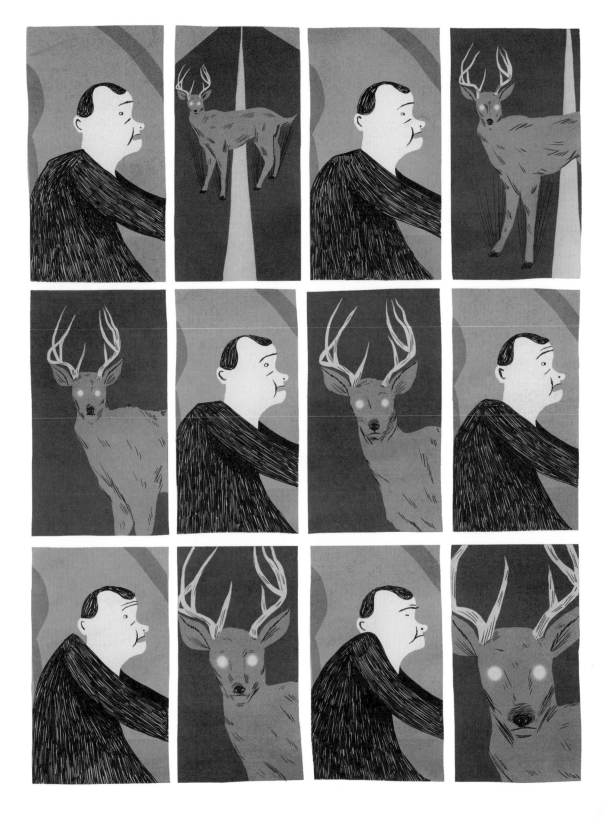

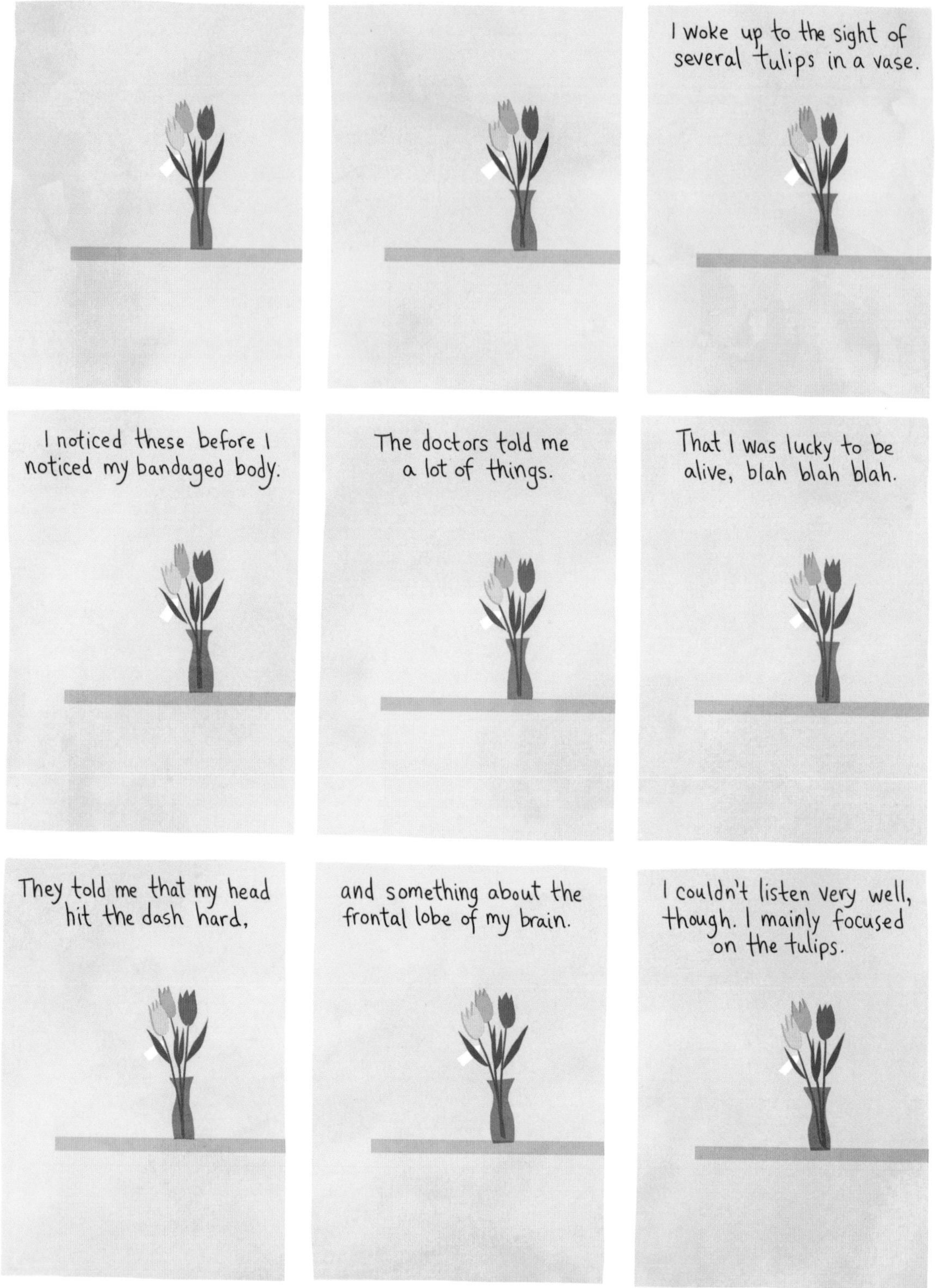
I woke up to the sight of several tulips in a vase.
I noticed these before I noticed my bandaged body.
The doctors told me a lot of things.
That I was lucky to be alive, blah blah blah.
They told me that my head hit the dash hard,
and something about the frontal lobe of my brain.
I couldn't listen very well, though. I mainly focused on the tulips.

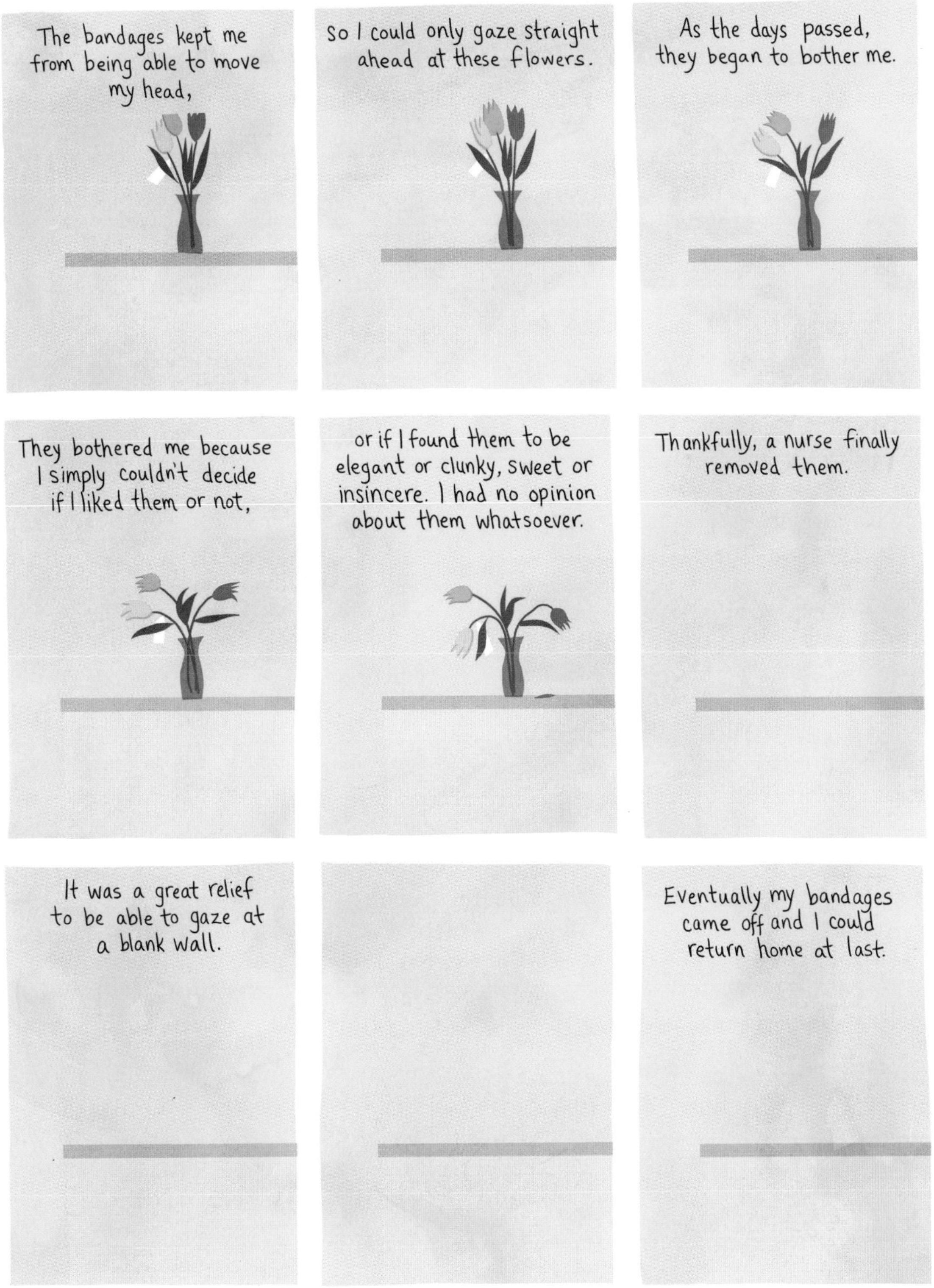
The bandages kept me from being able to move my head,
So I could only gaze straight ahead at these flowers.
As the days passed, they began to bother me.
They bothered me because I simply couldn't decide if I liked them or not,
or if I found them to be elegant or clunky, sweet or insincere. I had no opinion about them whatsoever.
Thankfully, a nurse finally removed them.
It was a great relief to be able to gaze at a blank wall.
Eventually my bandages came off and I could return home at last.

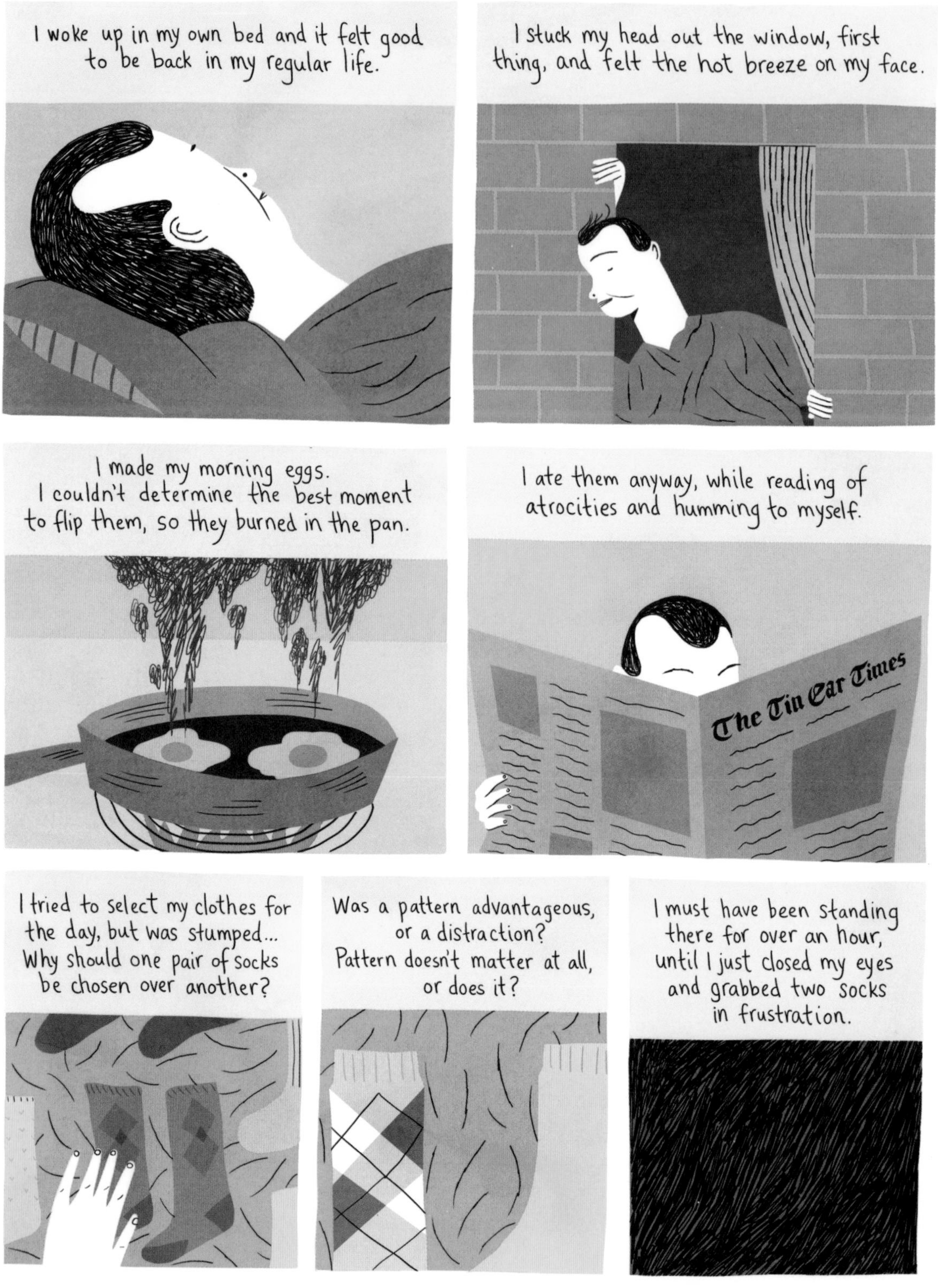
I woke up in my own bed and it felt good to be back in my regular life.
I stuck my head out the window, first thing, and felt the hot breeze on my face.
I made my morning eggs. I couldn't determine the best moment to flip them, so they burned in the pan.
I ate them anyway, while reading of atrocities and humming to myself.
The Tin Ear Times
I tried to select my clothes for the day, but was stumped... Why should one pair of socks be chosen over another?
Was a pattern advantageous, or a distraction? Pattern doesn't matter at all, or does it?
I must have been standing there for over an hour, until I just closed my eyes and grabbed two socks in frustration.

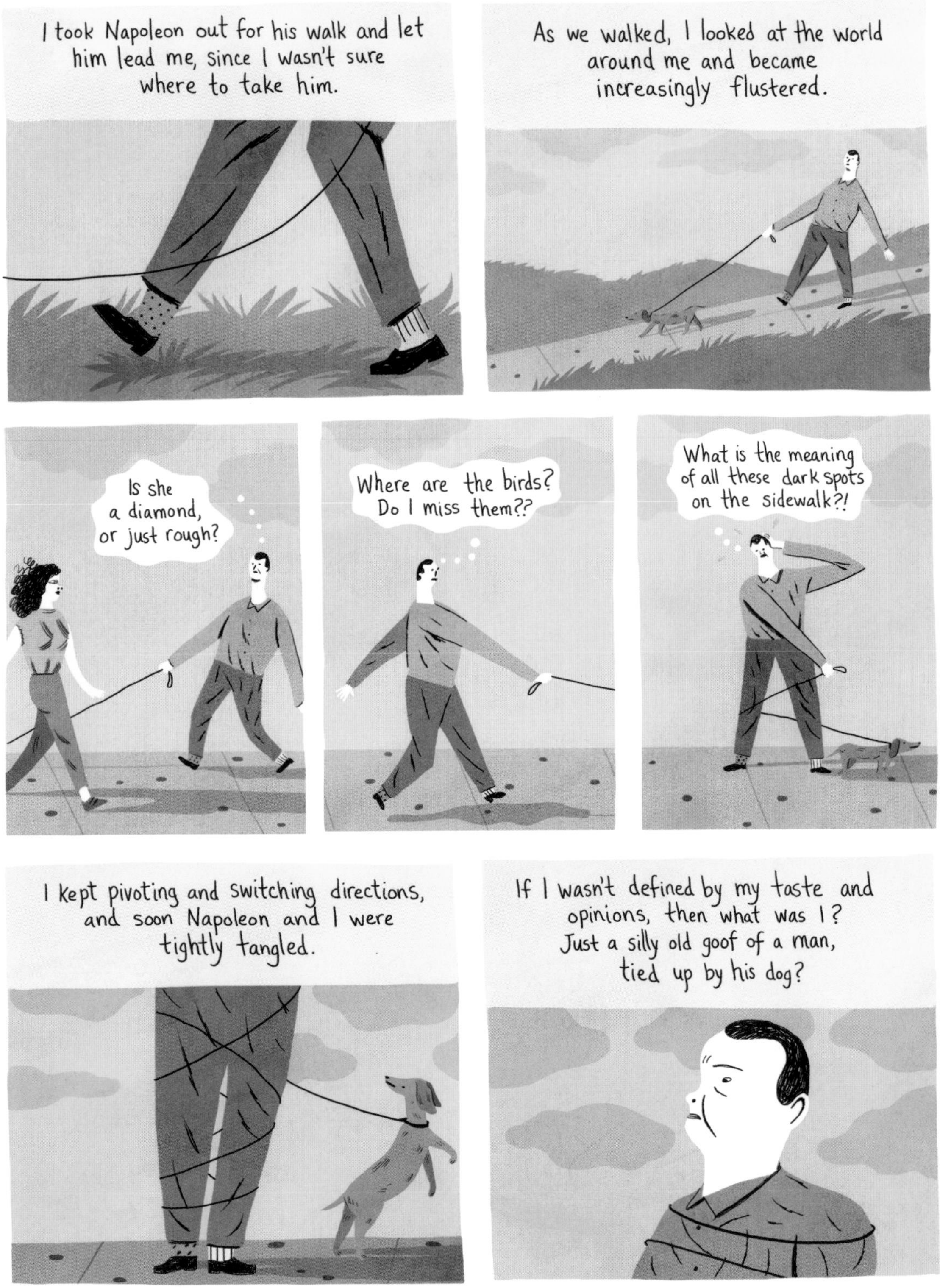
I took Napoleon out for his walk and let him lead me, since I wasn't sure where to take him.
As we walked, I looked at the world around me and became increasingly flustered.
Is she a diamond, or just rough?
Where are the birds? Do I miss them??
What is the meaning of all these dark spots on the sidewalk?!
I kept pivoting and switching directions, and soon Napoleon and I were tightly tangled.
If I wasn't defined by my taste and opinions, then what was I? Just a silly old goof of a man, tied up by his dog?

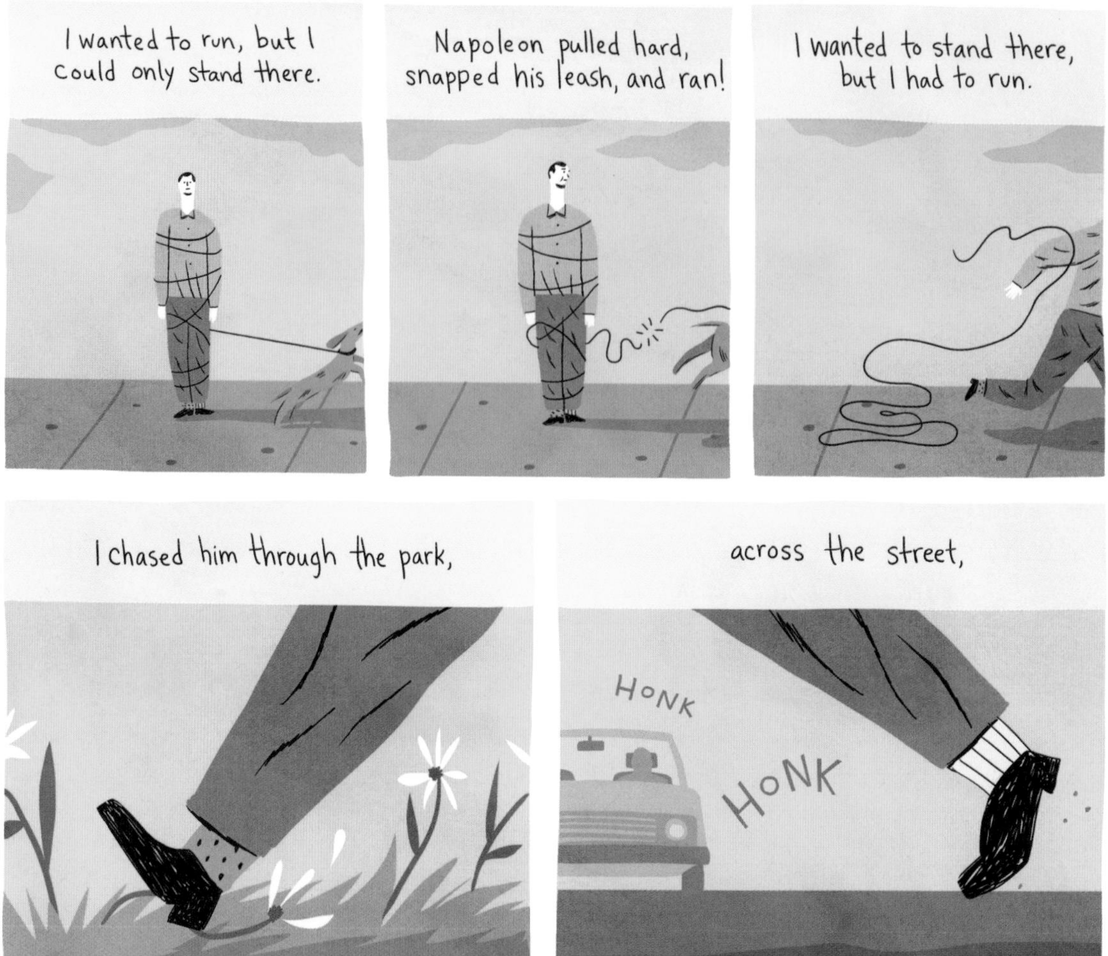
I wanted to run, but I could only stand there.
Napoleon pulled hard, snapped his leash, and ran!
I wanted to stand there, but I had to run.
I chased him through the park,
across the street,
HONK
HONK
down the hill,
all the way to the shore.

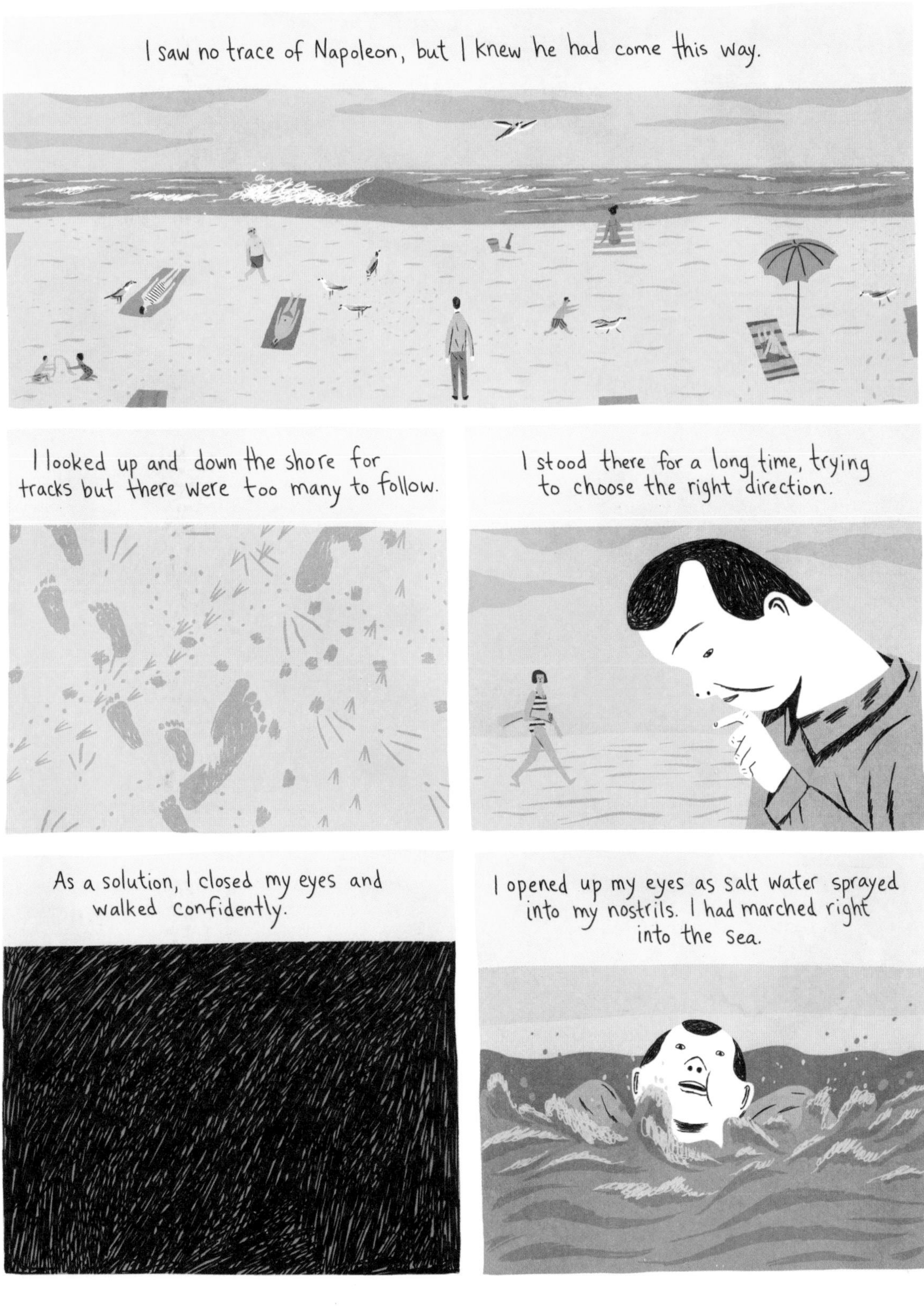
I saw no trace of Napoleon, but I knew he had come this way.
I looked up and down the shore for tracks but there were too many to follow.
I stood there for a long time, trying to choose the right direction.
As a solution, I closed my eyes and walked confidently.
I opened up my eyes as salt water sprayed into my nostrils. I had marched right into the sea.

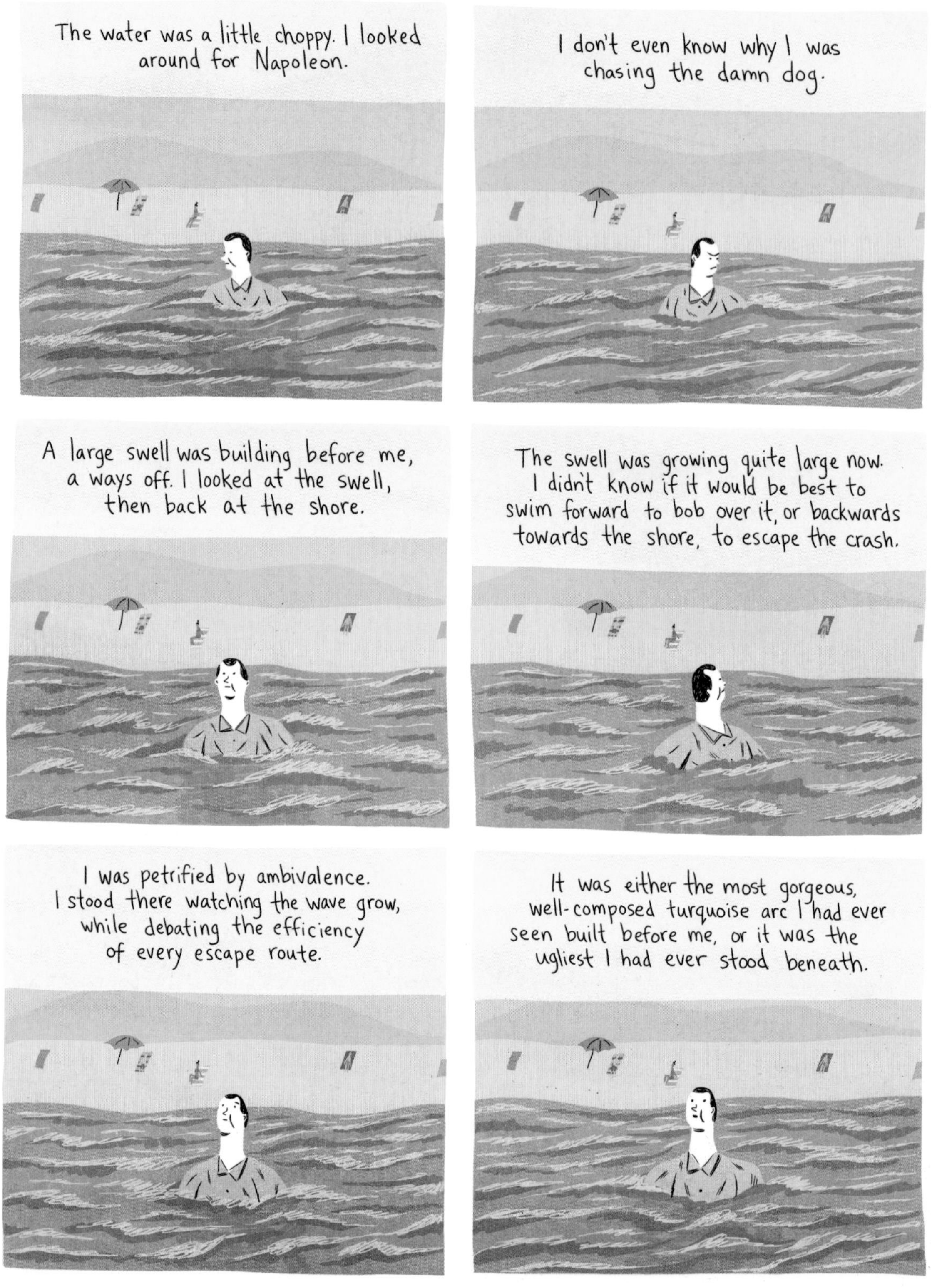
The water was a little choppy. I looked around for Napoleon.
I don't even know why I was chasing the damn dog.
A large swell was building before me, a ways off. I looked at the swell, then back at the shore.
The swell was growing quite large now. I didn't know if it would be best to swim forward to bob over it, or backwards towards the shore, to escape the crash.
I was petrified by ambivalence. I stood there watching the wave grow, while debating the efficiency of every escape route.
It was either the most gorgeous, well-composed turquoise arc I had ever seen built before me, or it was the ugliest I had ever stood beneath.

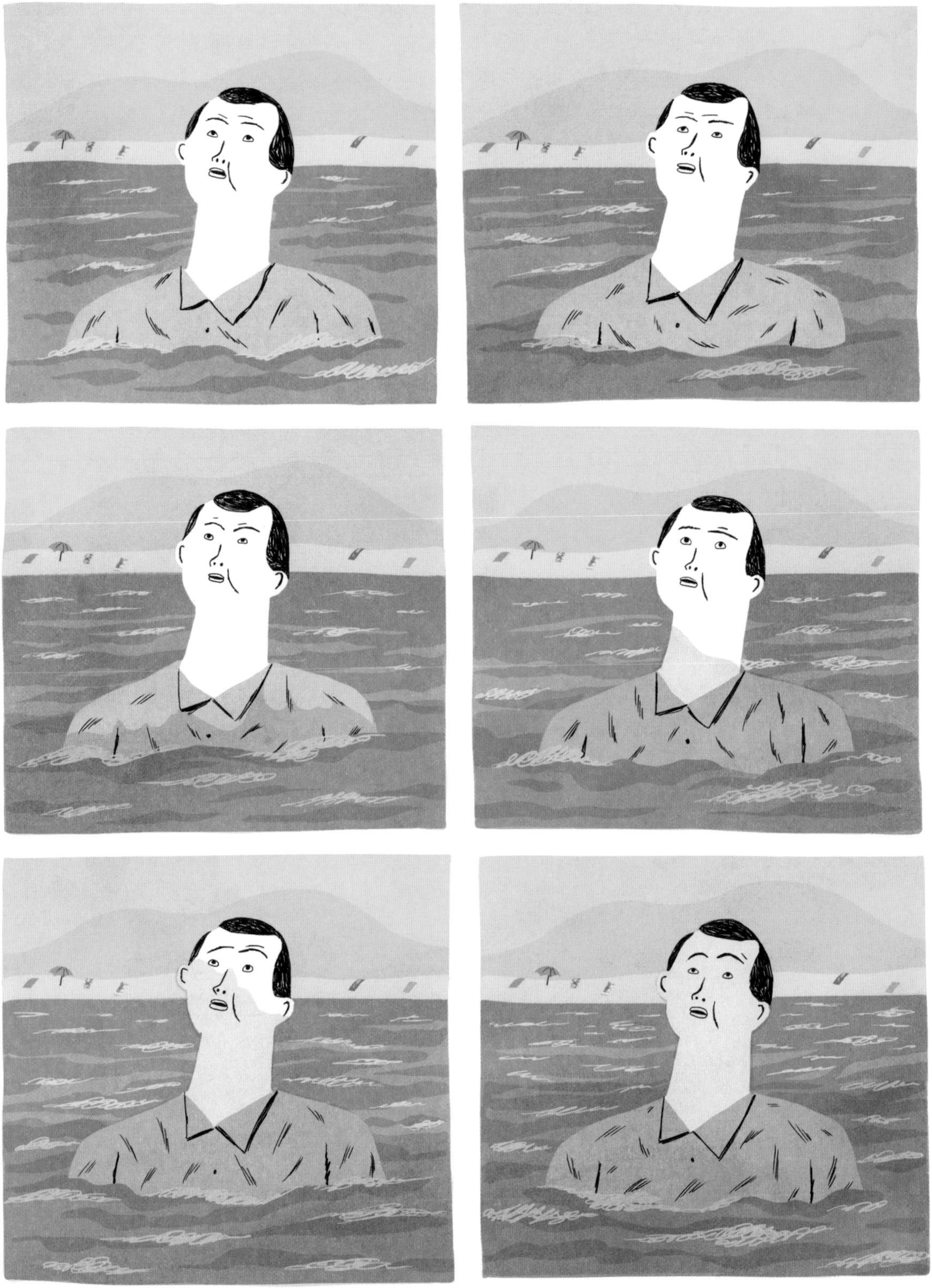

into
the
night

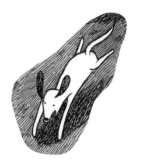

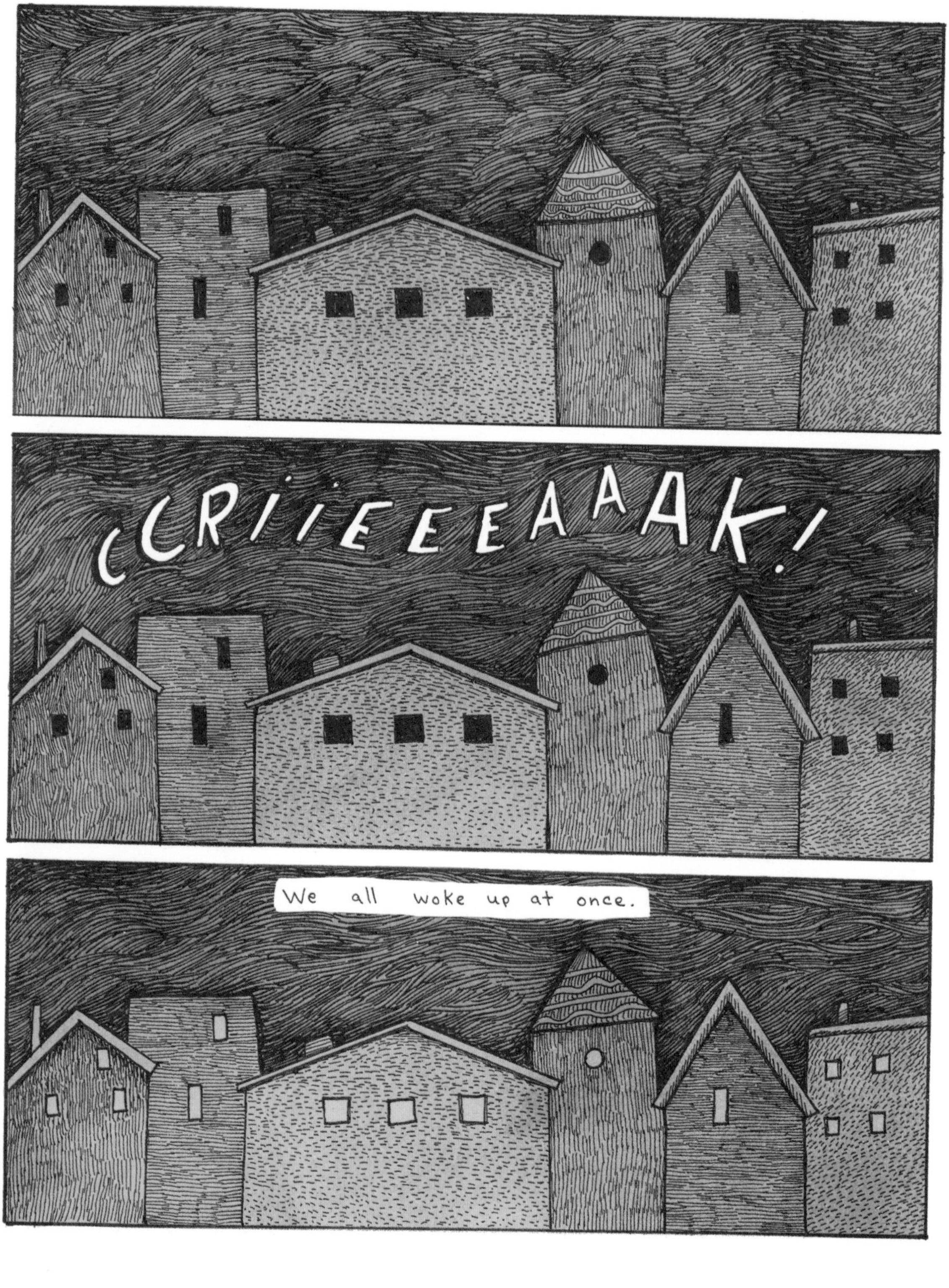
CCRIIEEEAAAK!
We all woke up at once.

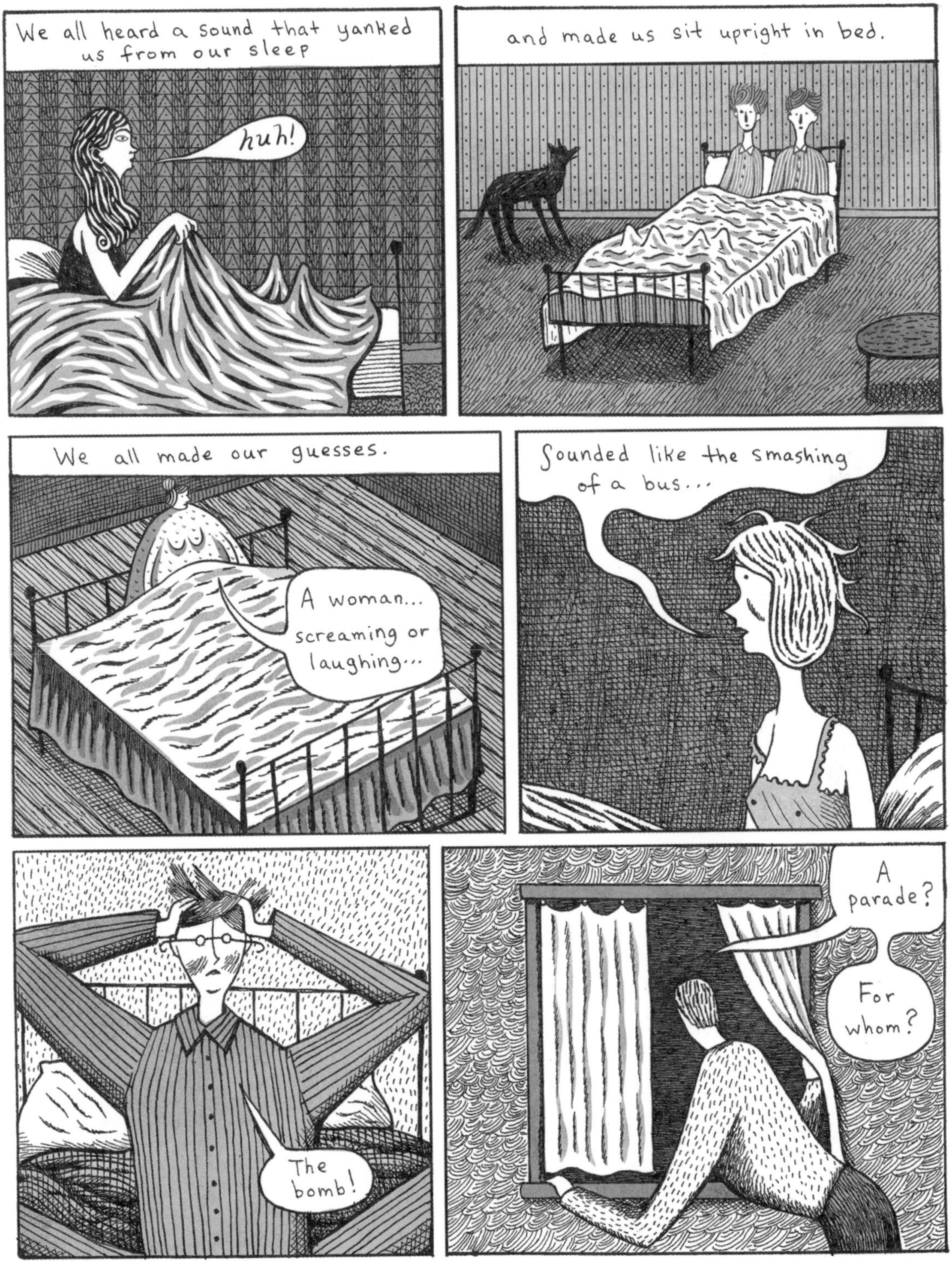
We all heard a sound that yanked us from our sleep
huh!
and made us sit upright in bed.
We all made our guesses.
A woman... screaming or laughing...
Sounded like the smashing of a bus...
The bomb!
A parade?
For whom?

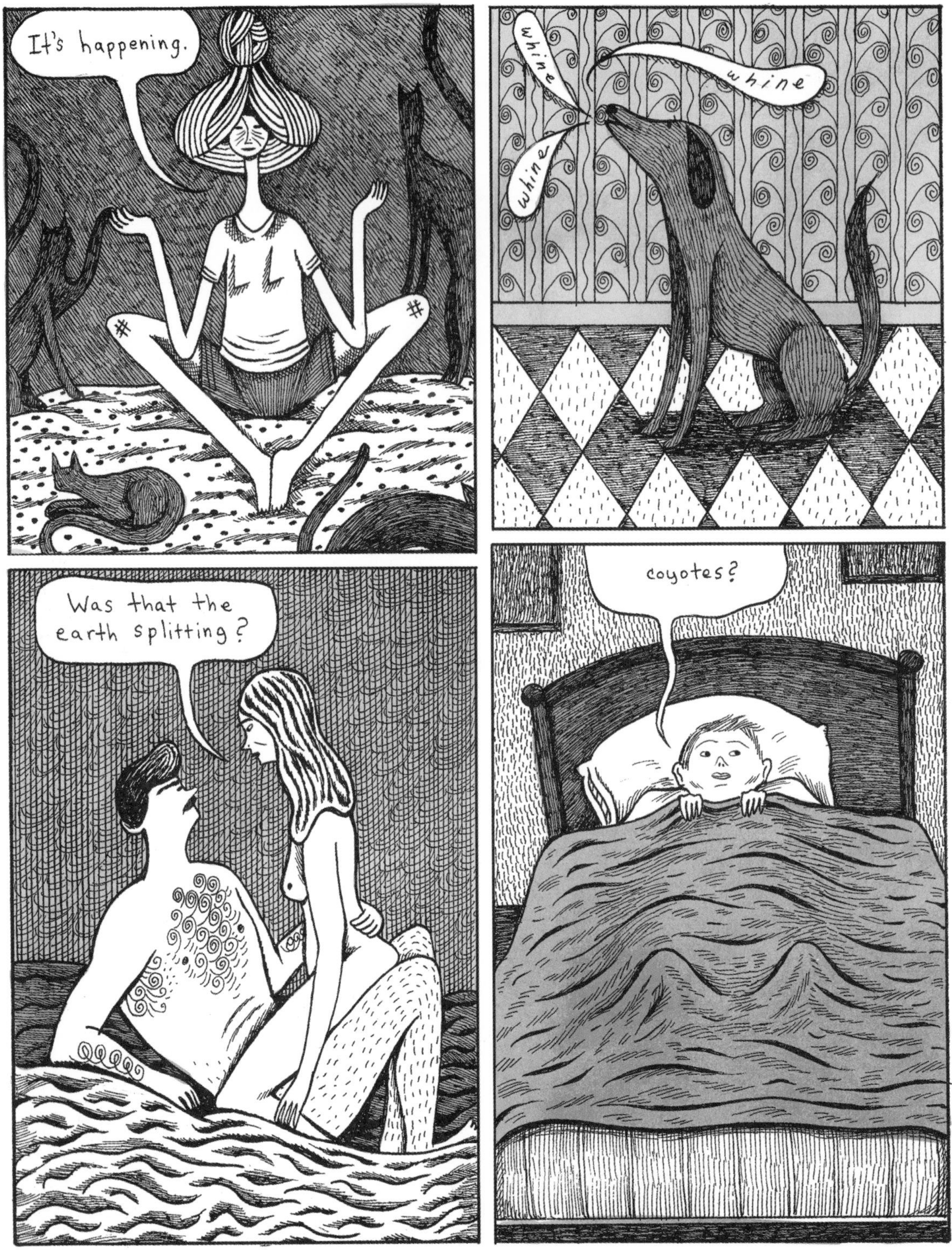
It's happening.
whine
whine
whine
Was that the earth splitting?
coyotes?

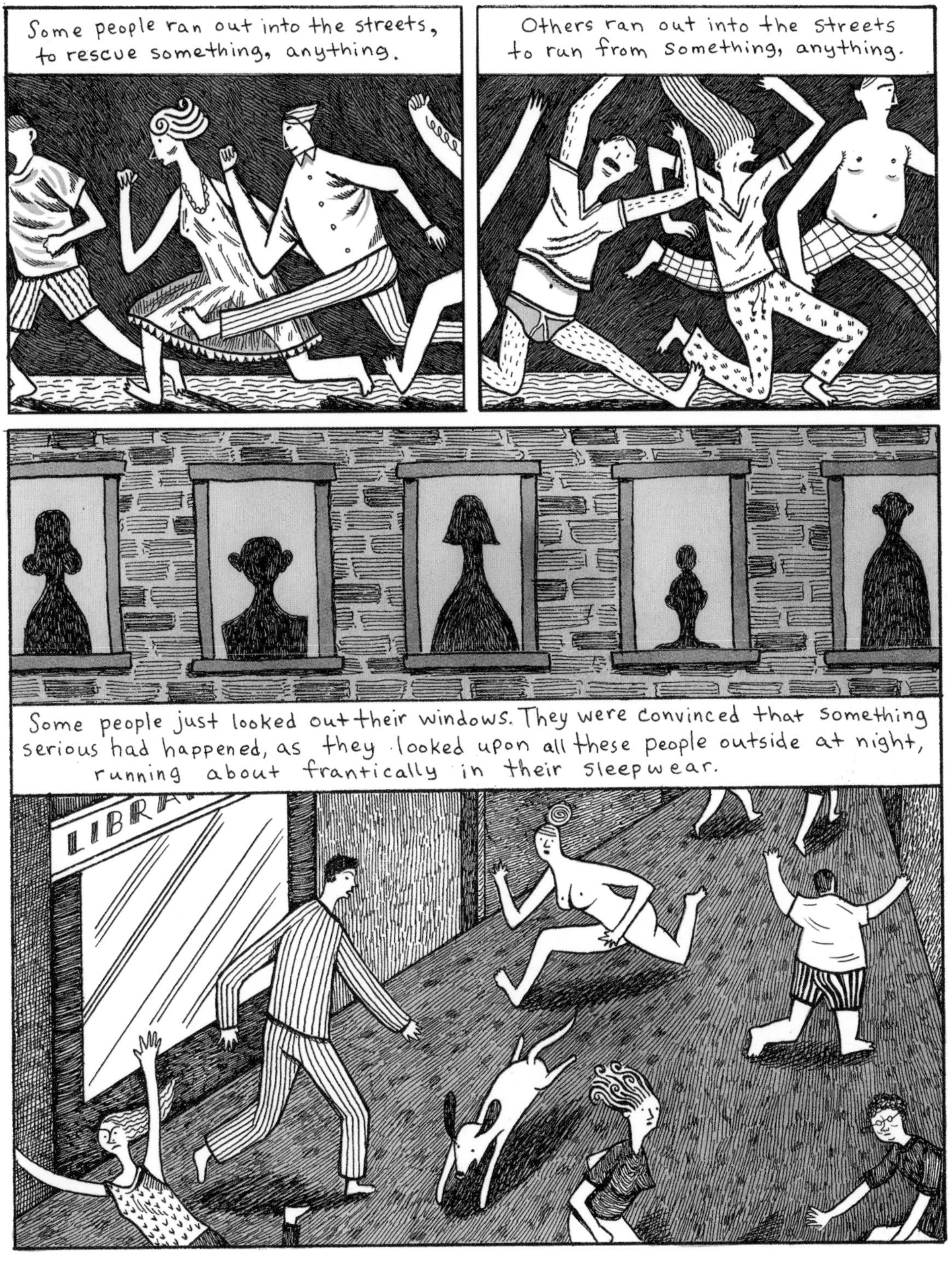
Some people ran out into the streets, to rescue something, anything.
Others ran out into the streets to run from something, anything.
Some people just looked out their windows. They were convinced that something serious had happened, as they looked upon all these people outside at night, running about frantically in their sleepwear.

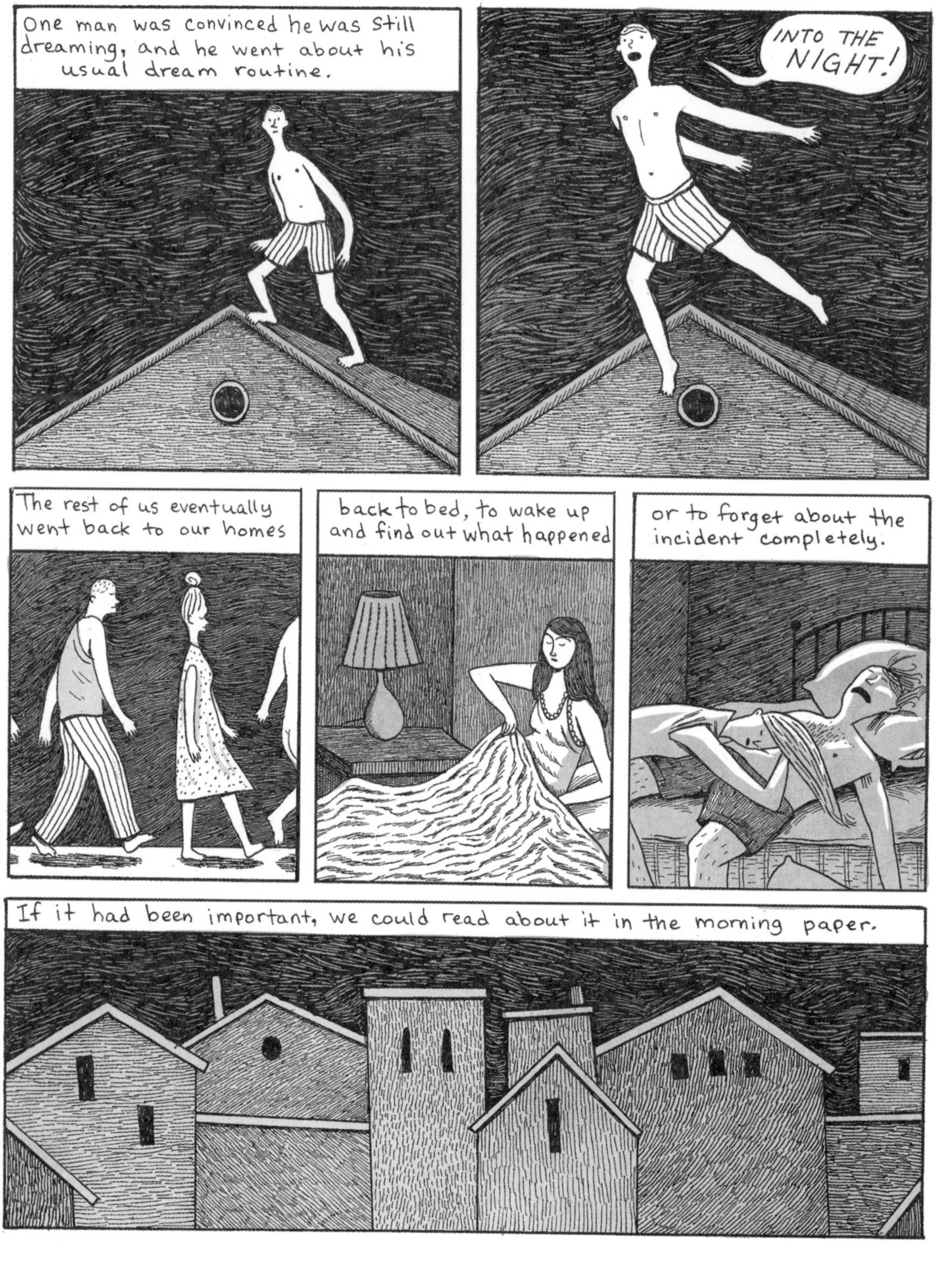
One man was convinced he was still dreaming, and he went about his usual dream routine.
INTO THE NIGHT!
The rest of us eventually went back to our homes
back to bed, to wake up and find out what happened
or to forget about the incident completely.
If it had been important, we could read about it in the morning paper.

We slept, as a man lay on his back in the street, listening to the sound of something getting closer.
CCRiiiiEAAK!
I wonder when I'll wake up from this one...

lilli carré

the thing about Madeline

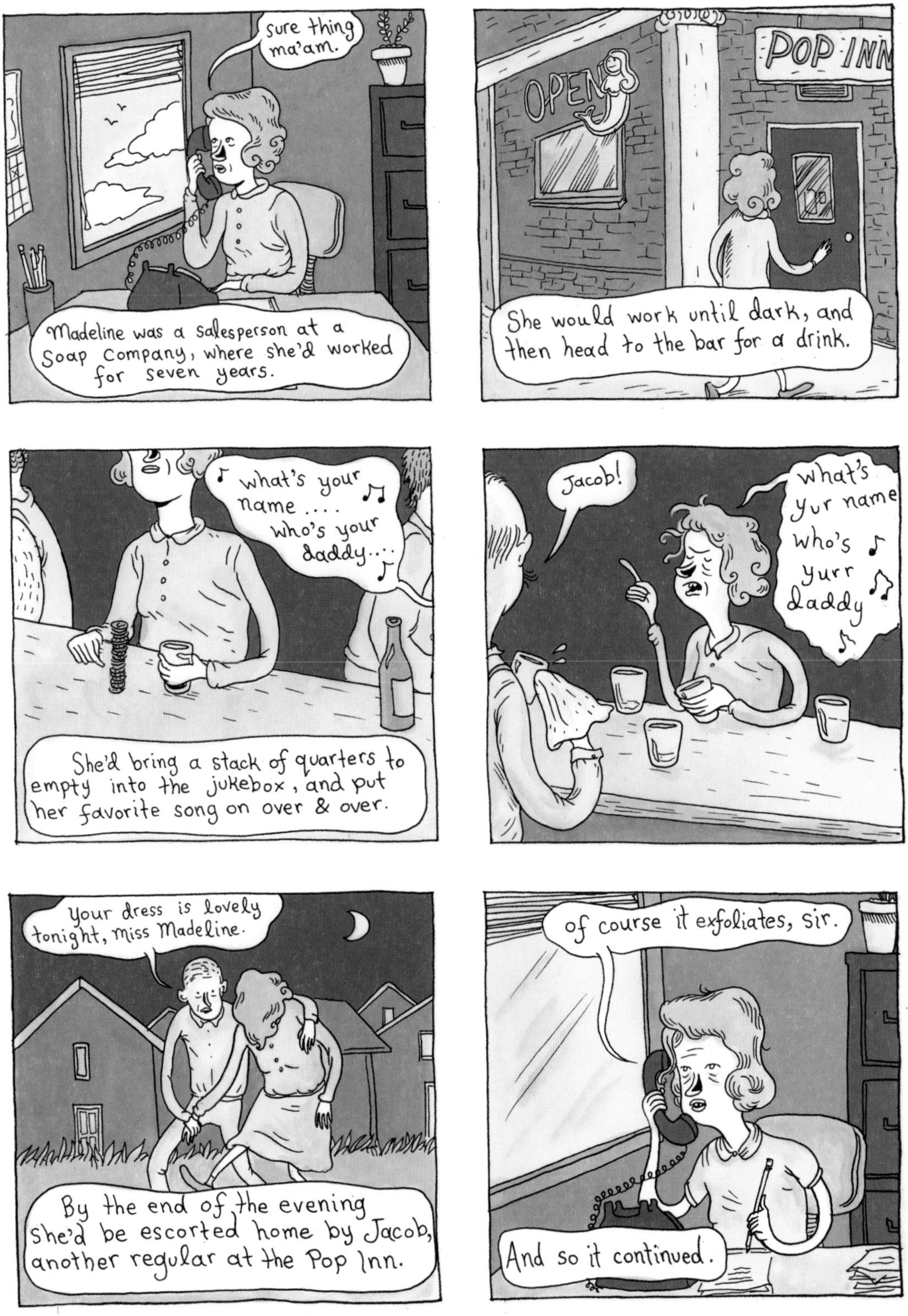
sure thing ma'am.
Madeline was a salesperson at a Soap Company, where she'd worked for seven years.
OPEN
POP INN
She would work until dark, and then head to the bar for a drink.
what's your name .... who's your daddy....
She'd bring a stack of quarters to empty into the jukebox, and put her favorite song on over & over.
Jacob!
what's yur name who's yurr daddy
Your dress is lovely tonight, miss Madeline.
By the end of the evening she'd be escorted home by Jacob, another regular at the Pop Inn.
of course it exfoliates, sir.
And so it continued.

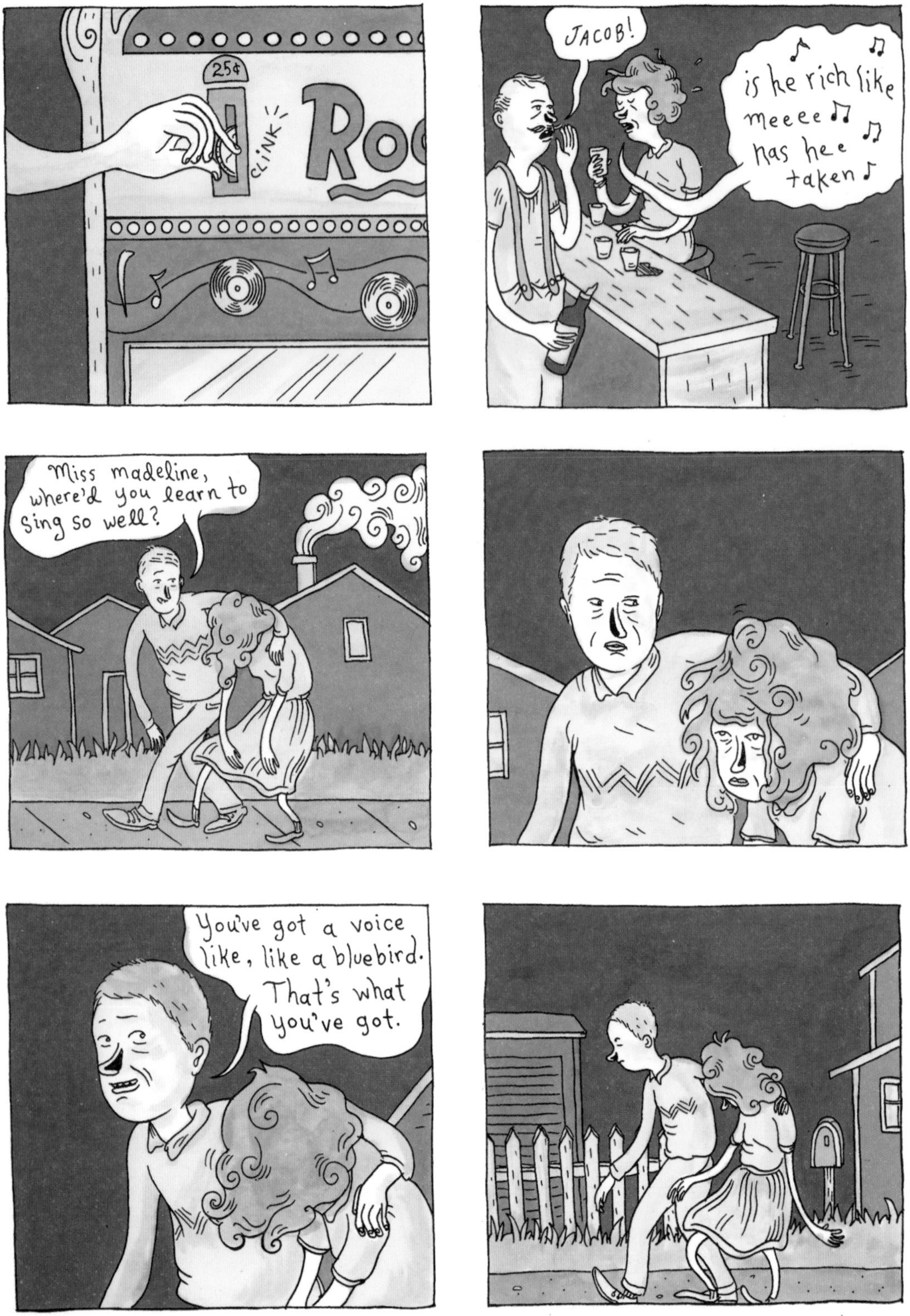
25¢
CLINK
Roc
JACOB!
is he rich like meeee has hee taken
Miss madeline, where'd you learn to sing so well?
You've got a voice like, like a bluebird. That's what you've got.

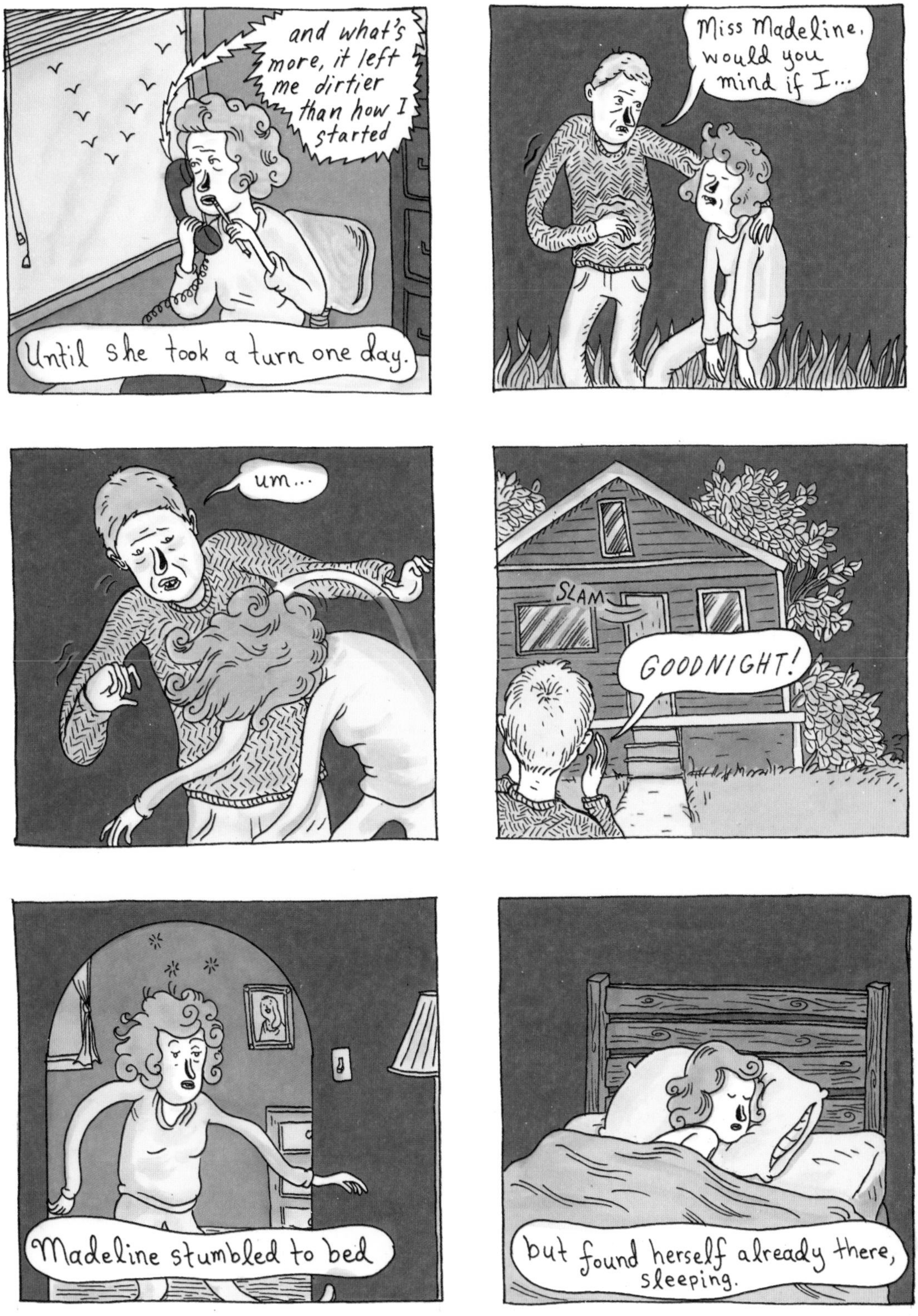
and what's more, it left me dirtier than how I started
Until she took a turn one day.
Miss Madeline, would you mind if I...
um...
SLAM
GOODNIGHT!
Madeline stumbled to bed
but found herself already there, sleeping.

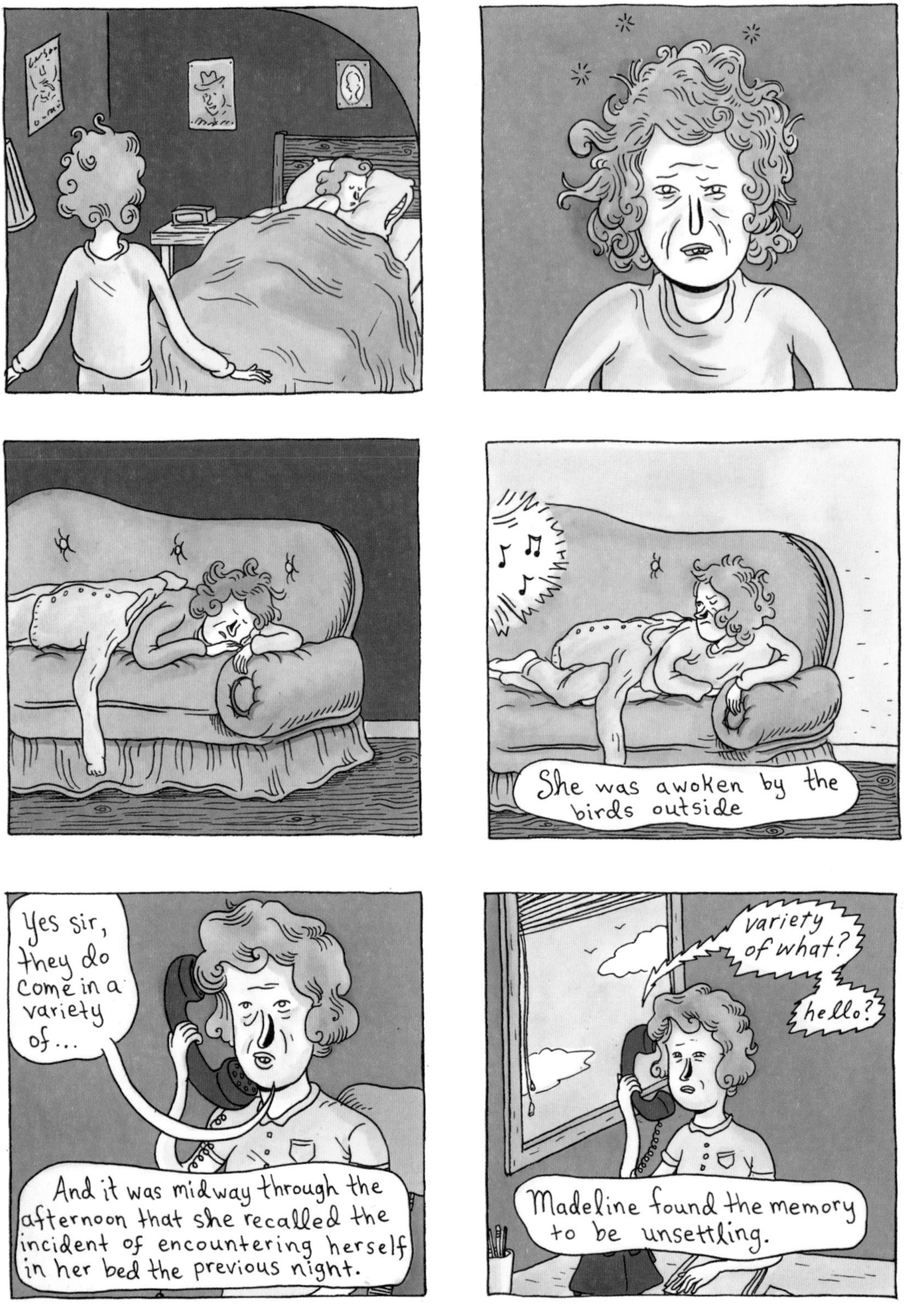
She was awoken by the birds outside
Yes sir, they do come in a variety of...
And it was midway through the afternoon that she recalled the incident of encountering herself in her bed the previous night.
variety of what?
hello?
Madeline found the memory to be unsettling.

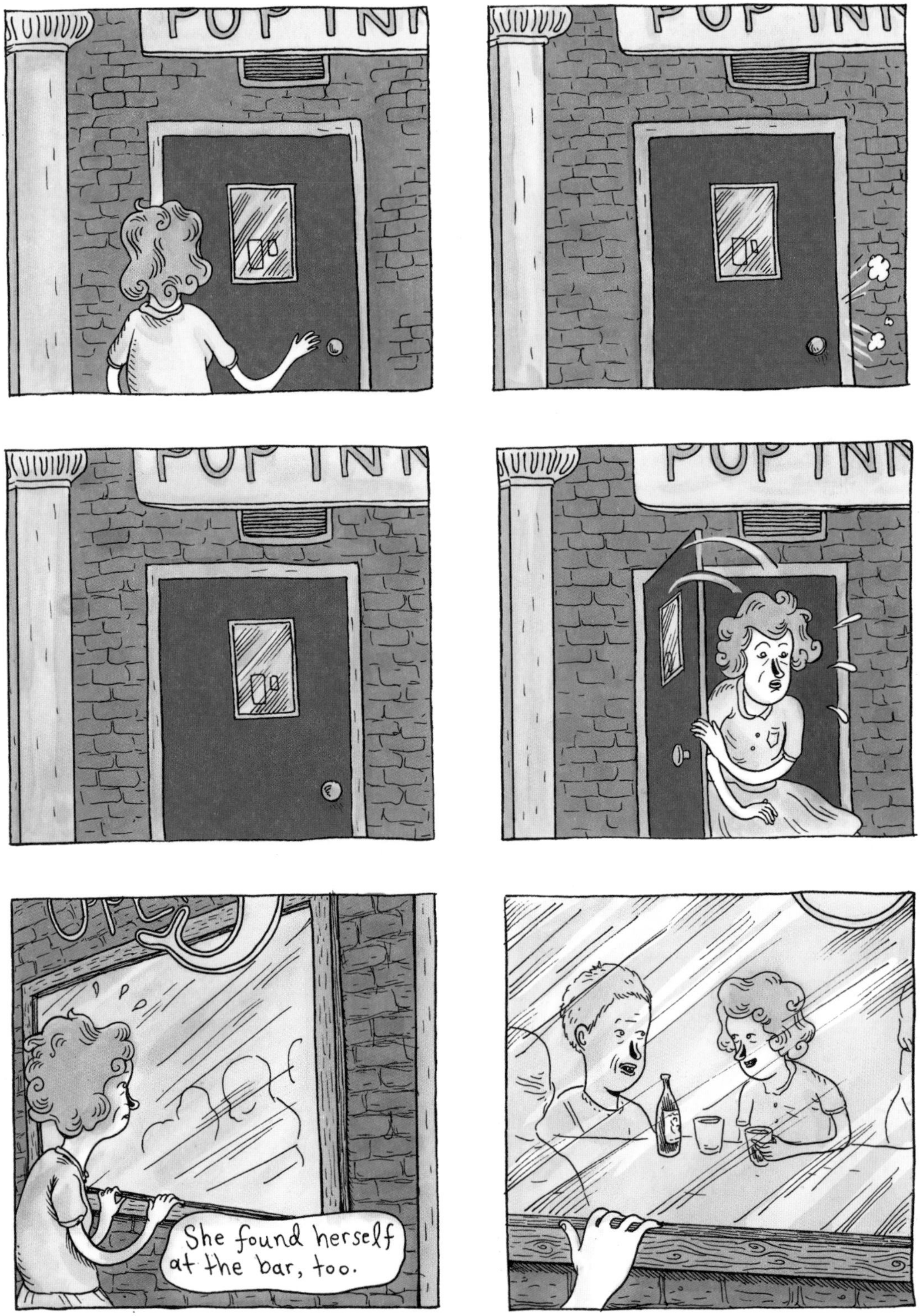
POP INN
POP INN
POP INN
POP INN
She found herself at the bar, too.

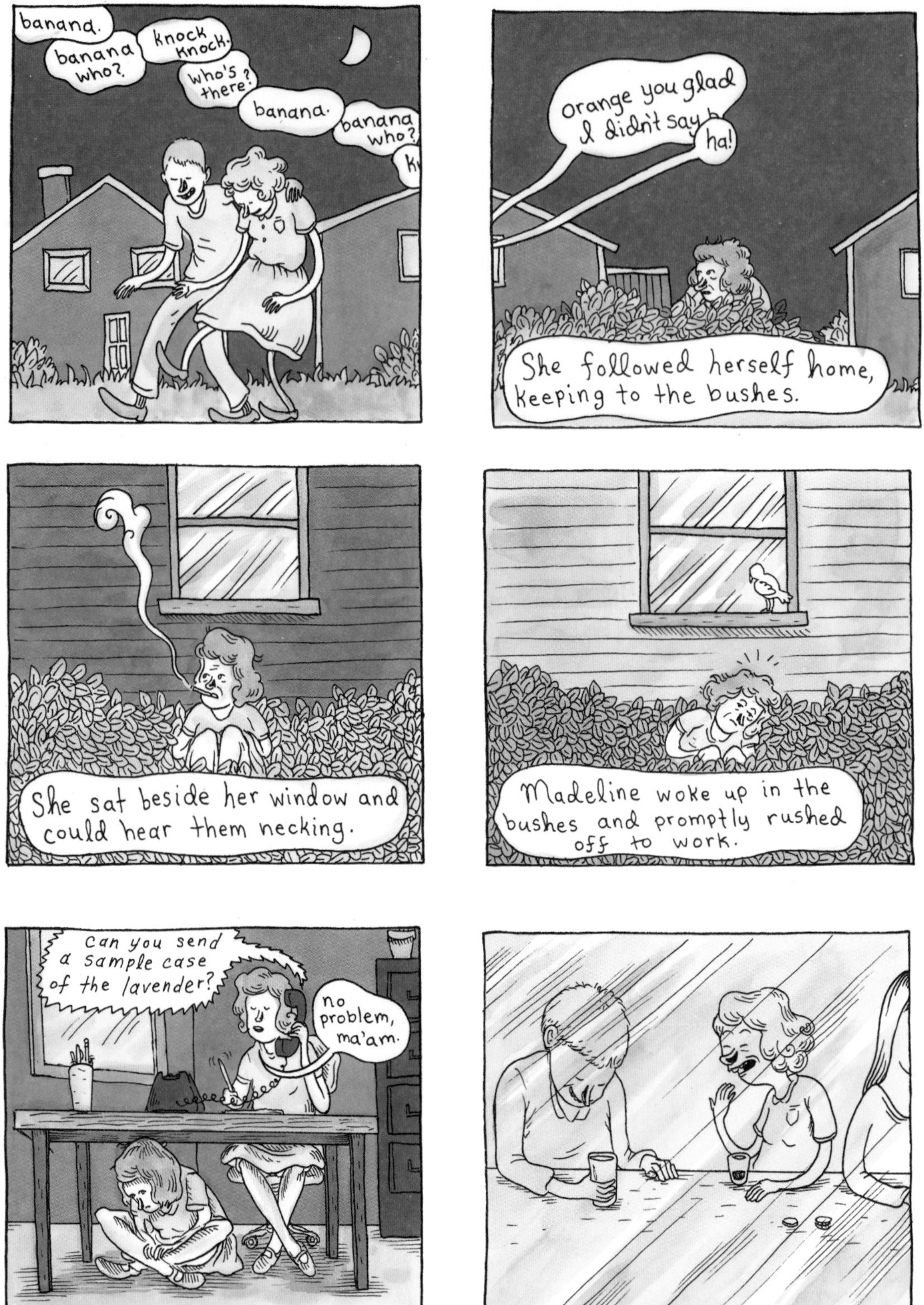
banana.
banana who?
knock knock.
who's there?
banana.
banana who?
Orange you glad I didn't say
ha!
She followed herself home, keeping to the bushes.
She sat beside her window and could hear them necking.
Madeline woke up in the bushes and promptly rushed off to work.
Can you send a sample case of the lavender?
no problem, ma'am.

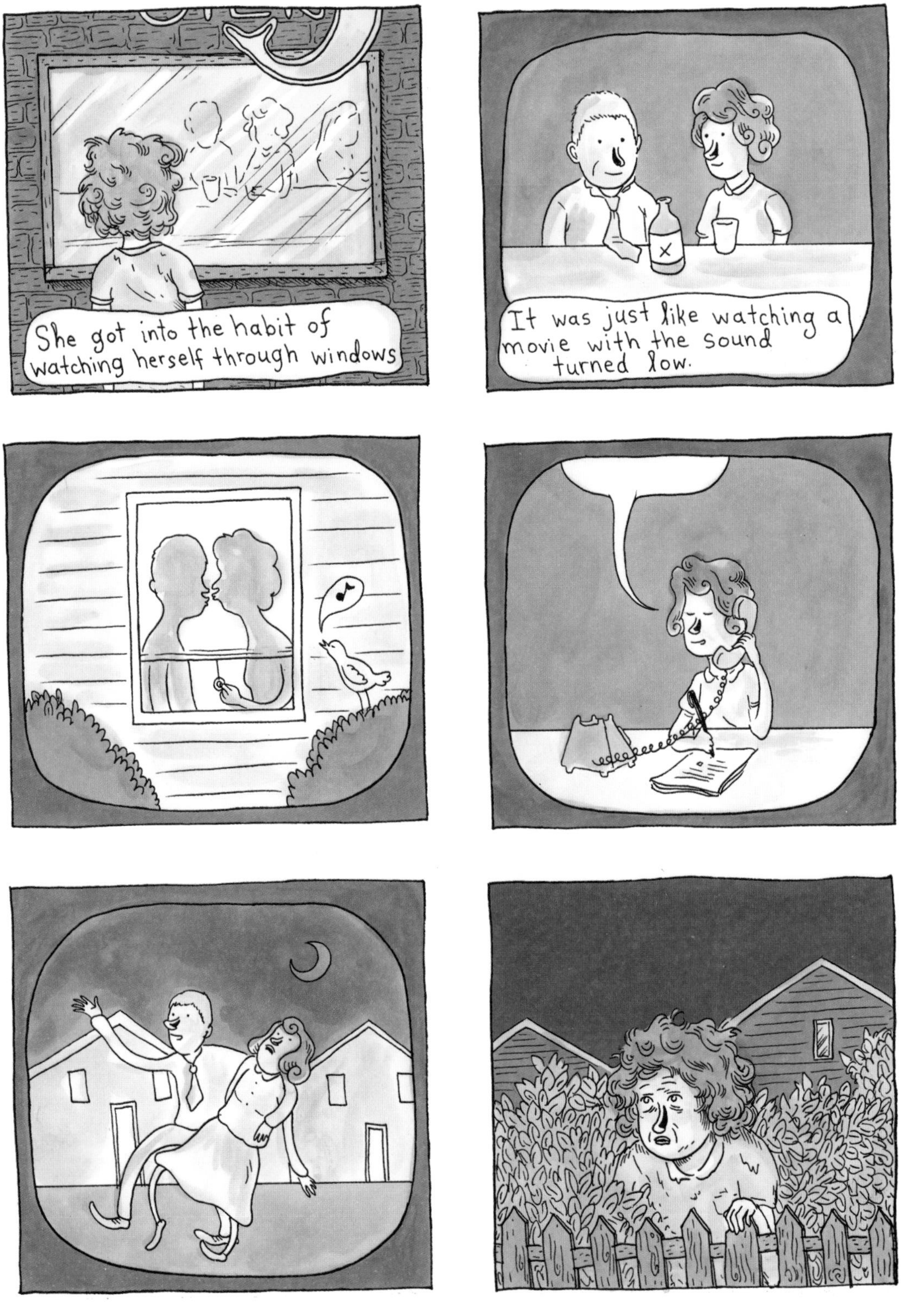
She got into the habit of watching herself through windows
It was just like watching a movie with the sound turned low.

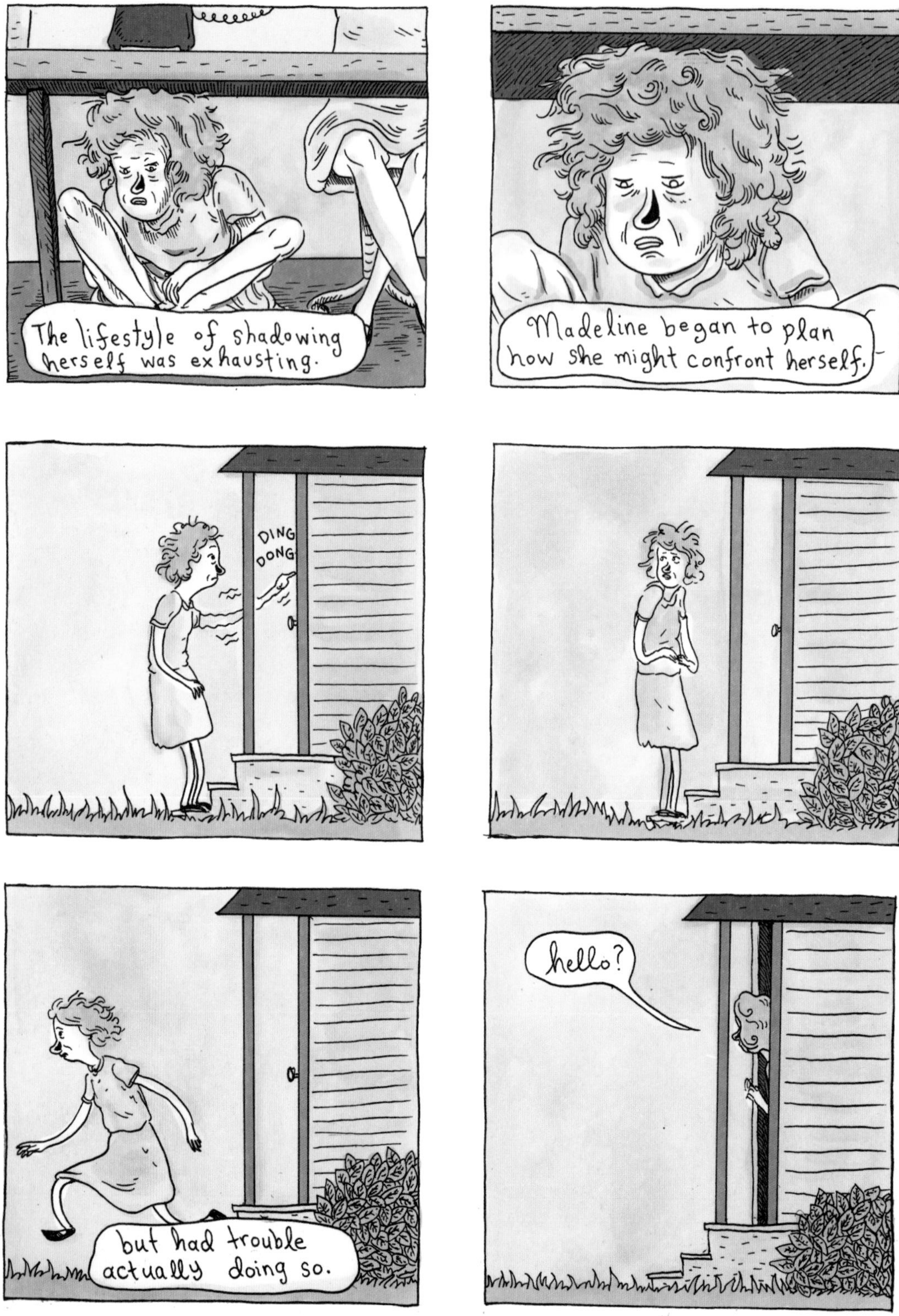
The lifestyle of shadowing herself was exhausting.
Madeline began to plan how she might confront herself.
DING DONG
but had trouble actually doing so.
hello?

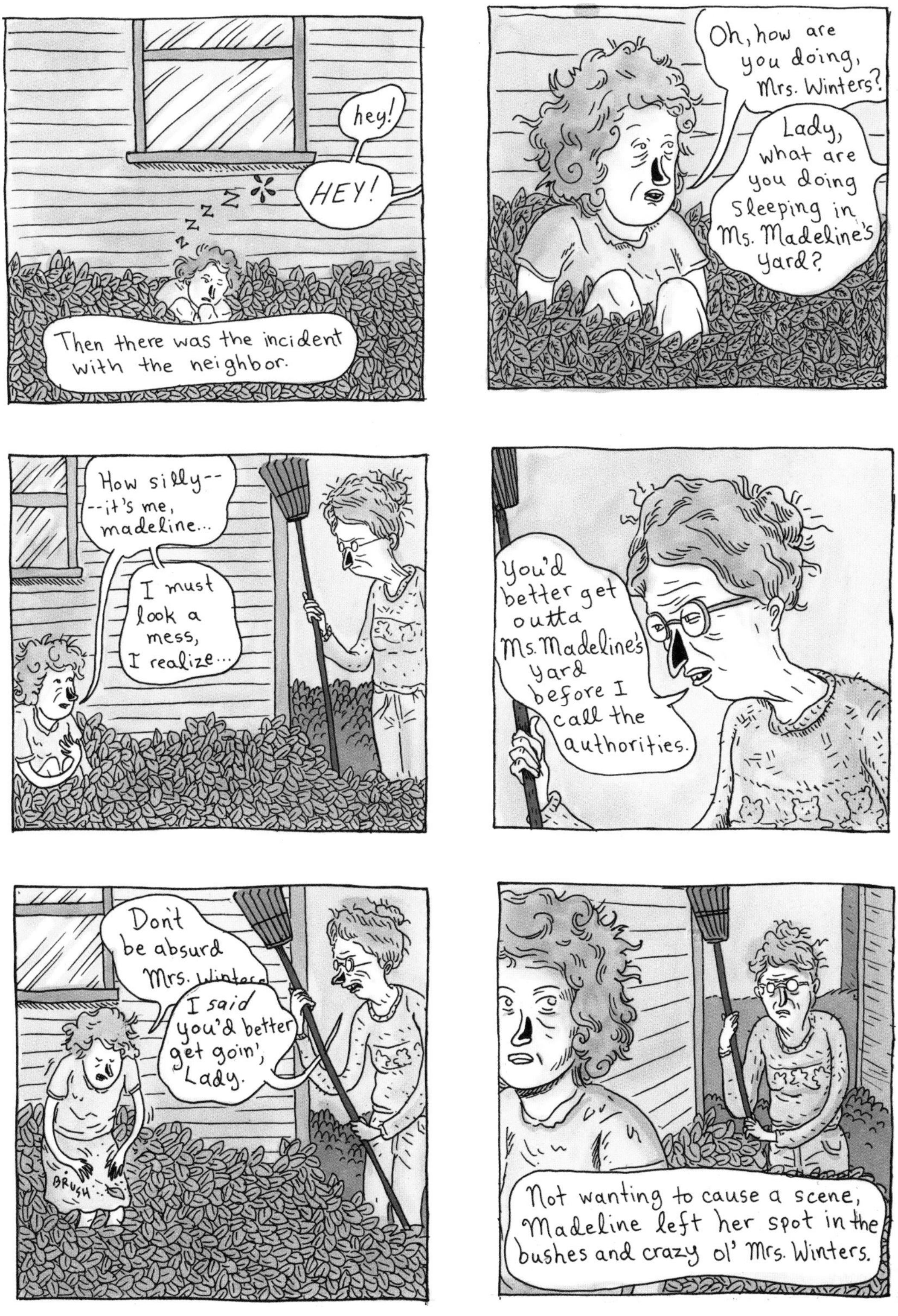
hey!
HEY!
Then there was the incident with the neighbor.
Oh, how are you doing, Mrs. Winters?
Lady, what are you doing sleeping in Ms. Madeline's yard?
How silly-- --it's me, madeline...
I must look a mess, I realize...
You'd better get outta Ms. Madeline's yard before I call the authorities.
Don't be absurd Mrs. Winters
I said you'd better get goin', Lady.
BRUSH
Not wanting to cause a scene, Madeline left her spot in the bushes and crazy ol' Mrs. Winters.

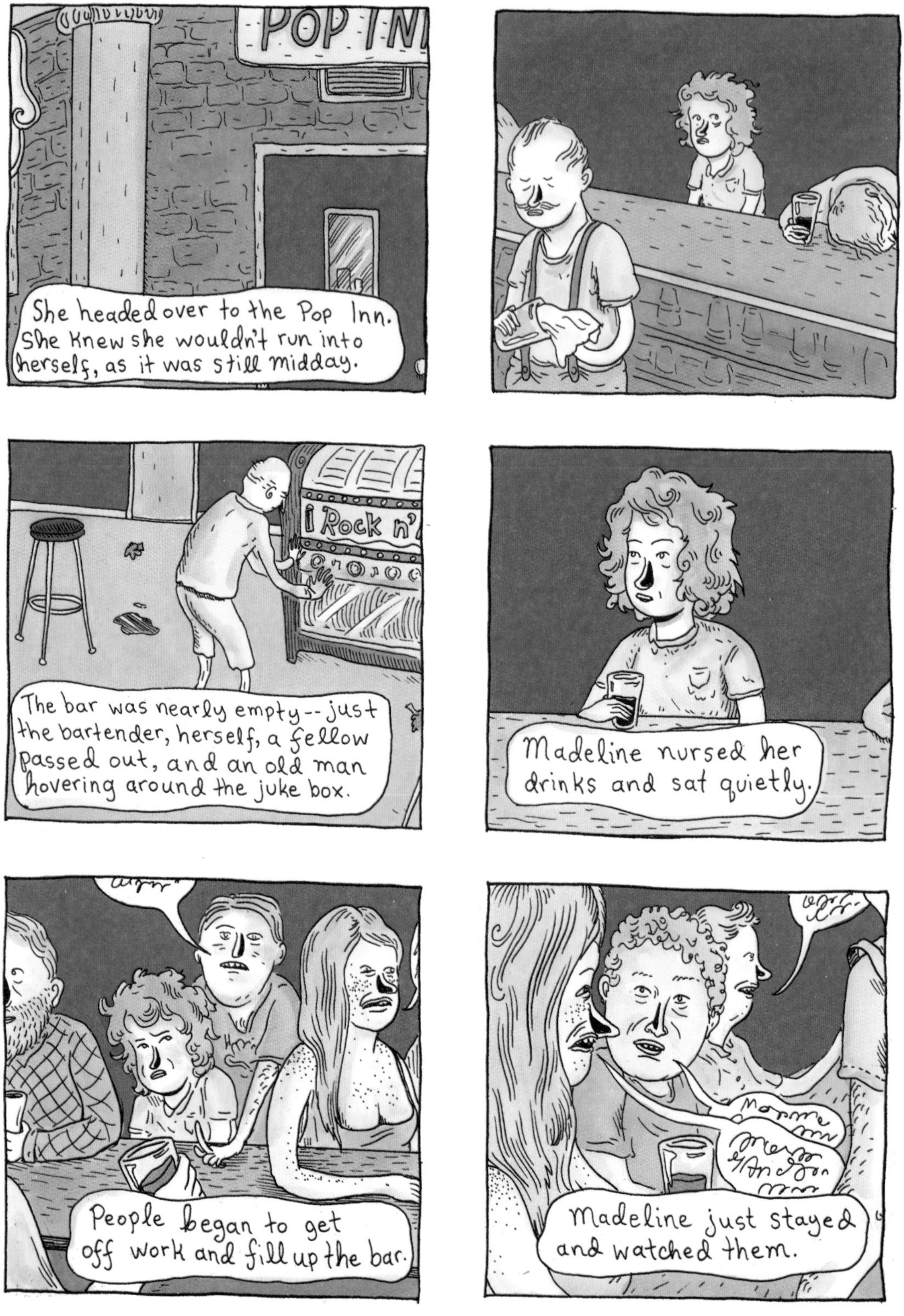
She headed over to the Pop Inn. She knew she wouldn't run into herself, as it was still midday.
The bar was nearly empty -- just the bartender, herself, a fellow passed out, and an old man hovering around the juke box.
Madeline nursed her drinks and sat quietly.
People began to get off work and fill up the bar.
Madeline just stayed and watched them.

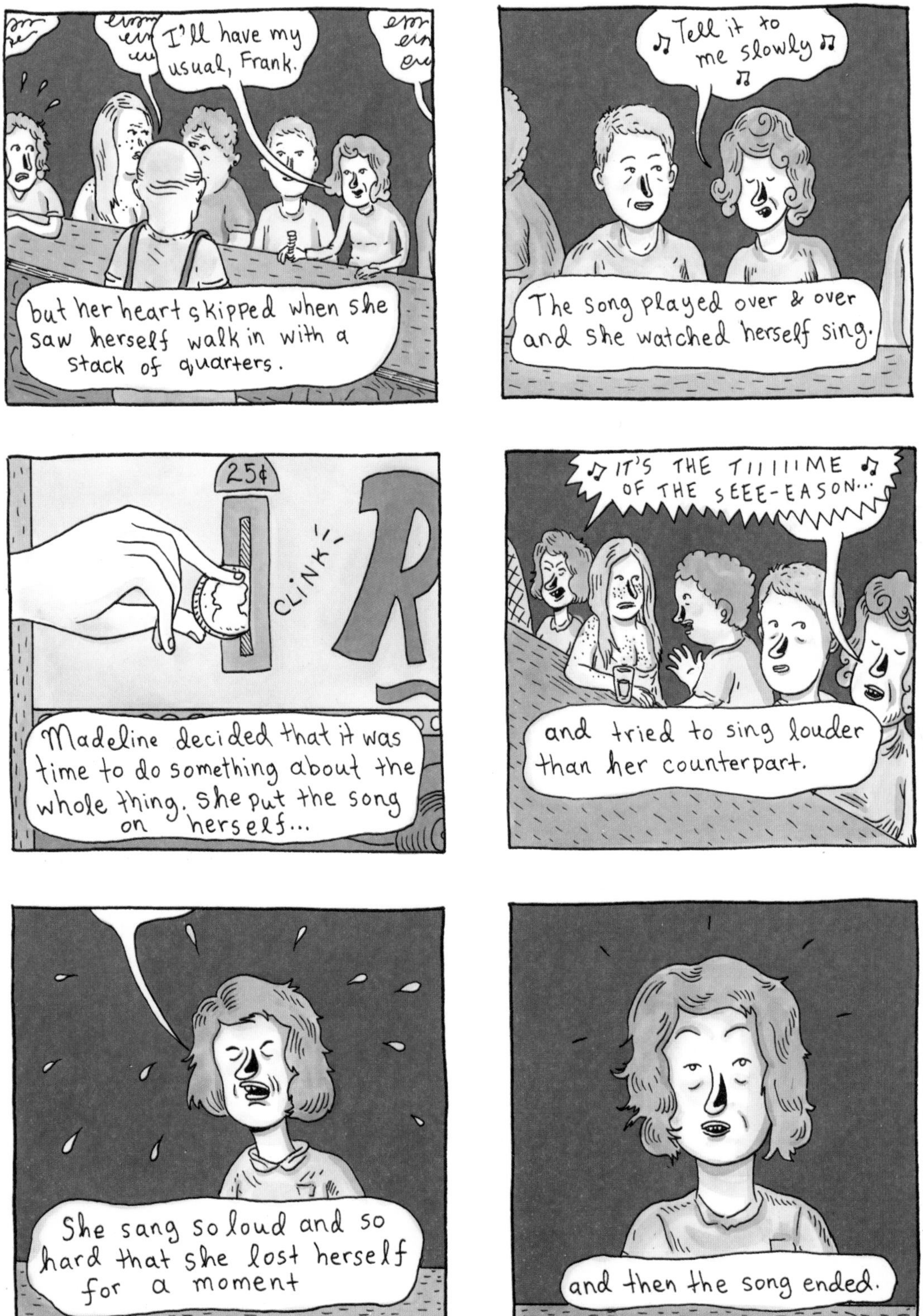

I'll have my usual, Frank.
but her heart skipped when she saw herself walk in with a stack of quarters.
♫ Tell it to me slowly ♫ ♫
The song played over & over and she watched herself sing.
25¢
CLINK
Madeline decided that it was time to do something about the whole thing. She put the song on herself...
♫ IT'S THE TIIIIIME OF THE SEEE-EASON... ♫
and tried to sing louder than her counterpart.
She sang so loud and so hard that she lost herself for a moment
and then the song ended.

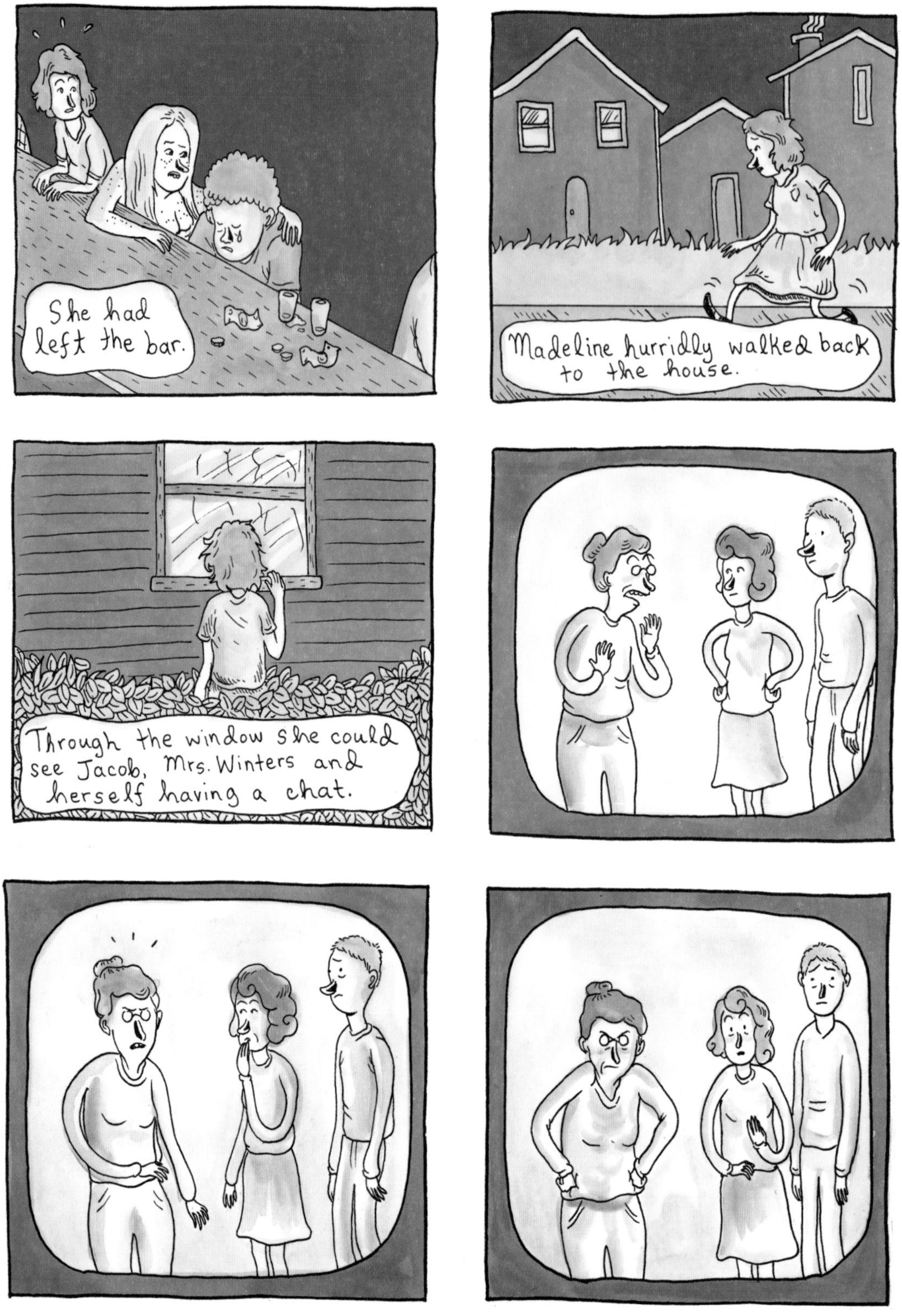
She had left the bar.
Madeline hurridly walked back to the house.
Through the window she could see Jacob, Mrs. Winters and herself having a chat.

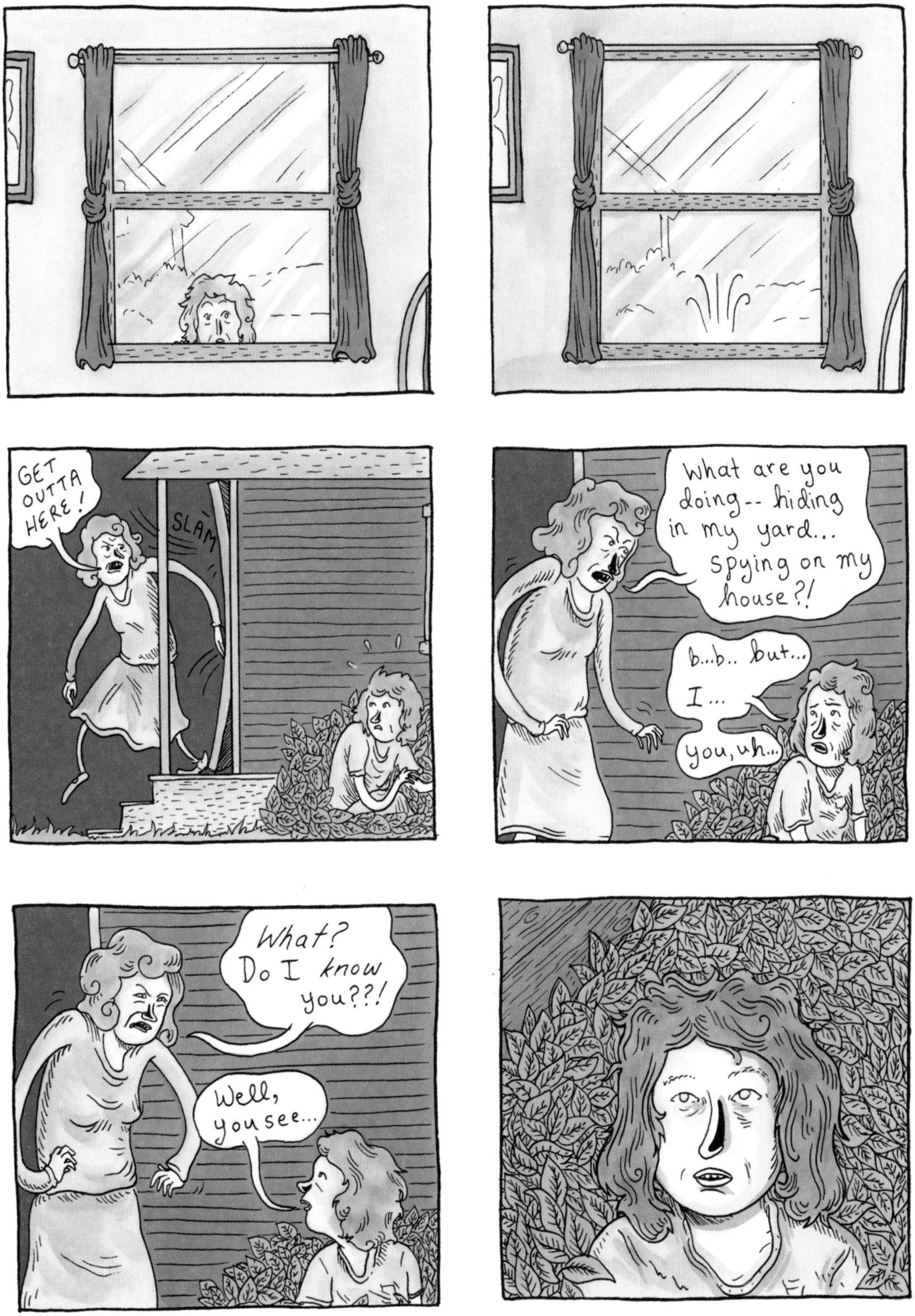
GET OUTTA HERE!
SLAM
What are you doing -- hiding in my yard... spying on my house?!
b...b.. but...
I...
you, uh...
What? Do I know you??!
Well, you see...

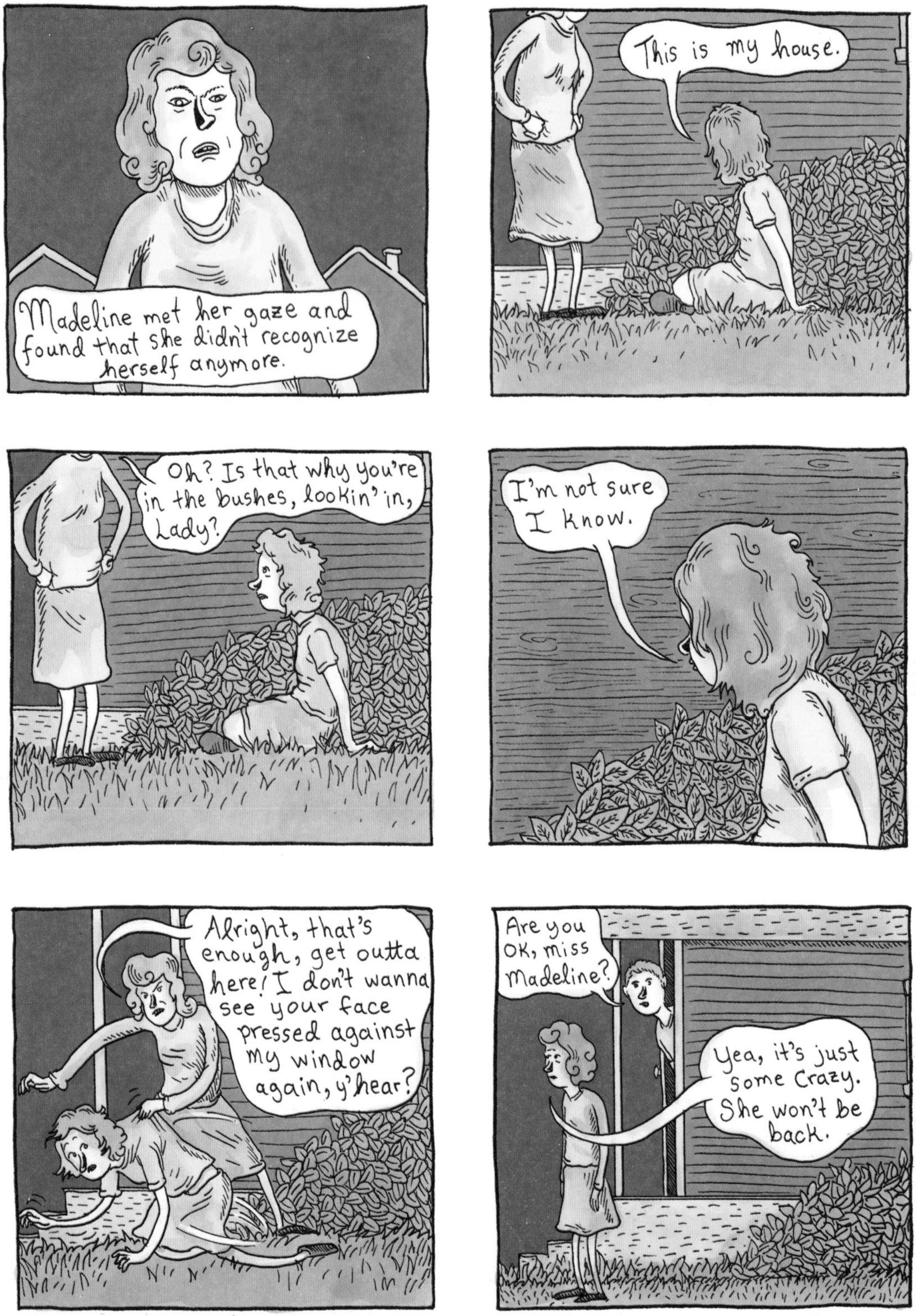
Madeline met her gaze and found that she didn't recognize herself anymore.
This is my house.
Oh? Is that why you're in the bushes, lookin' in, Lady?
I'm not sure I know.
Alright, that's enough, get outta here! I don't wanna see your face pressed against my window again, y'hear?
Are you OK, miss Madeline?
Yea, it's just some Crazy. She won't be back.

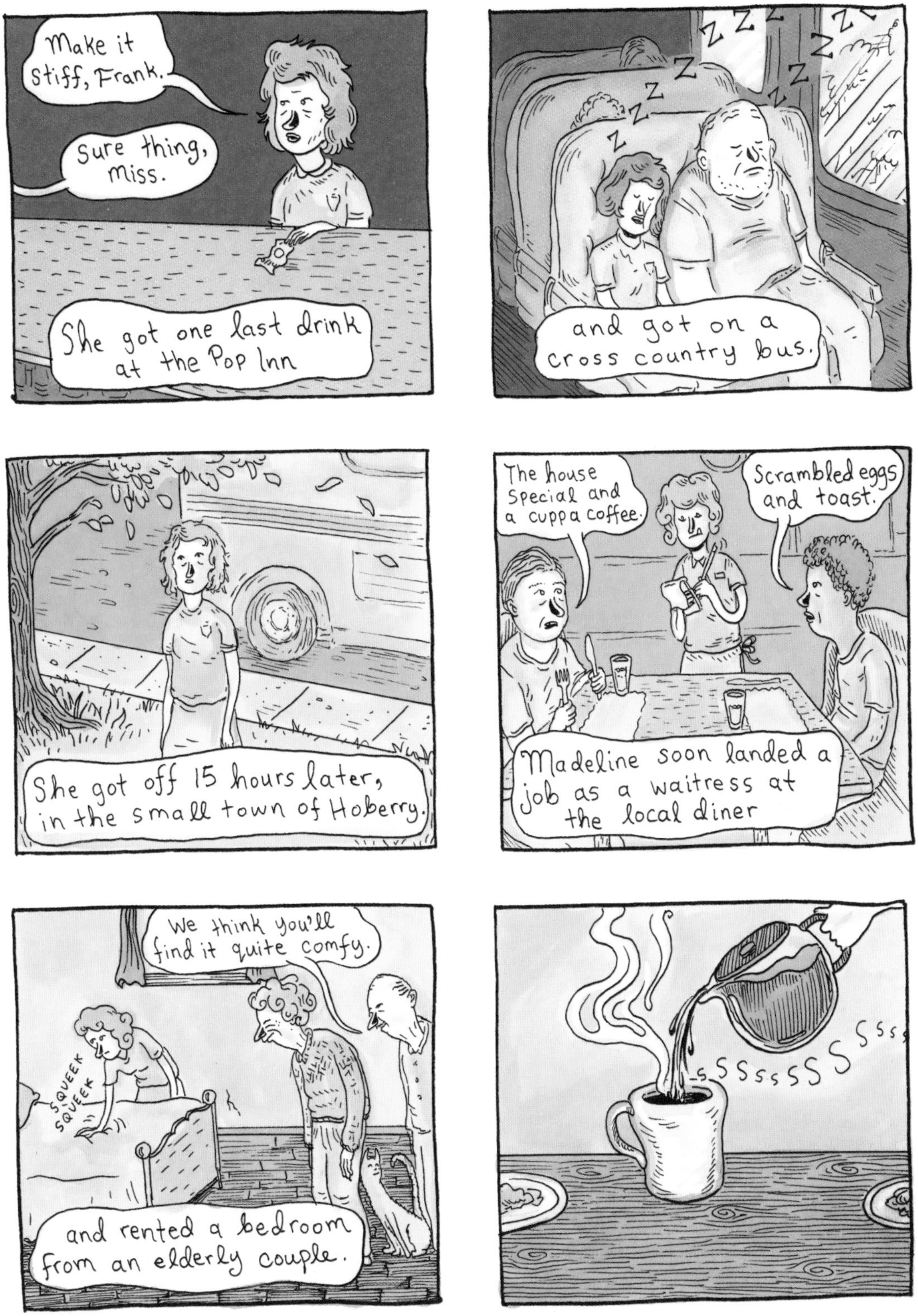
Make it stiff, Frank.
Sure thing, miss.
She got one last drink at the Pop Inn
Z Z Z Z Z Z Z Z Z Z
and got on a cross country bus.
She got off 15 hours later, in the small town of Hoberry.
The house Special and a cuppa coffee.
Scrambled eggs and toast.
Madeline soon landed a job as a waitress at the local diner
We think you'll find it quite comfy.
SQUEEK SQUEEK
and rented a bedroom from an elderly couple.
sSSssSSSSss

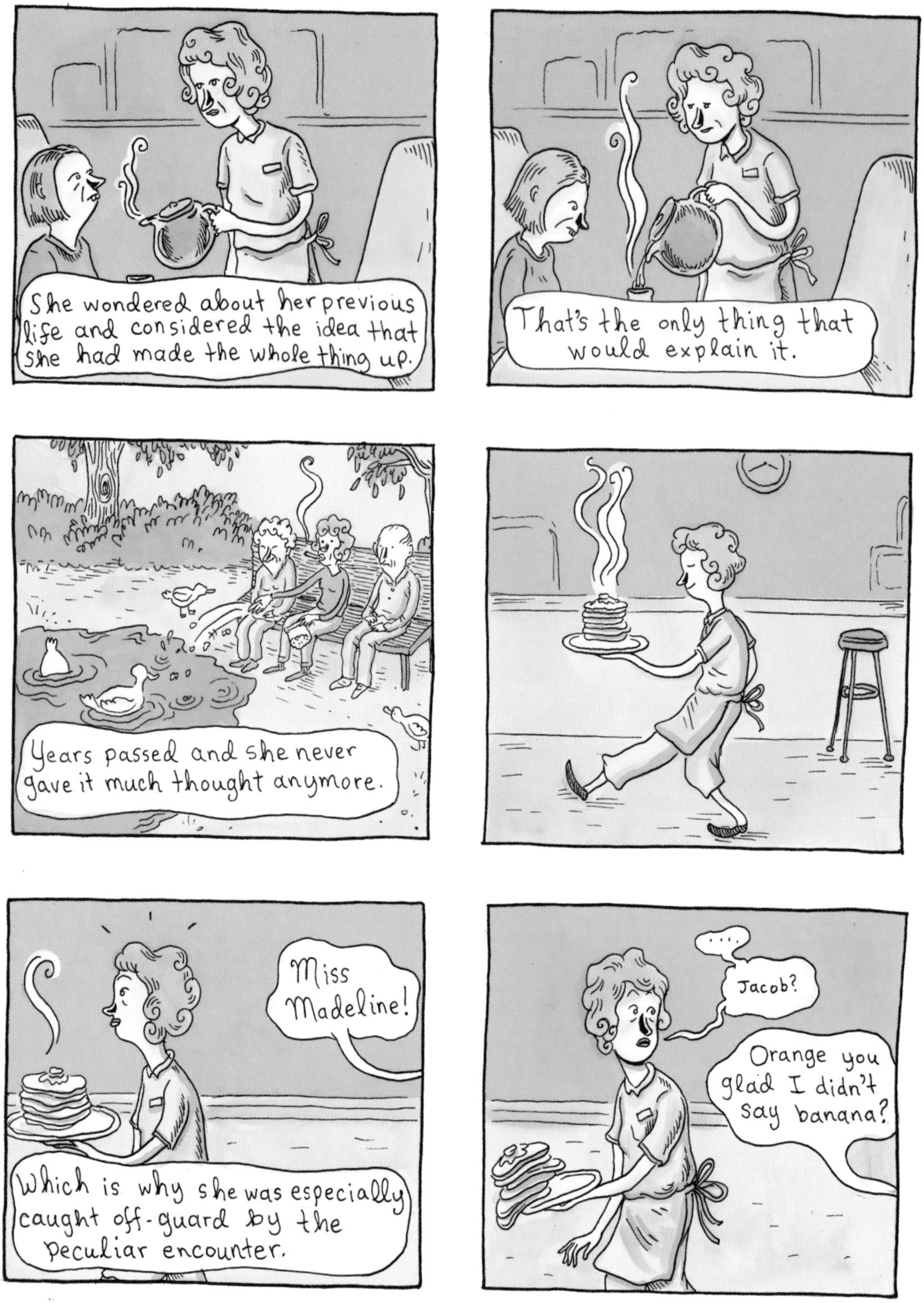
She wondered about her previous life and considered the idea that she had made the whole thing up.
That's the only thing that would explain it.
Years passed and she never gave it much thought anymore.
Miss Madeline!
Which is why she was especially caught off-guard by the peculiar encounter.
...
Jacob?
Orange you glad I didn't say banana?

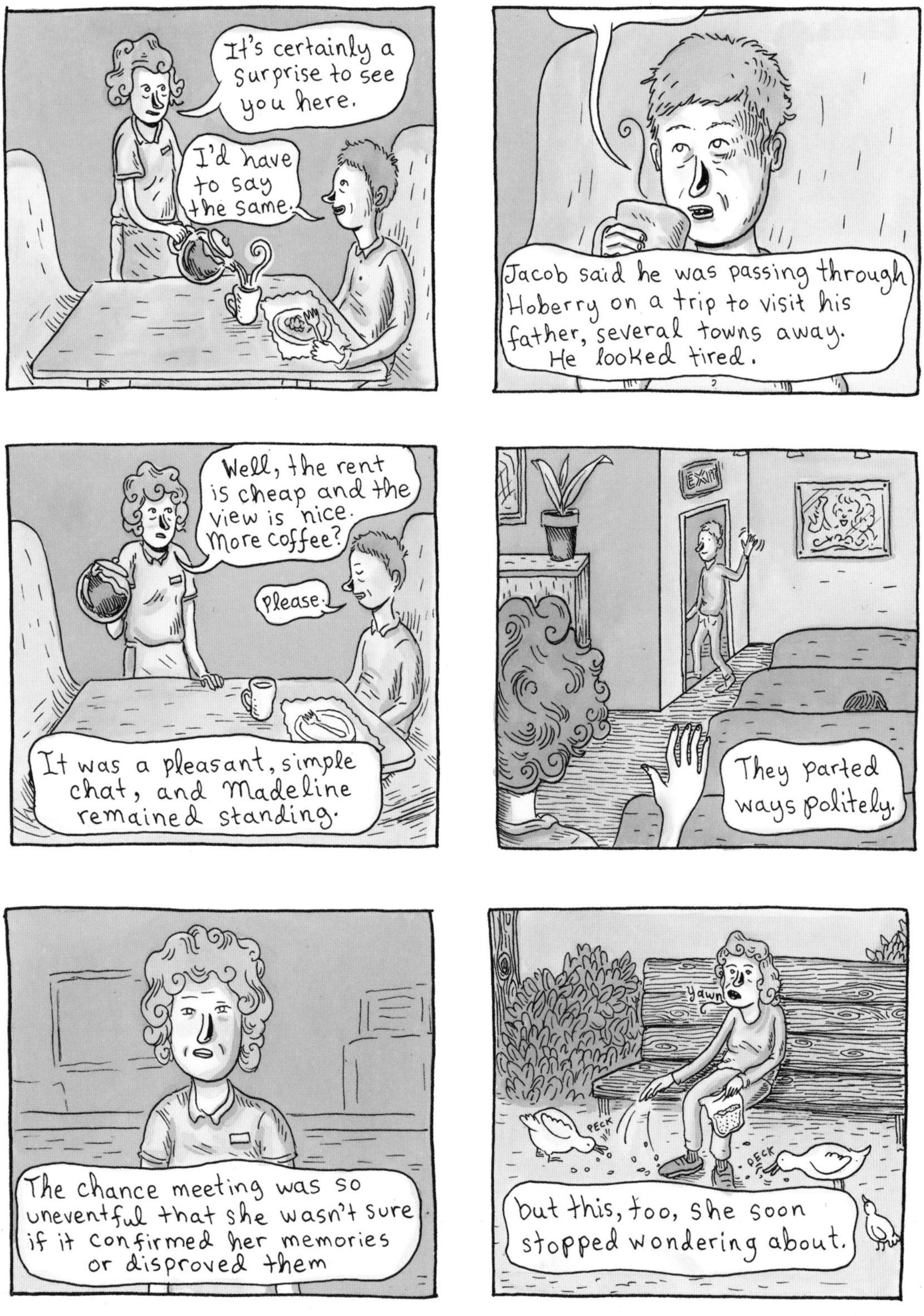
It's certainly a surprise to see you here.
I'd have to say the same.
Jacob said he was passing through Hoberry on a trip to visit his father, several towns away. He looked tired.
Well, the rent is cheap and the view is nice. More coffee?
Please.
It was a pleasant, simple chat, and Madeline remained standing.
EXIT
They parted ways politely.
The chance meeting was so uneventful that she wasn't sure if it confirmed her memories or disproved them
yawn
PECK
PECK
but this, too, she soon stopped wondering about.

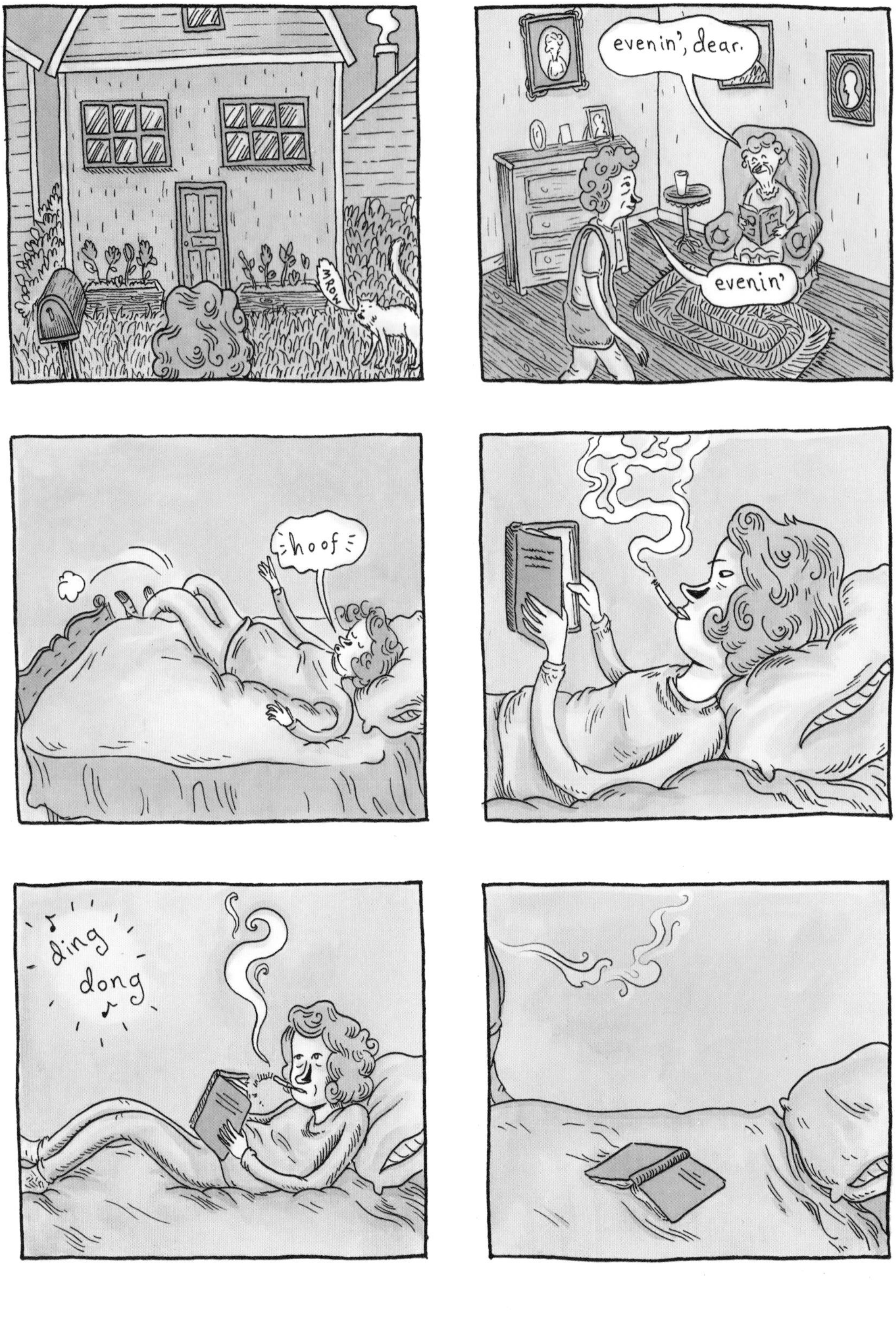
MROW
evenin', dear.
evenin'
hoof
ding dong

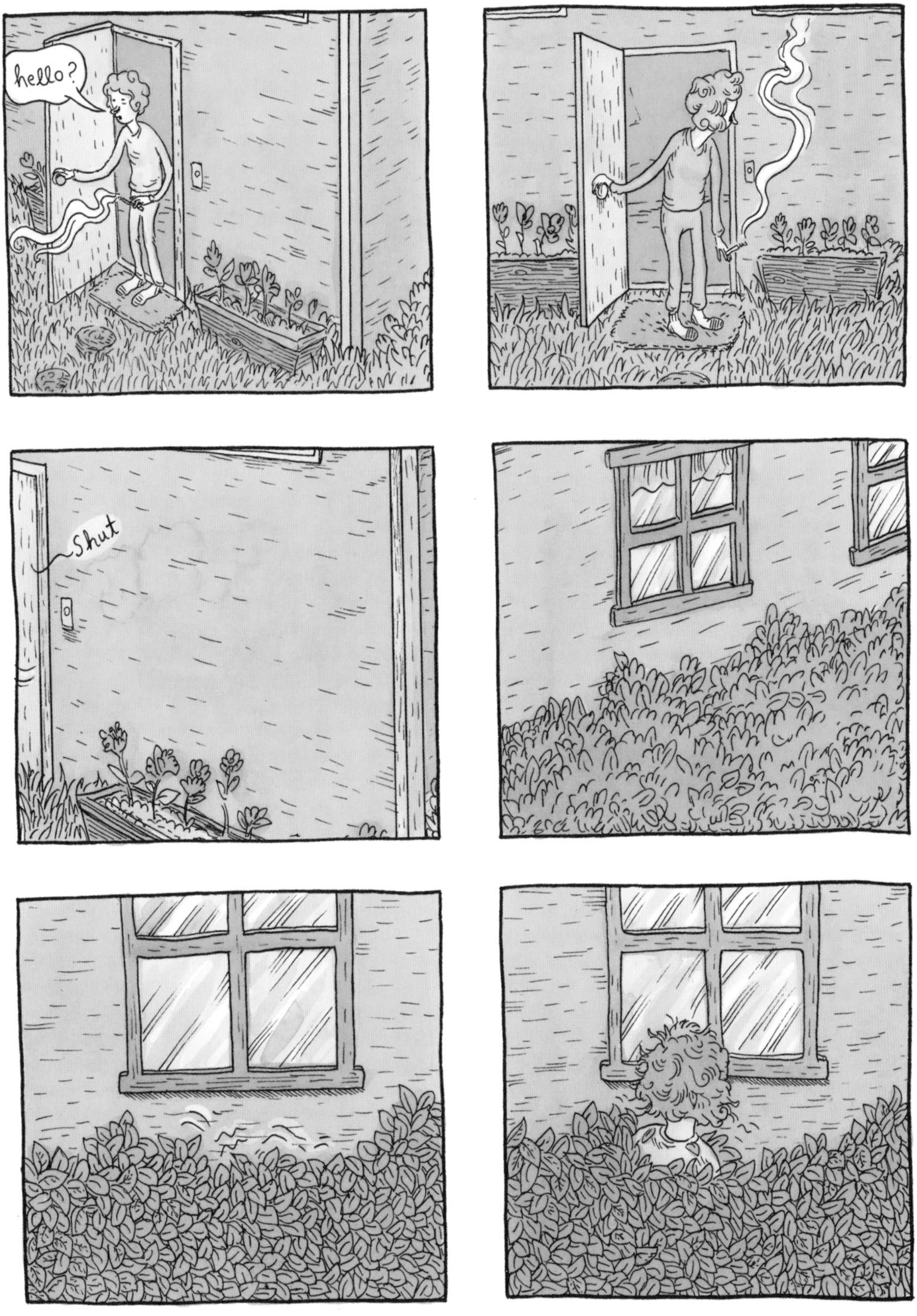
hello?
Shut

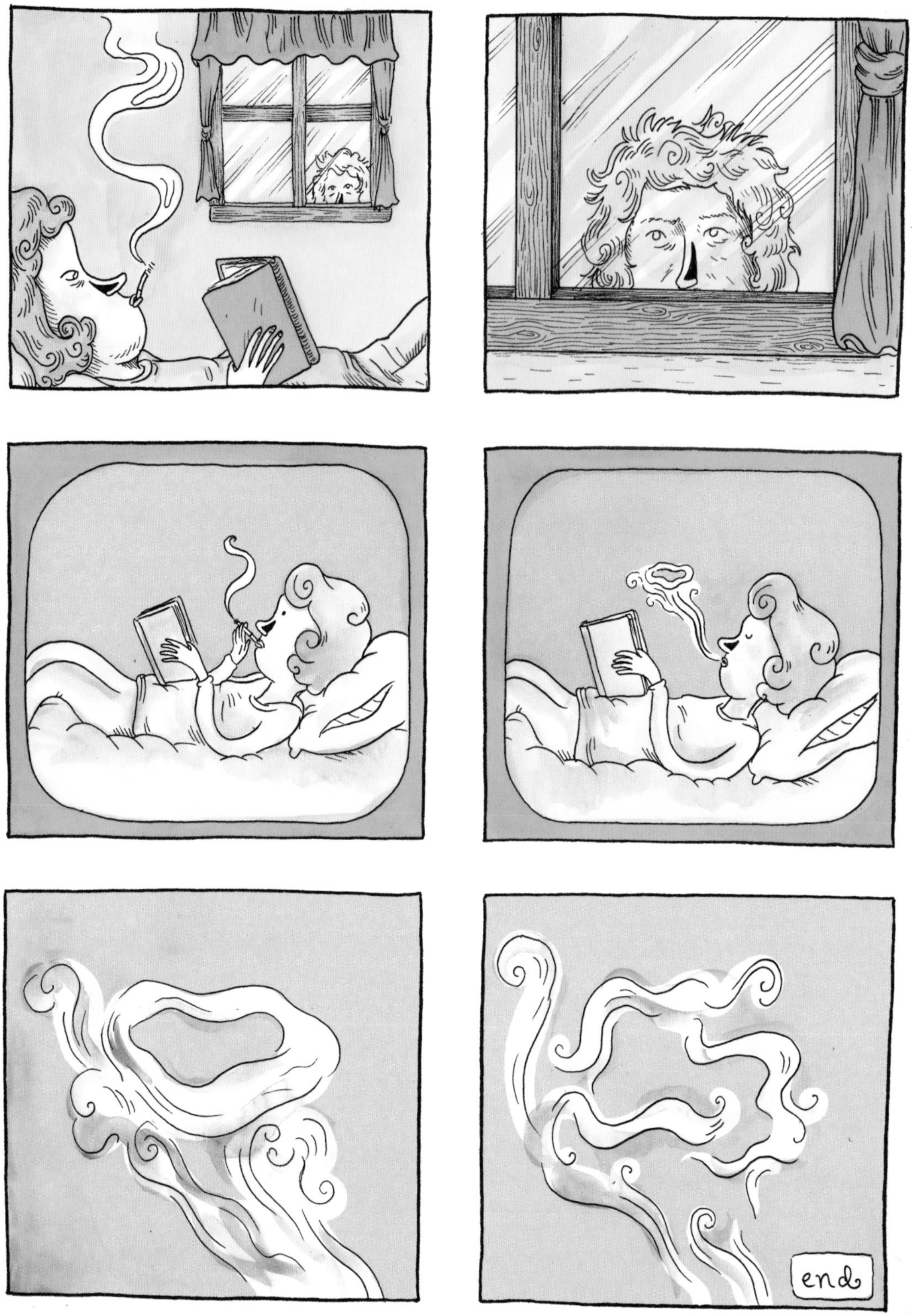
end

the
Carnival

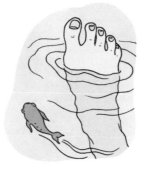

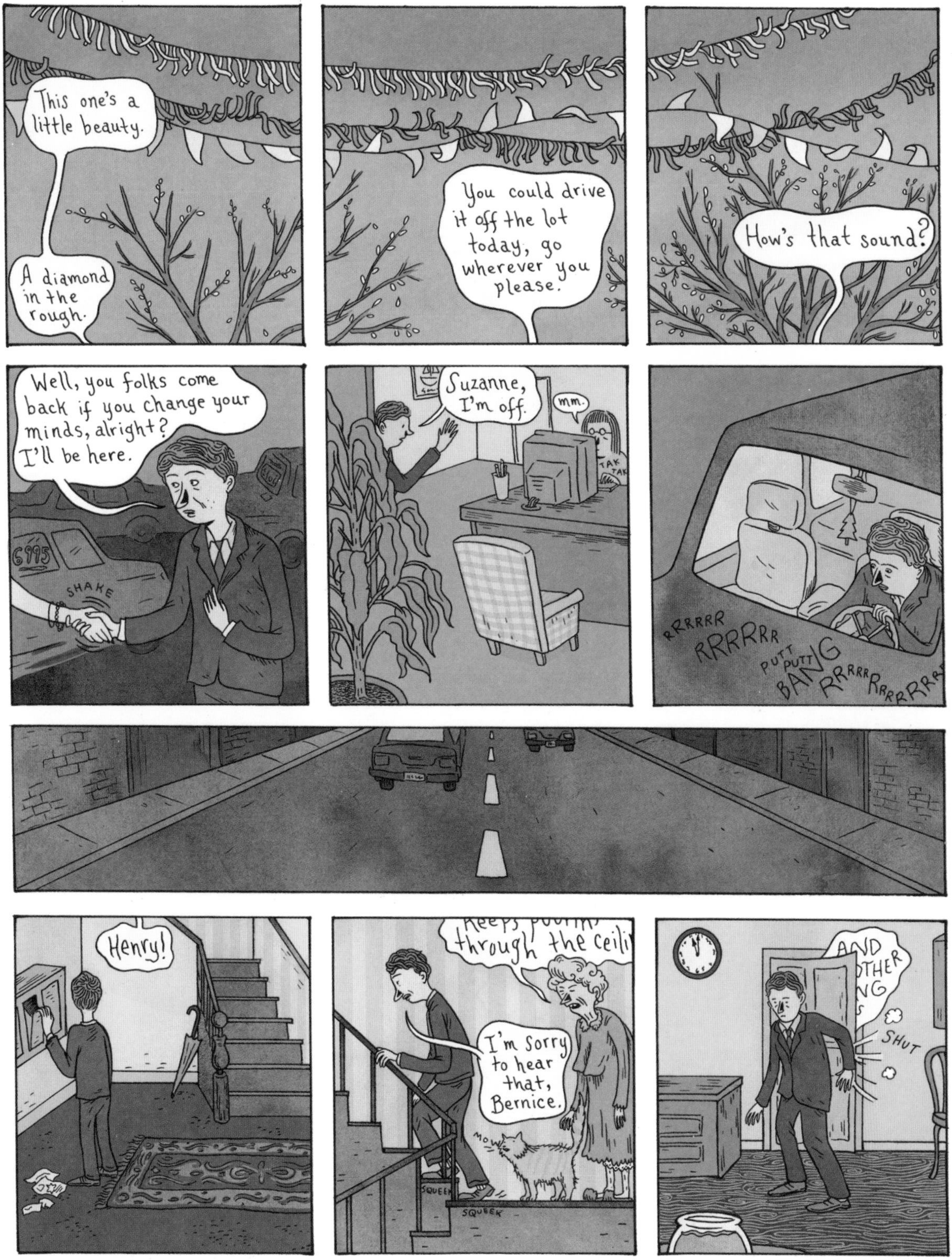
This one's a little beauty.
A diamond in the rough.
You could drive it off the lot today, go wherever you please.
How's that sound?
Well, you folks come back if you change your minds, alright? I'll be here.
6995
SHAKE
Suzanne, I'm off.
mm.
TAK TAK
RRRRRR
RRRRRR
PUTT PUTT
BANG
RRRRRRRRRRRR
Henry!
through the ceili
I'm sorry to hear that, Bernice.
MOW
SQUEEK
SQUEEK
SHUT

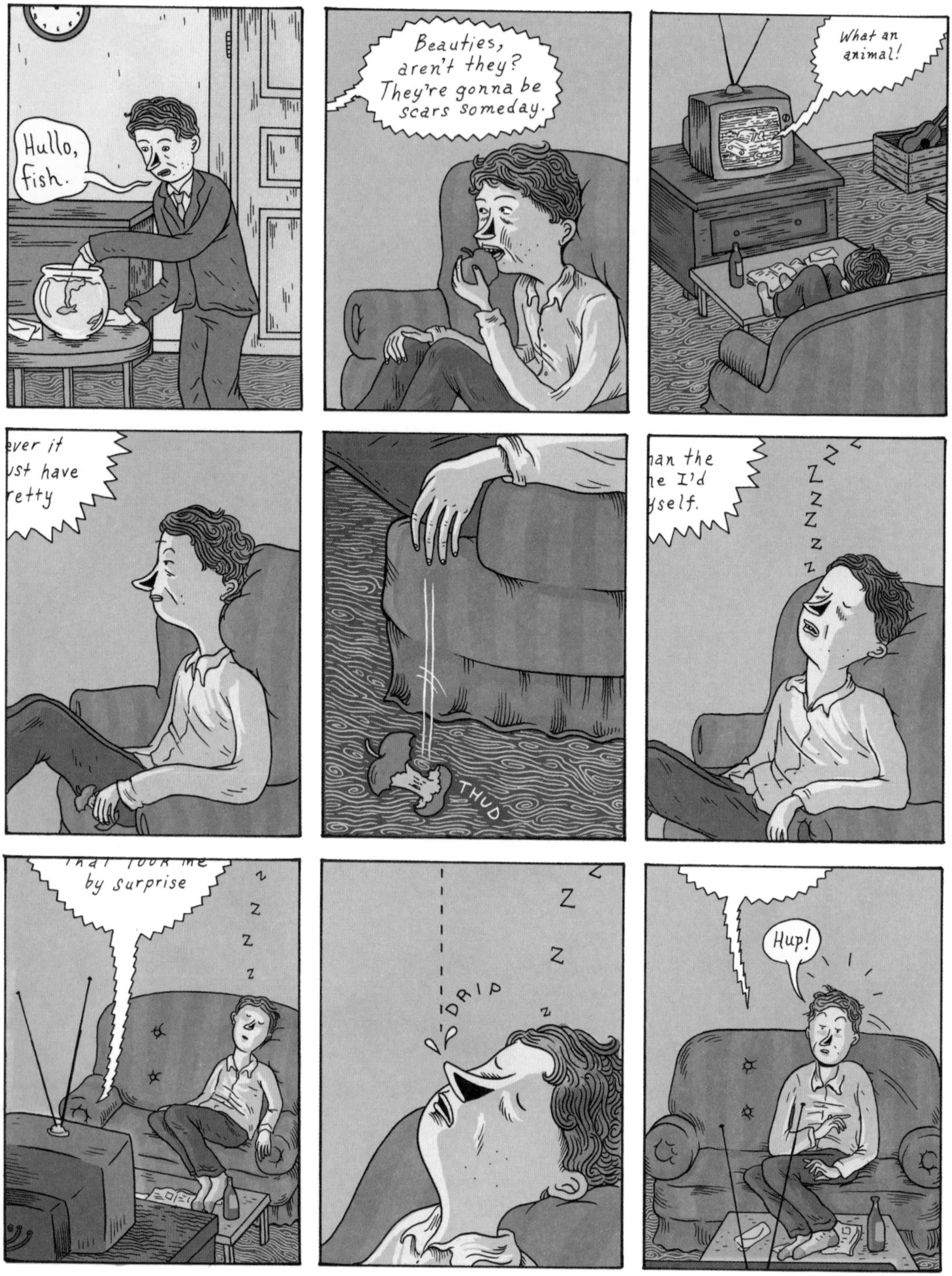
Hullo, fish.
Beauties, aren't they? They're gonna be scars someday.
What an animal!
ever it
ust have
retty
THUD
an the
e I'd
yself.
Z Z Z Z Z Z Z
by surprise
Z Z Z Z
Z Z Z
DRIP
Z
Hup!

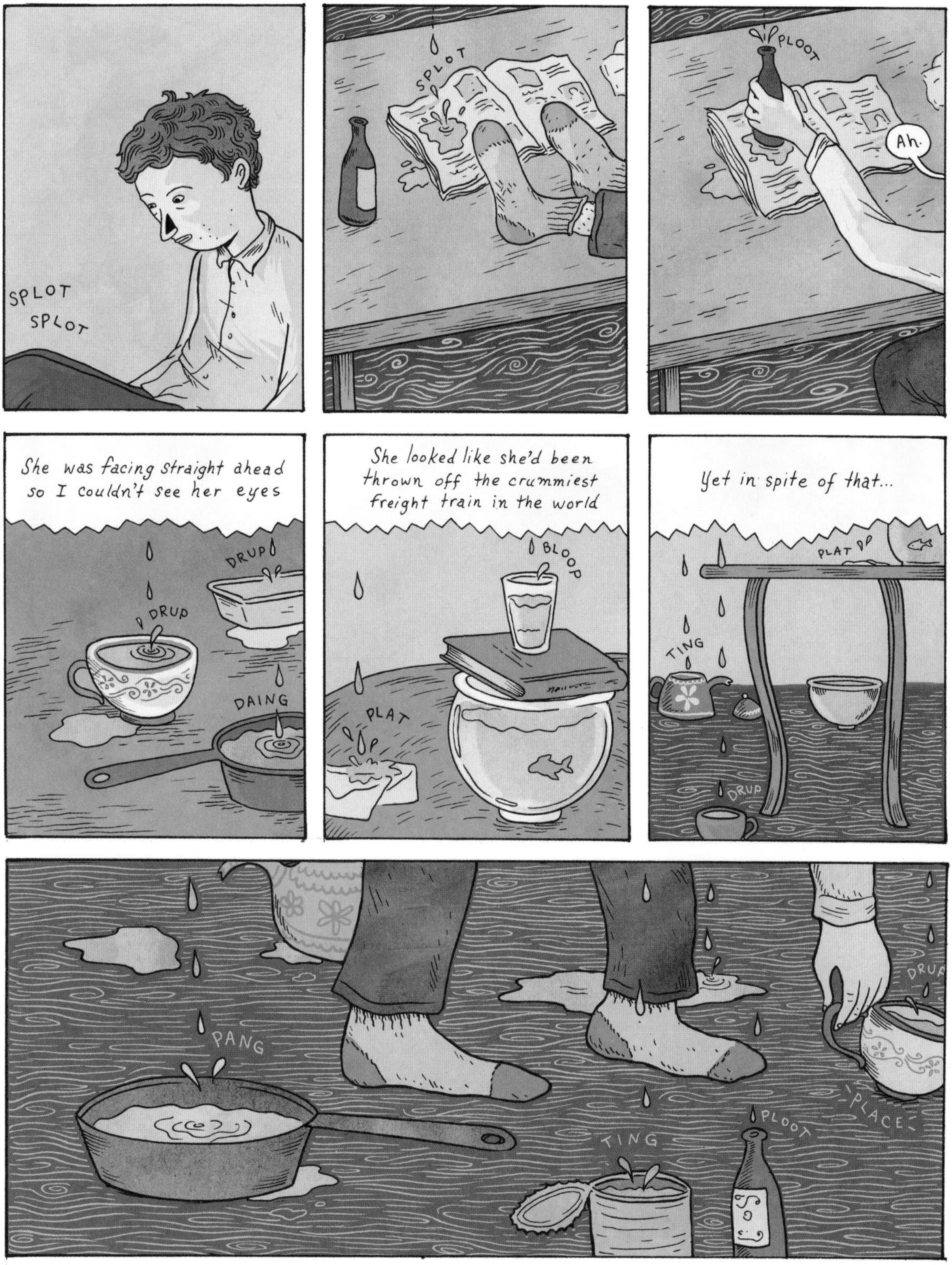
SPLOT
SPLOT
SPLOT
PLOOT
Ah.
She was facing straight ahead so I couldn't see her eyes
DRUP
DRUP
DAING
She looked like she'd been thrown off the crummiest freight train in the world
BLOOP
PLAT
Yet in spite of that...
PLAT
TING
DRUP
PANG
DRUP
TING
PLOOT
PLACE

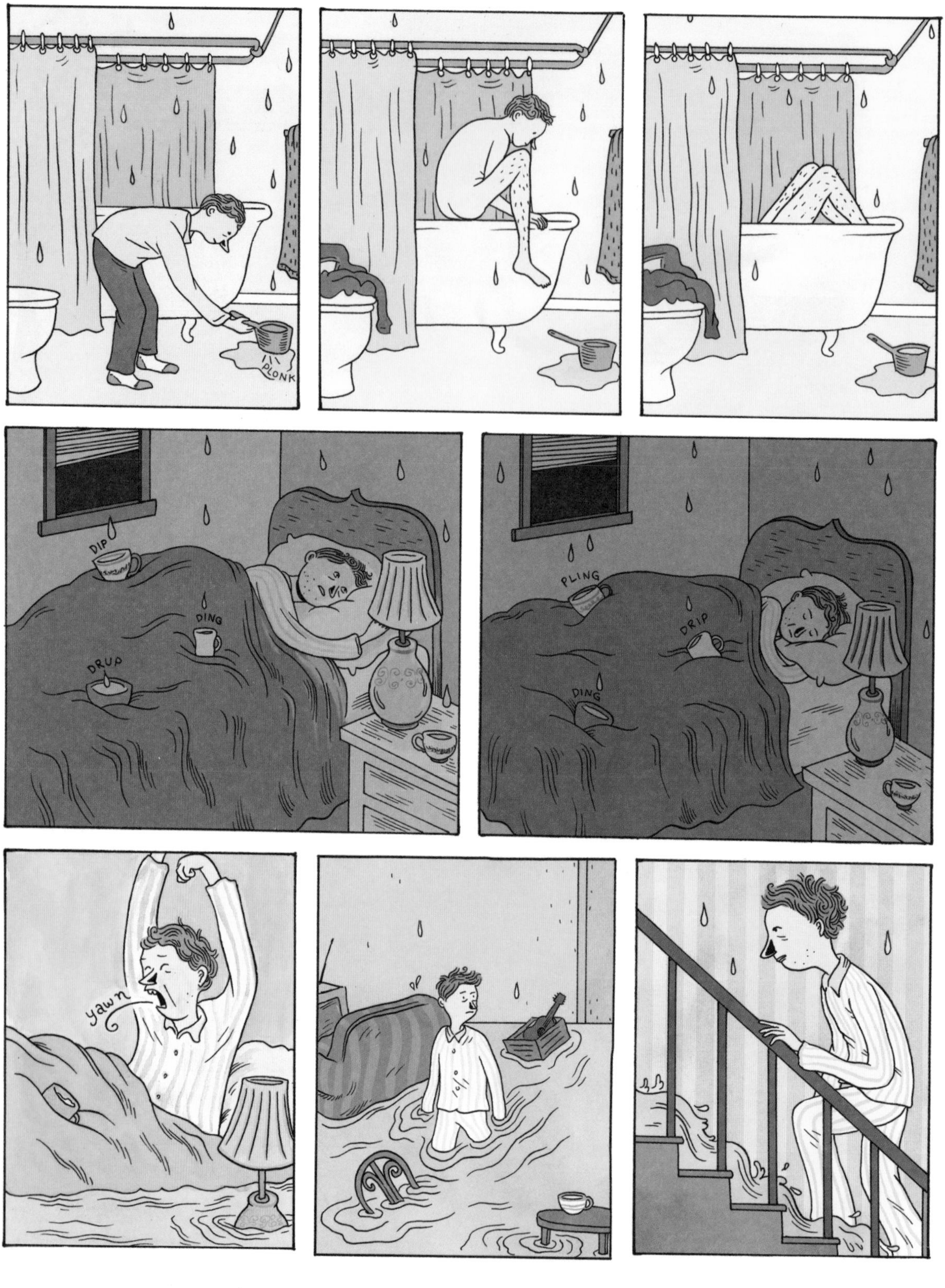
PLONK
DIP
DING
DRUP
PLING
DRIP
DING
yawn

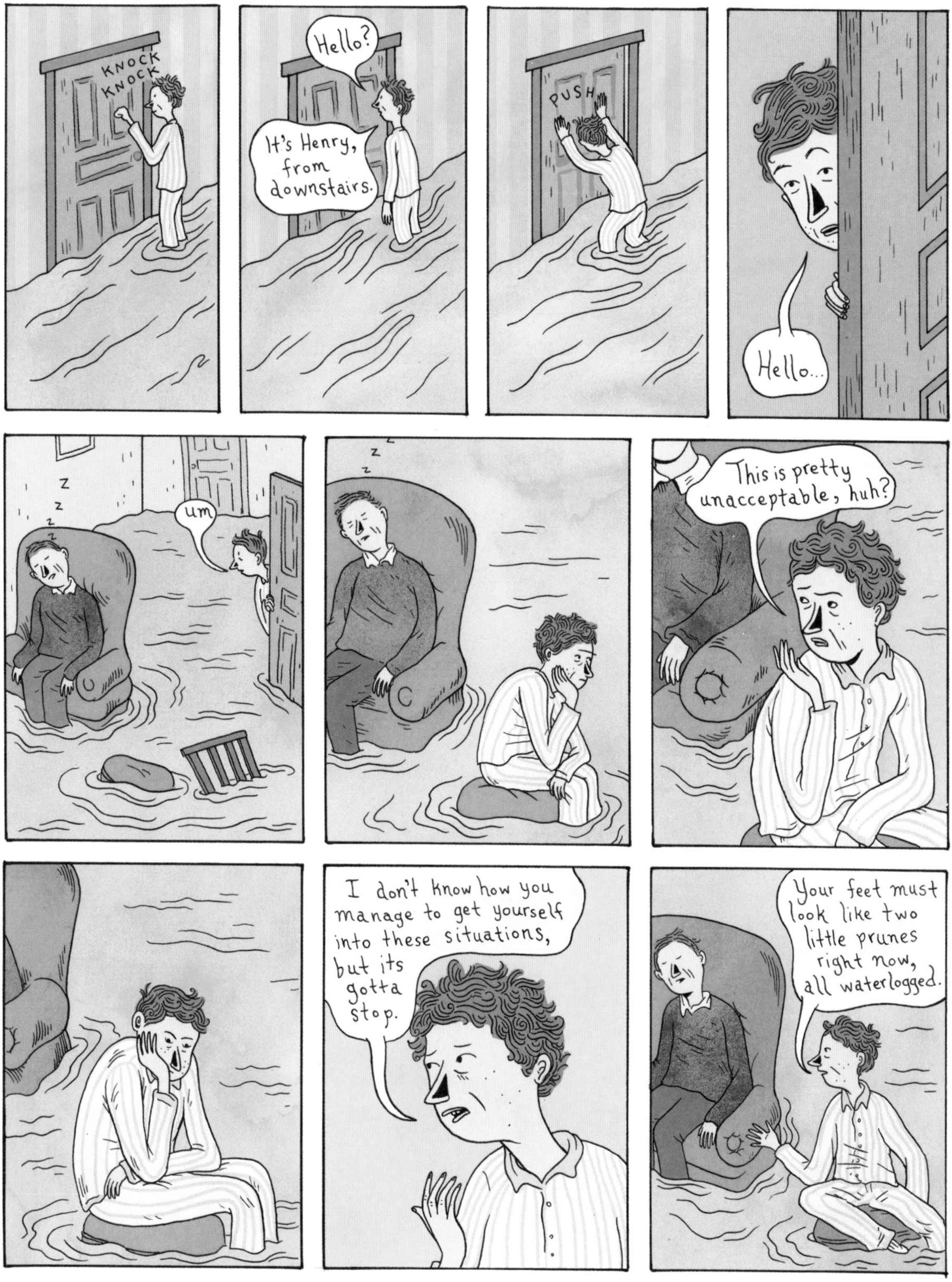
KNOCK KNOCK
Hello?
It's Henry, from downstairs.
PUSH
Hello...
z z z z
um
z z
This is pretty unacceptable, huh?
I don't know how you manage to get yourself into these situations, but its gotta stop.
Your feet must look like two little prunes right now, all waterlogged.

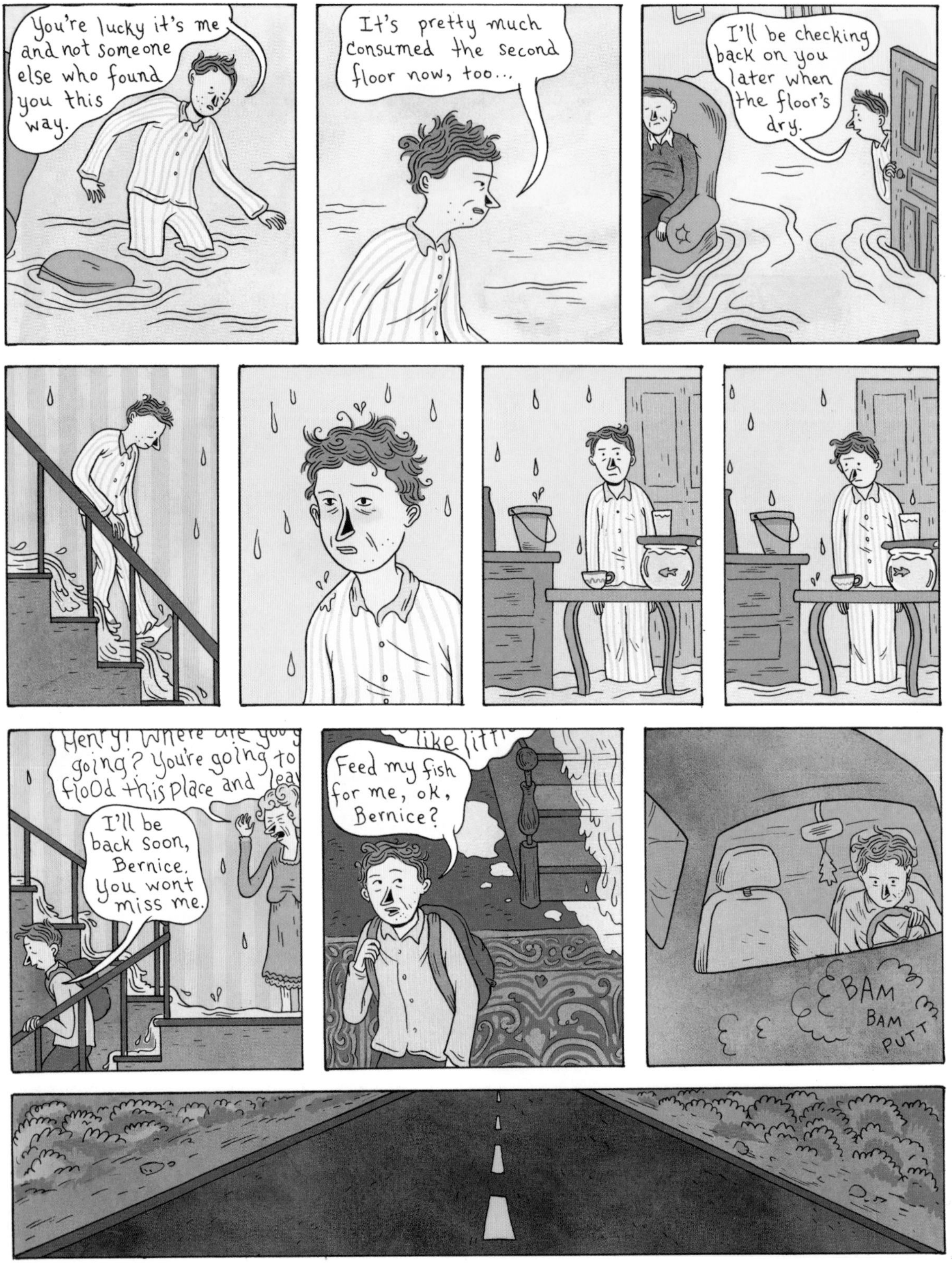
You're lucky it's me and not someone else who found you this way.
It's pretty much consumed the second floor now, too...
I'll be checking back on you later when the floor's dry.
going? You're going to flood this place and
I'll be back soon, Bernice. You wont miss me.
Feed my fish for me, ok, Bernice?
BAM
BAM
PUTT

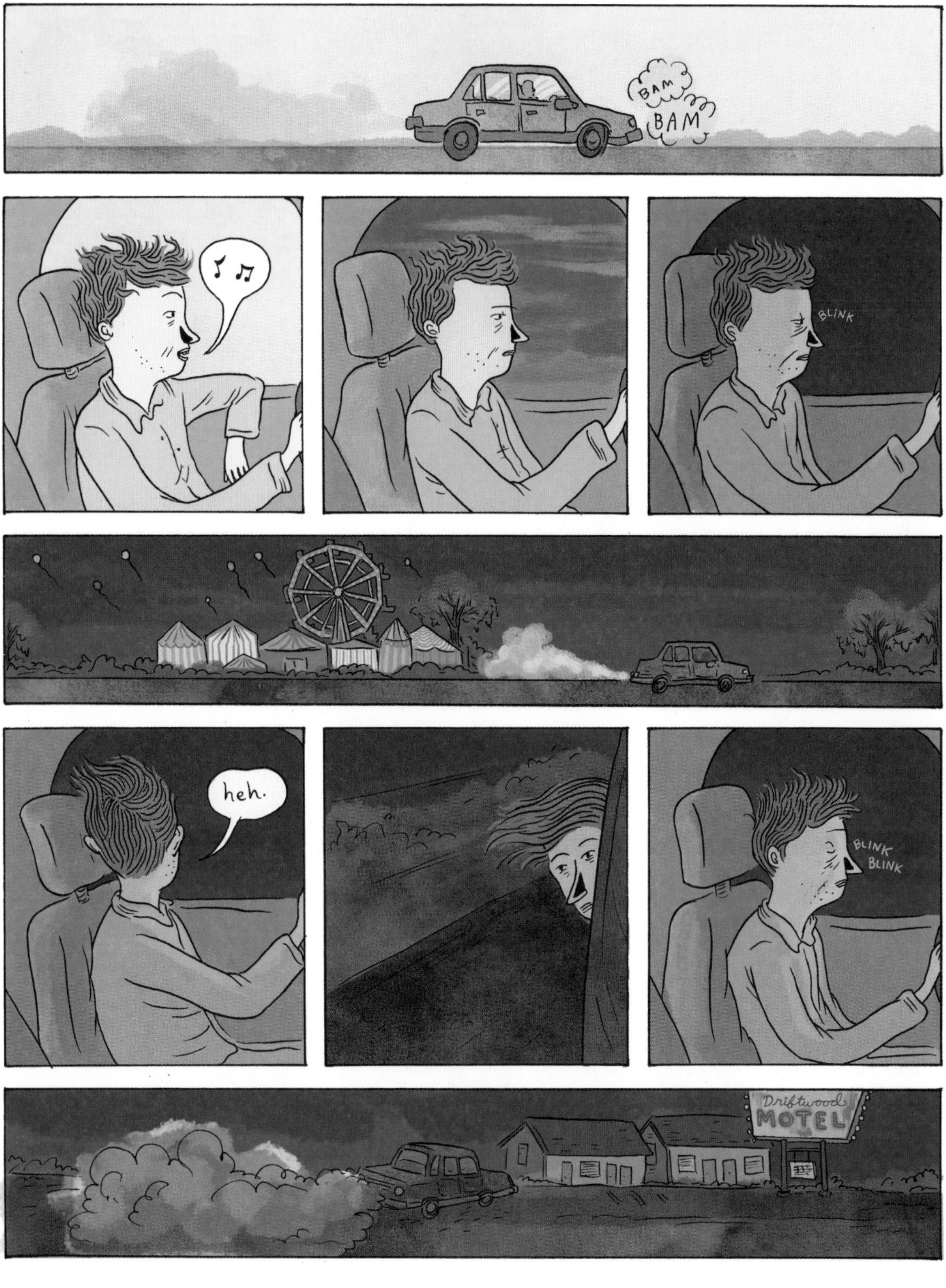
BAM
BAM
♪ ♫
BLINK
heh.
BLINK
BLINK
Driftwood
MOTEL

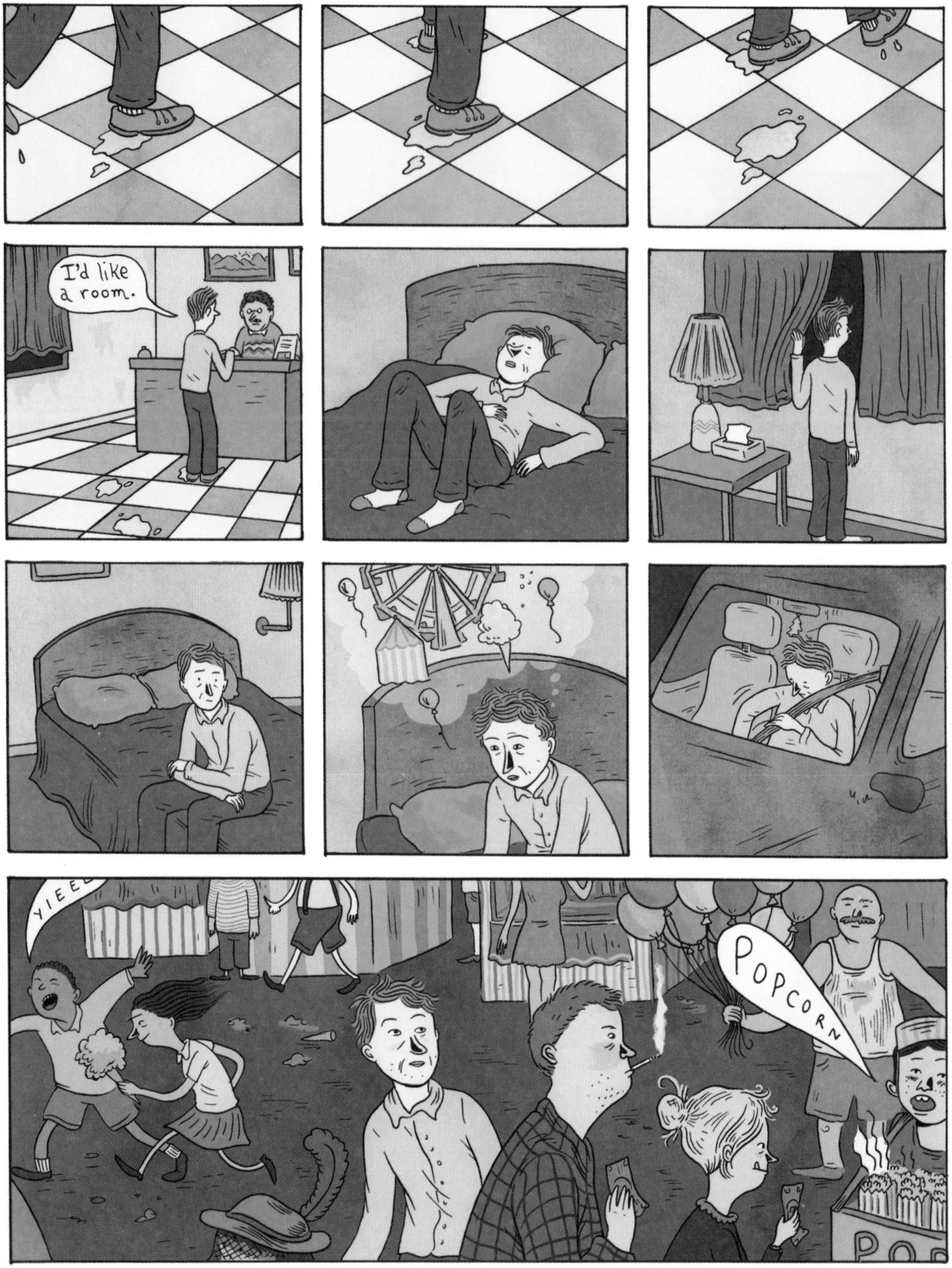
I'd like a room.
POPCORN

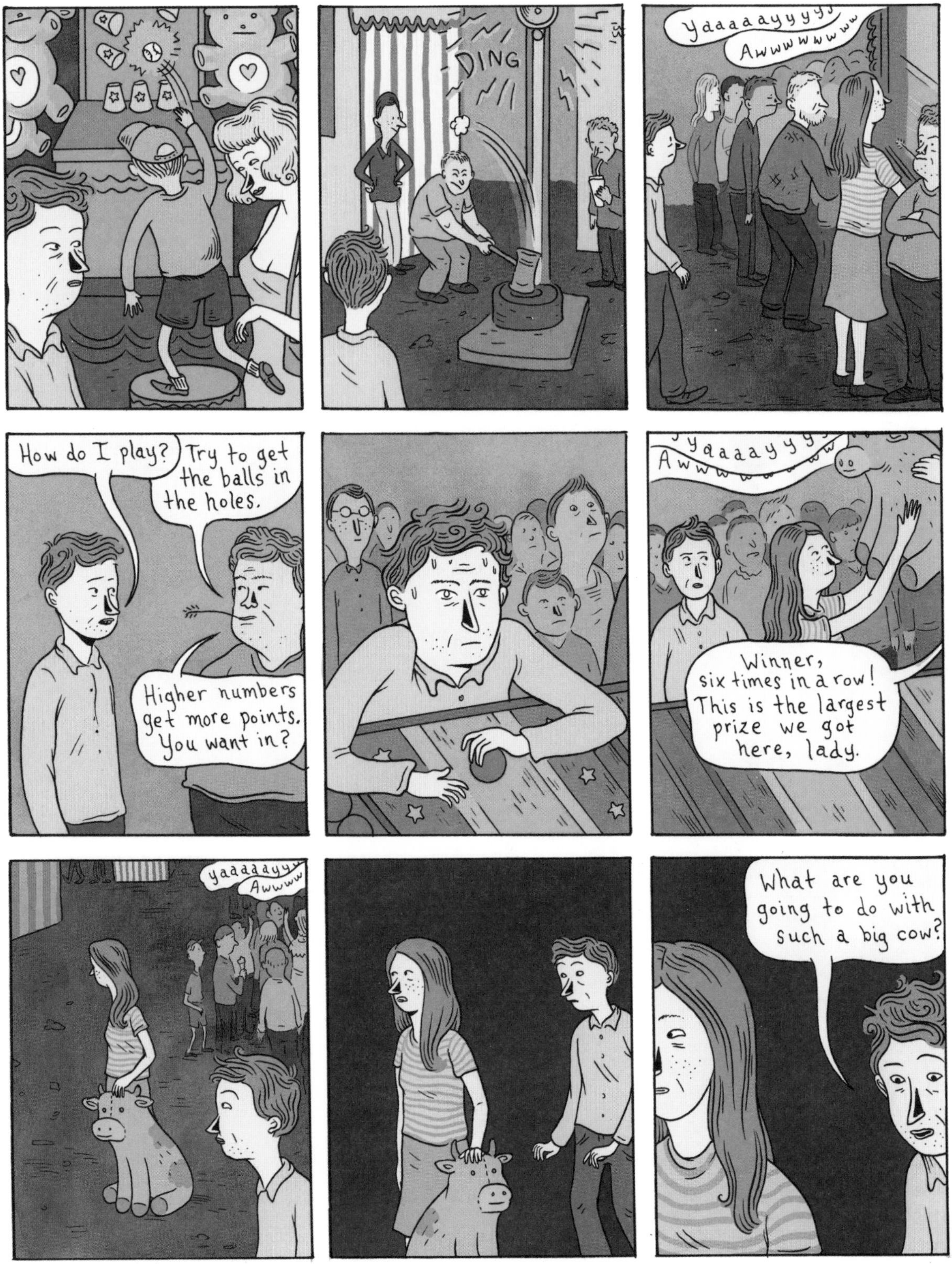
DING
Yaaaaayyyyy
Awwwwwwww
How do I play?
Try to get the balls in the holes.
Higher numbers get more points. You want in?
Yaaaayyyy
Awwwwwwww
Winner, six times in a row! This is the largest prize we got here, lady.
yaaaaayyy
Awwww
What are you going to do with such a big cow?

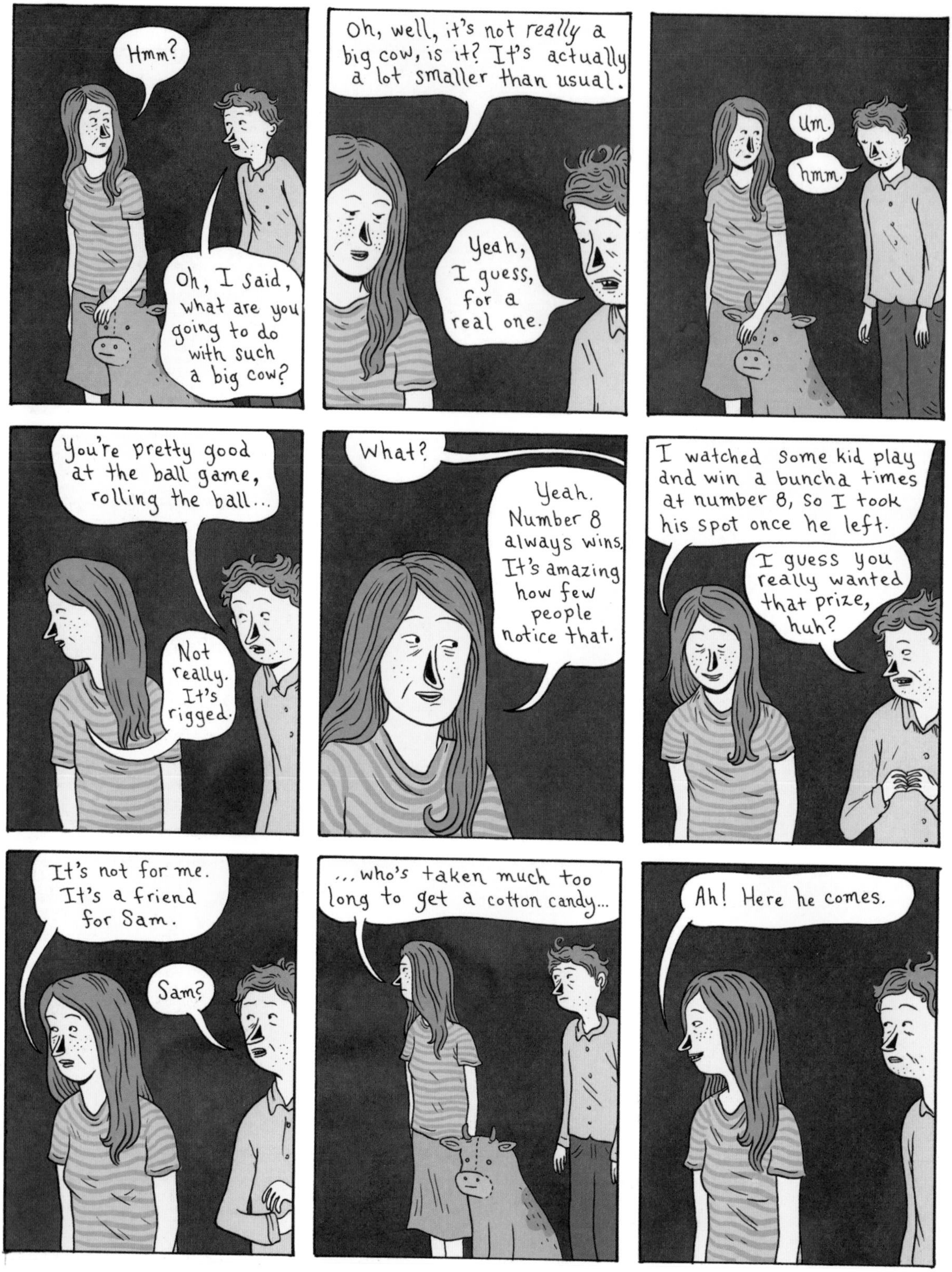

Hmm?
Oh, I said, what are you going to do with such a big cow?
Oh, well, it's not really a big cow, is it? It's actually a lot smaller than usual.
Yeah, I guess, for a real one.
Um.
hmm.
You're pretty good at the ball game, rolling the ball...
Not really. It's rigged.
What?
Yeah. Number 8 always wins. It's amazing how few people notice that.
I watched some kid play and win a buncha times at number 8, so I took his spot once he left.
I guess you really wanted that prize, huh?
It's not for me. It's a friend for Sam.
Sam?
...who's taken much too long to get a cotton candy...
Ah! Here he comes.

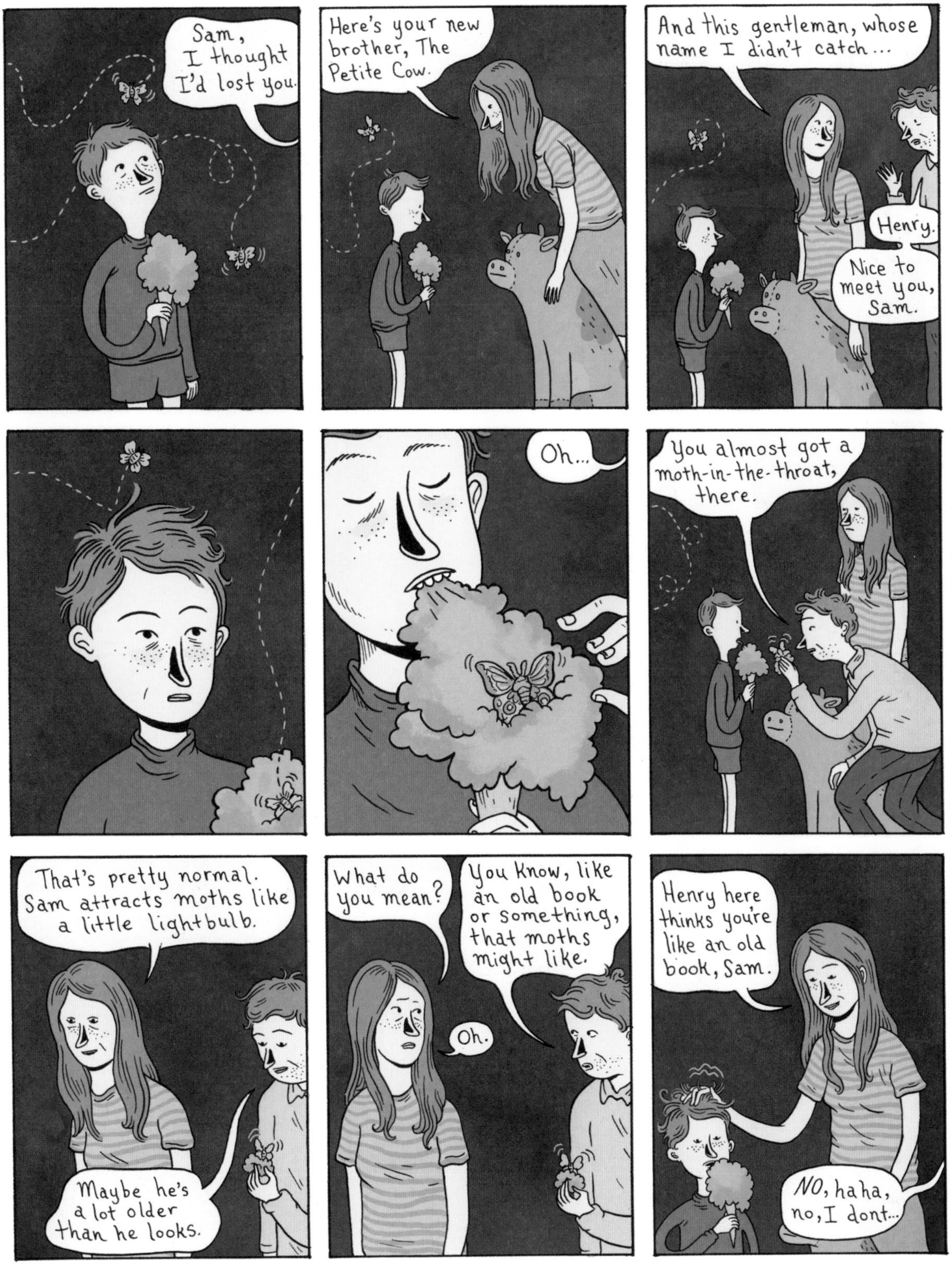
Sam, I thought I'd lost you.
Here's your new brother, The Petite Cow.
And this gentleman, whose name I didn't catch...
Henry.
Nice to meet you, Sam.
Oh...
You almost got a moth-in-the-throat, there.
That's pretty normal. Sam attracts moths like a little lightbulb.
Maybe he's a lot older than he looks.
What do you mean?
You know, like an old book or something, that moths might like.
Oh.
Henry here thinks you're like an old book, Sam.
NO, haha, no, I dont...

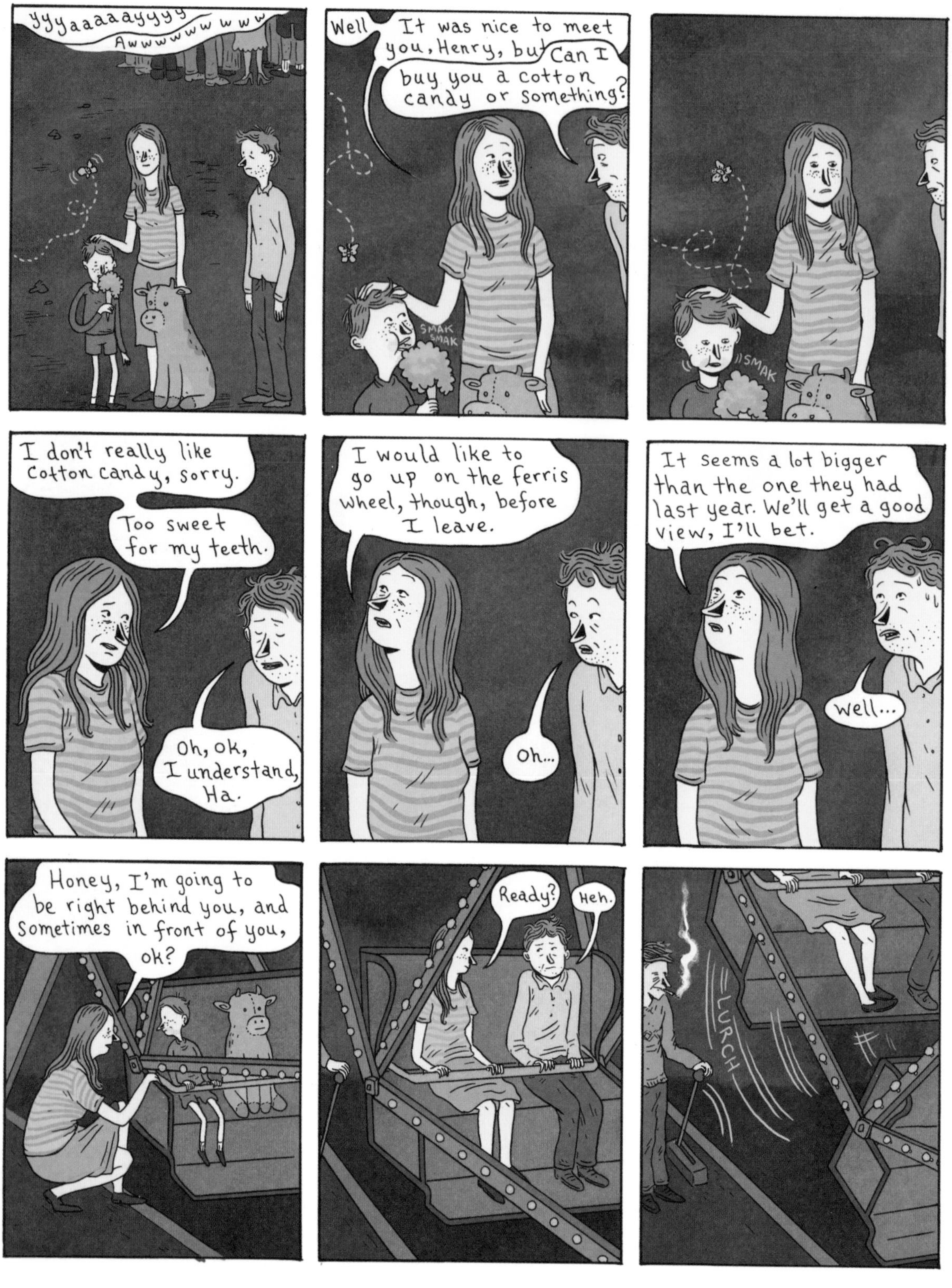
yyyaaaaayyyy
Awwwwwwwww
Well
It was nice to meet you, Henry, but
Can I buy you a cotton candy or something?
SMAK SMAK
SMAK
I don't really like cotton candy, sorry.
Too sweet for my teeth.
Oh, ok, I understand, Ha.
I would like to go up on the ferris wheel, though, before I leave.
Oh...
It seems a lot bigger than the one they had last year. We'll get a good view, I'll bet.
well...
Honey, I'm going to be right behind you, and sometimes in front of you, ok?
Ready?
Heh.
LURCH

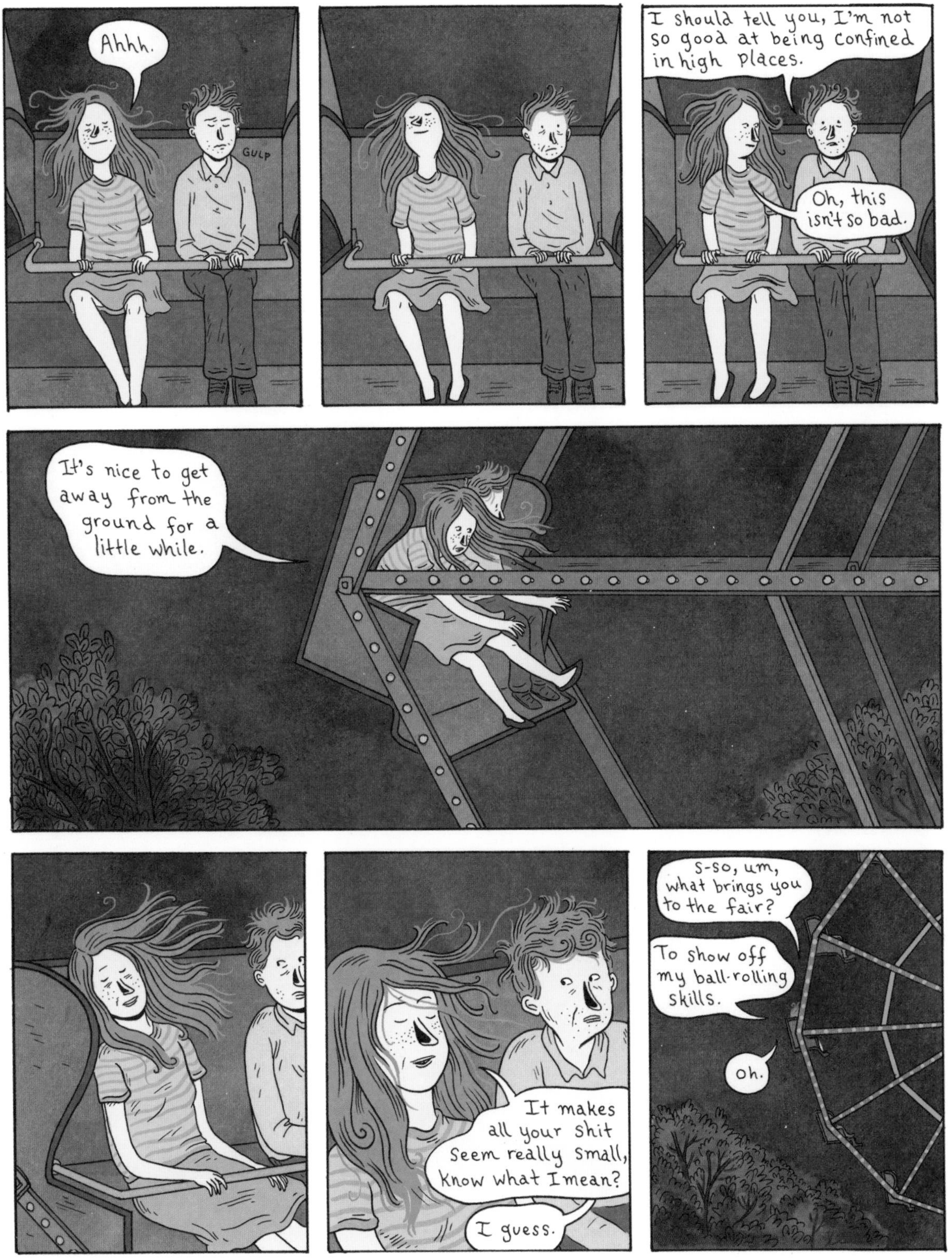
Ahhh.
GULP
I should tell you, I'm not so good at being confined in high places.
Oh, this isn't so bad.
It's nice to get away from the ground for a little while.
It makes all your shit seem really small, know what I mean?
I guess.
S-so, um, what brings you to the fair?
To show off my ball-rolling skills.
Oh.

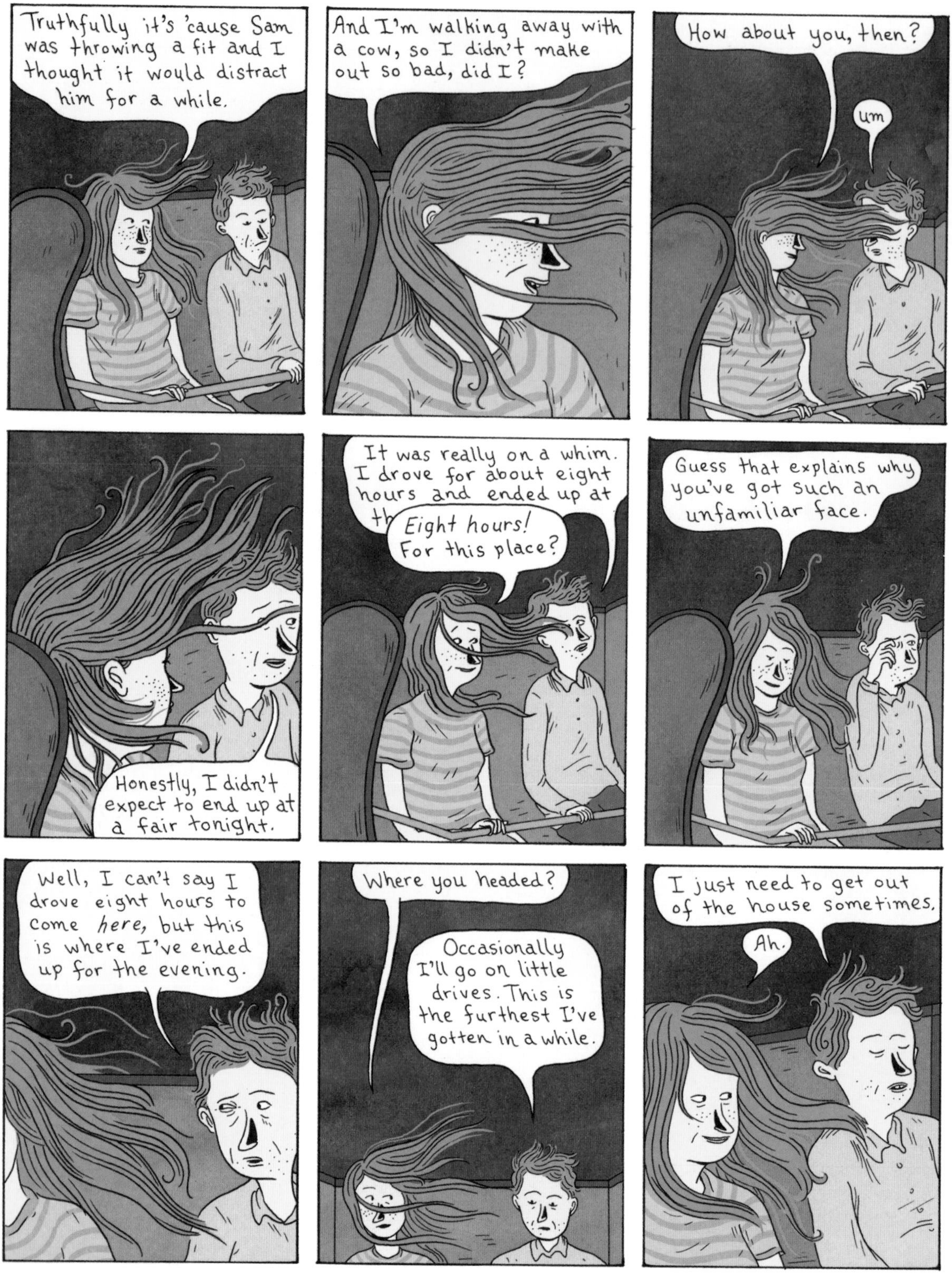
Truthfully it's 'cause Sam was throwing a fit and I thought it would distract him for a while.
And I'm walking away with a cow, so I didn't make out so bad, did I?
How about you, then?
um
Honestly, I didn't expect to end up at a fair tonight.
It was really on a whim. I drove for about eight hours and ended up at th
Eight hours! For this place?
Guess that explains why you've got such an unfamiliar face.
Well, I can't say I drove eight hours to come *here*, but this is where I've ended up for the evening.
Where you headed?
Occasionally I'll go on little drives. This is the furthest I've gotten in a while.
I just need to get out of the house sometimes.
Ah.

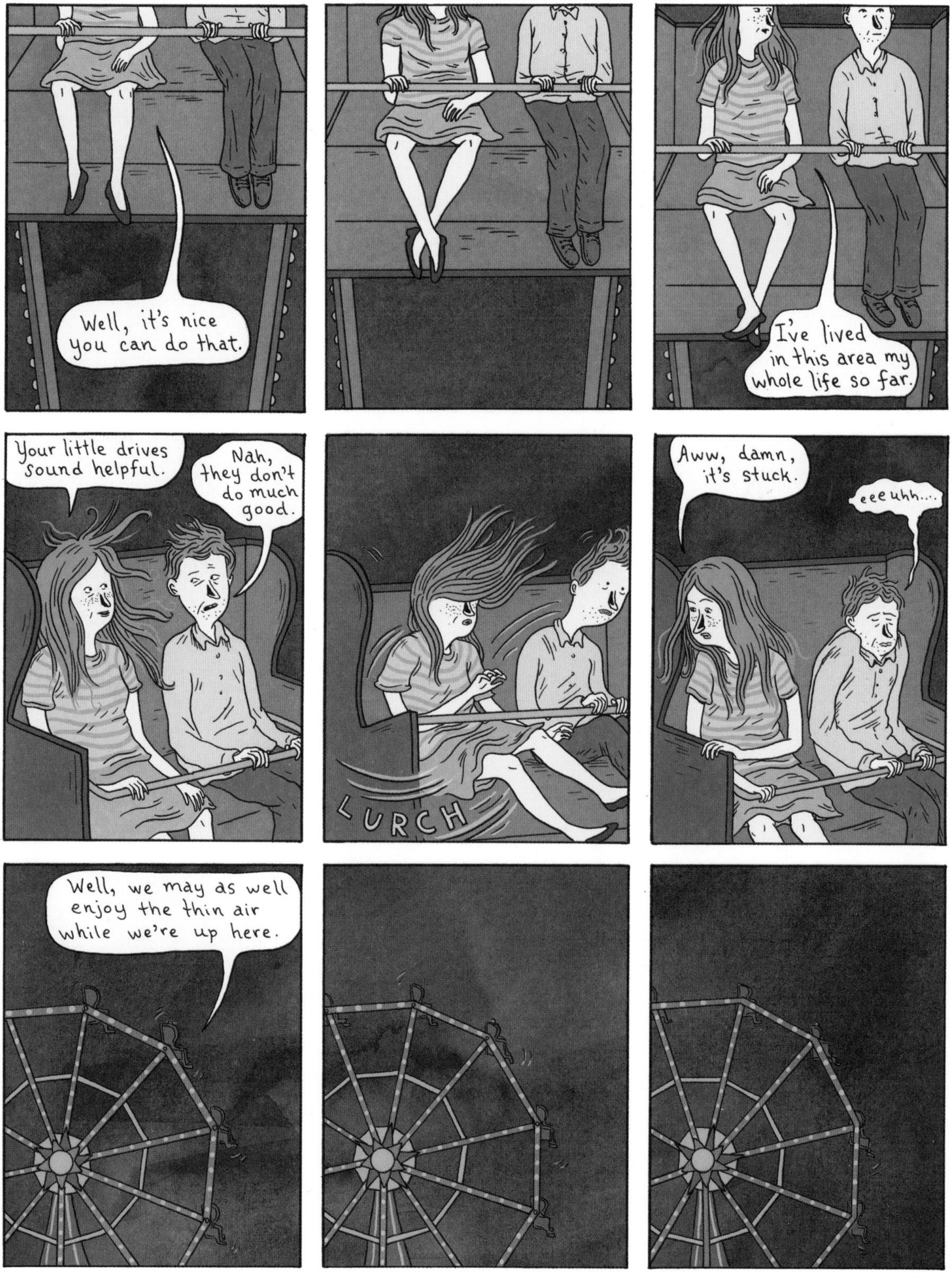
Well, it's nice you can do that.
I've lived in this area my whole life so far.
Your little drives sound helpful.
Nah, they don't do much good.
LURCH
Aww, damn, it's stuck.
eee uhh....
Well, we may as well enjoy the thin air while we're up here.

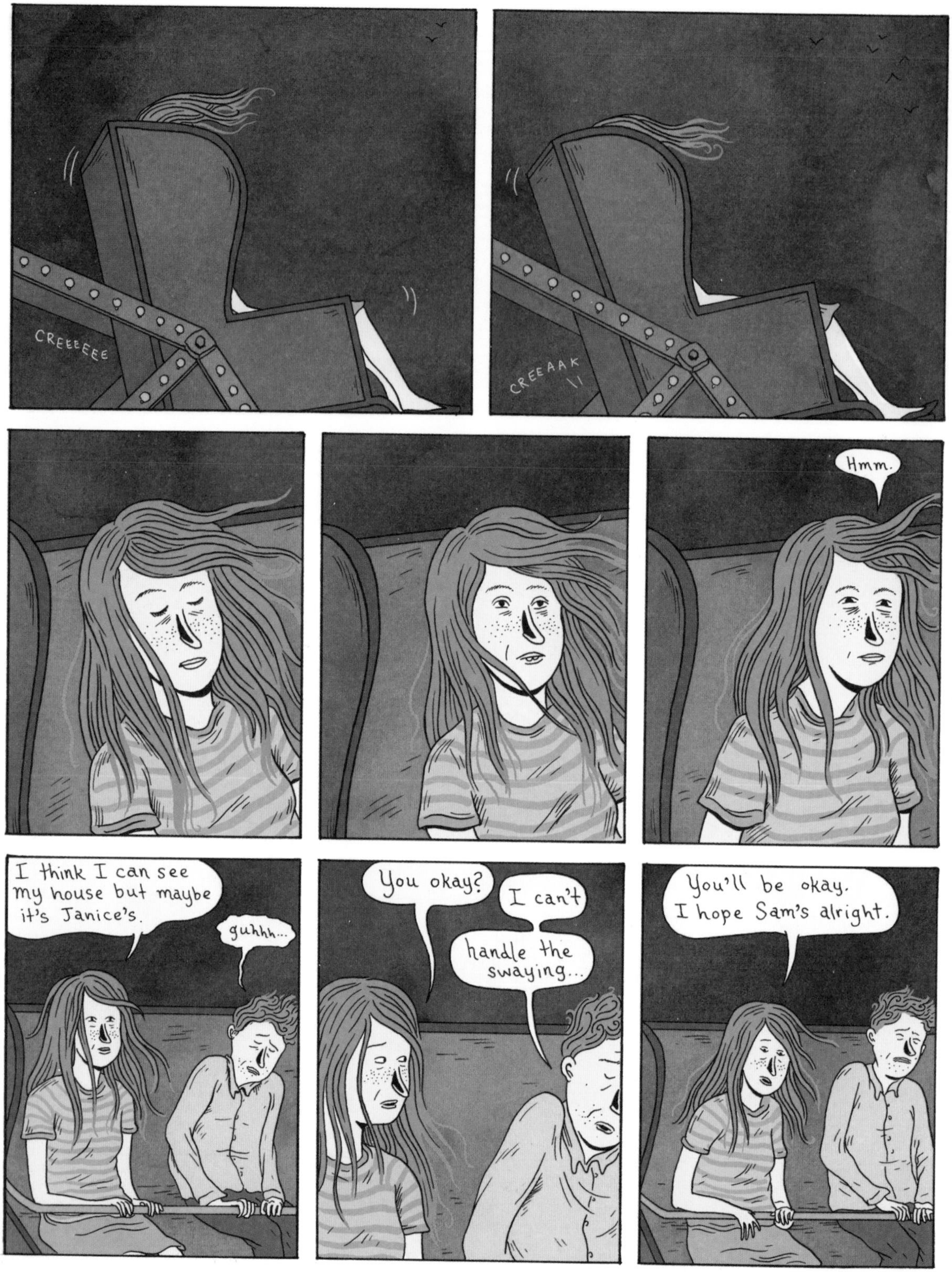
CREEEEEE
CREEAAK
Hmm.
I think I can see my house but maybe it's Janice's.
guhhh...
You okay?
I can't handle the swaying...
You'll be okay. I hope Sam's alright.

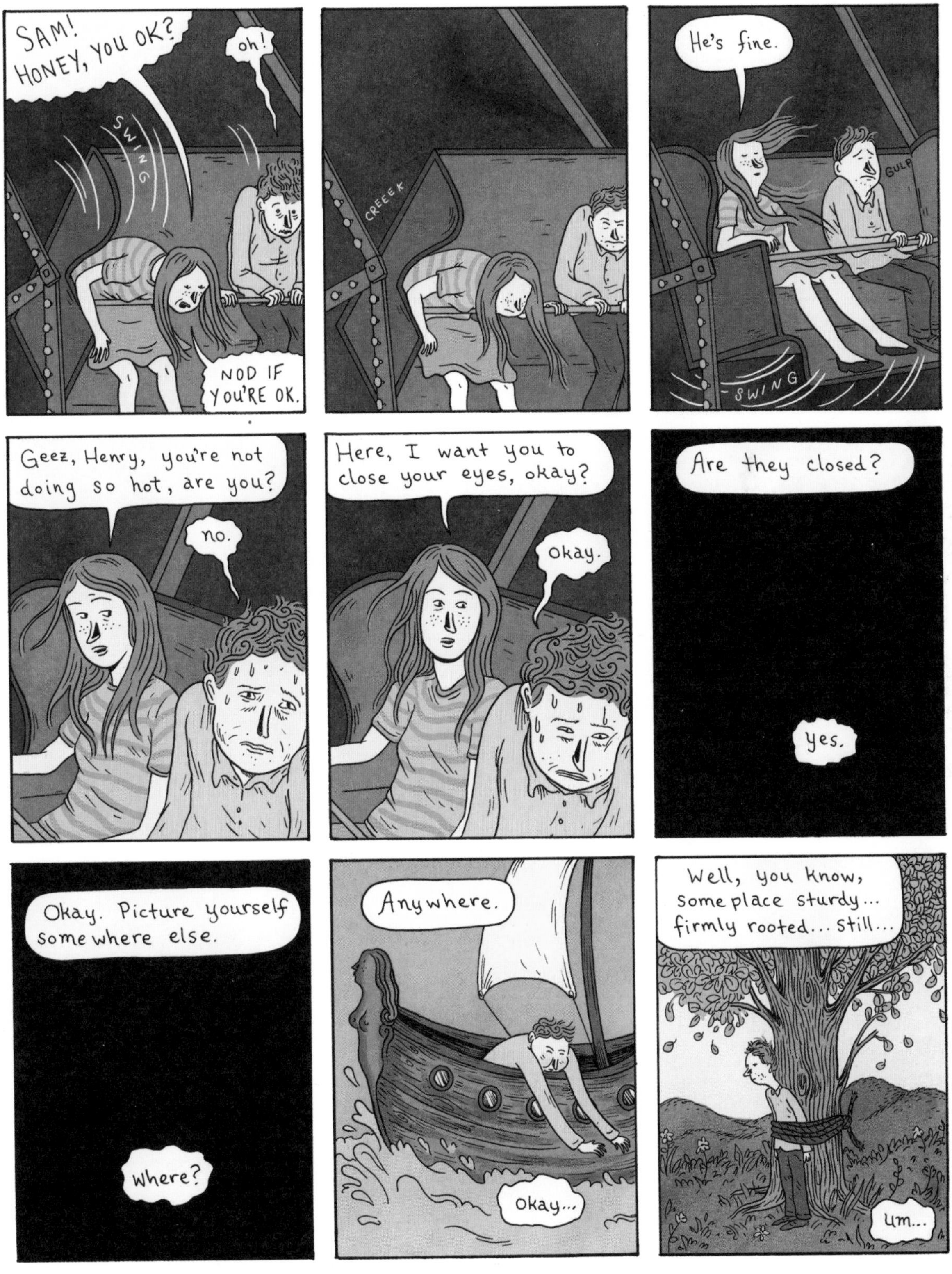
SAM! HONEY, YOU OK?
oh!
SWING
NOD IF YOU'RE OK.
CREEEK
He's fine.
GULP
SWING
Geez, Henry, you're not doing so hot, are you?
no.
Here, I want you to close your eyes, okay?
okay.
Are they closed?
yes.
Okay. Picture yourself somewhere else.
Where?
Anywhere.
okay...
Well, you know, some place sturdy... firmly rooted... still...
um...

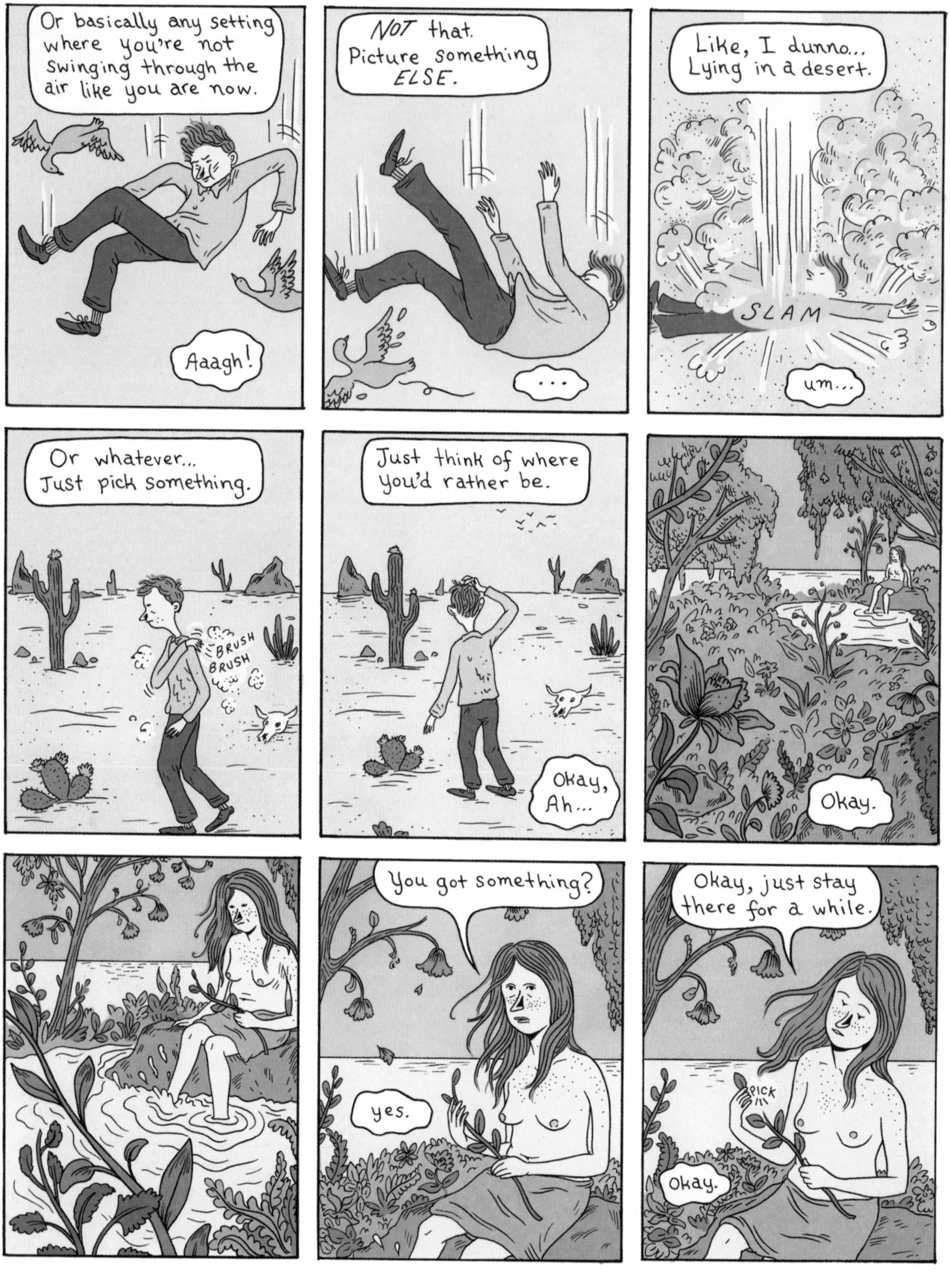
Or basically any setting where you're not swinging through the air like you are now.
Aaagh!
NOT that. Picture something ELSE.
...
Like, I dunno... Lying in a desert.
SLAM
um...
Or whatever... Just pick something.
BRUSH
BRUSH
Just think of where you'd rather be.
Okay, Ah...
Okay.
You got something?
yes.
Okay, just stay there for a while.
PICK
Okay.

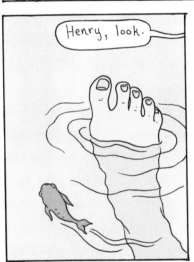

Henry, look.

Hey...

You're on firm ground again.

You still look queasy, Henry. Do you need a ride back anywhere?

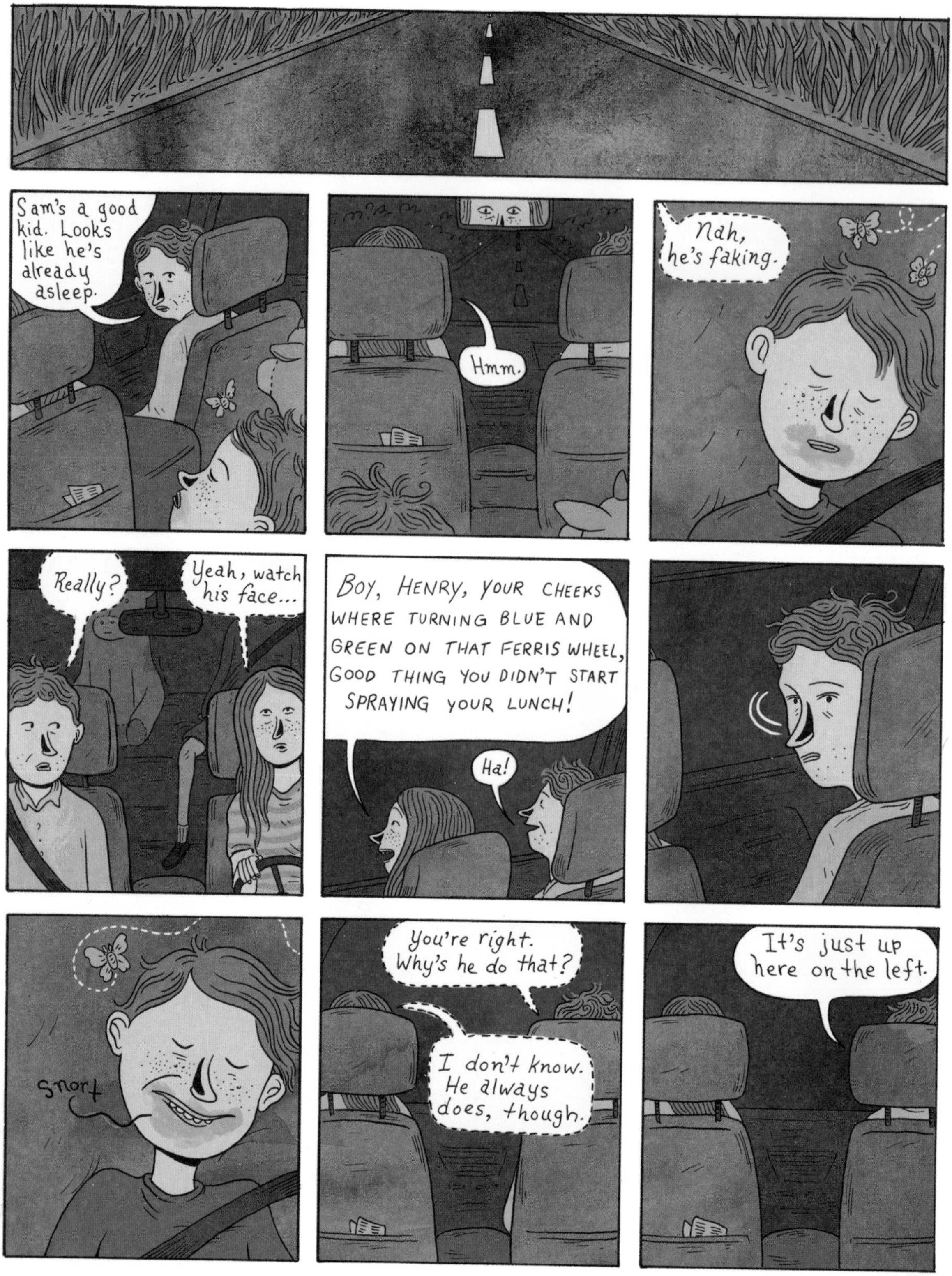
Sam's a good kid. Looks like he's already asleep.
Hmm.
Nah, he's faking.
Really?
Yeah, watch his face...
BOY, HENRY, YOUR CHEEKS WHERE TURNING BLUE AND GREEN ON THAT FERRIS WHEEL, GOOD THING YOU DIDN'T START SPRAYING YOUR LUNCH!
Ha!
Snort
You're right. Why's he do that?
I don't know. He always does, though.
It's just up here on the left.

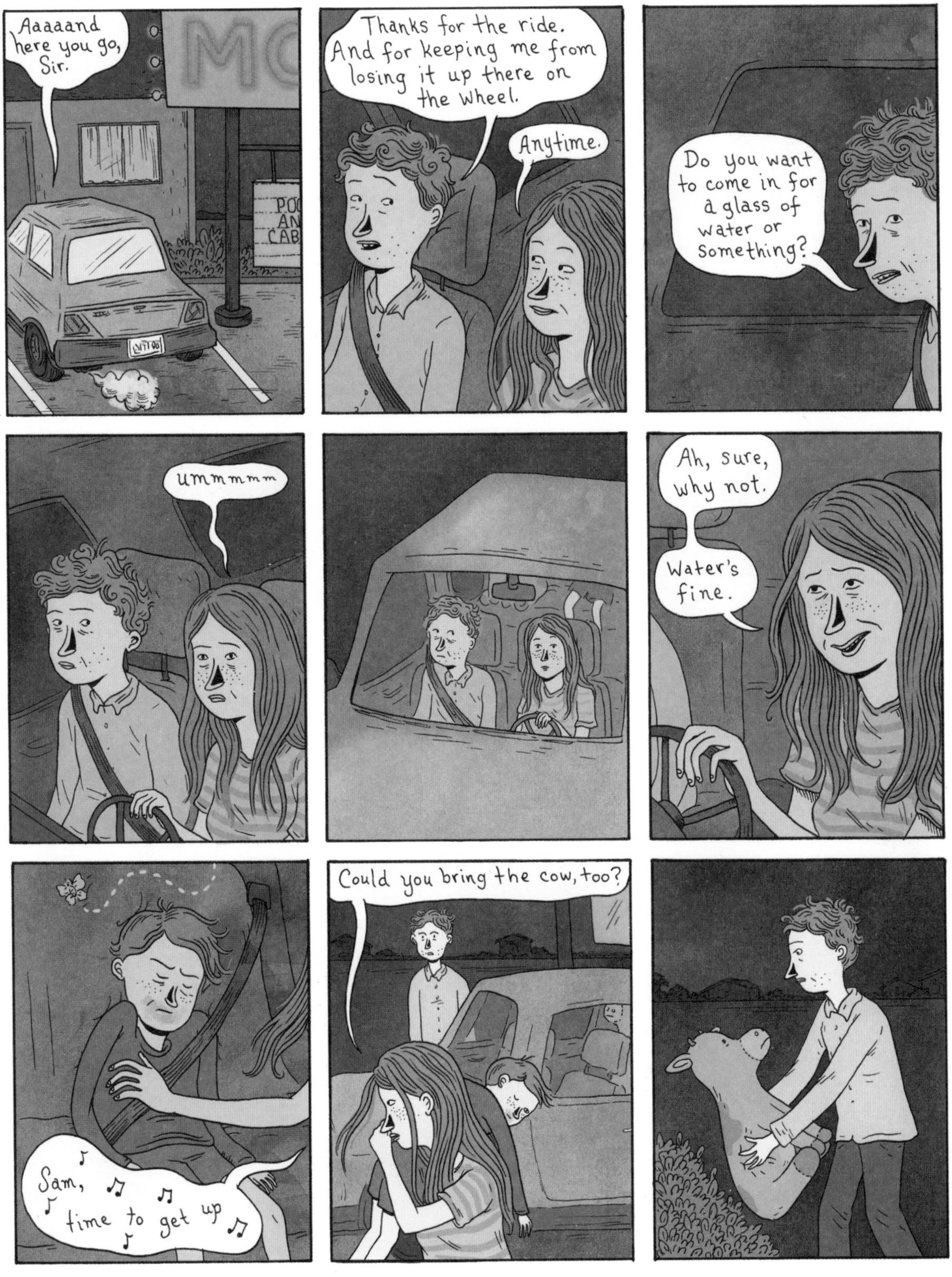
Aaaaand here you go, Sir.
Thanks for the ride. And for keeping me from losing it up there on the wheel.
Anytime.
Do you want to come in for a glass of water or something?
Ummmmm
Ah, sure, why not.
Water's fine.
Sam, time to get up
Could you bring the cow, too?

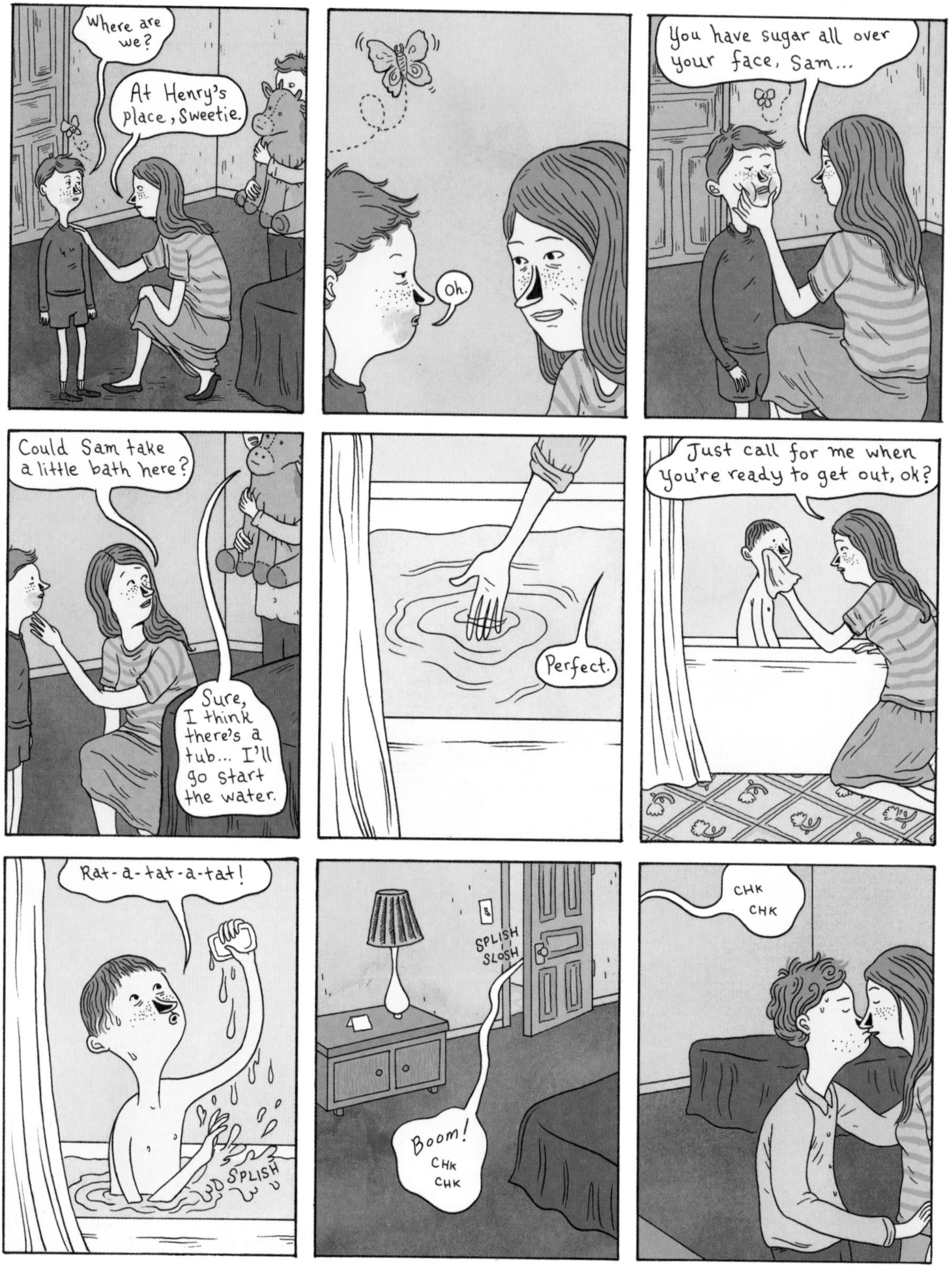
Where are we?
At Henry's place, Sweetie.
Oh.
You have sugar all over your face, Sam...
Could Sam take a little bath here?
Sure, I think there's a tub... I'll go start the water.
Perfect.
Just call for me when you're ready to get out, ok?
Rat-a-tat-a-tat!
SPLISH
SPLISH SLOSH
Boom! CHK CHK
CHK CHK

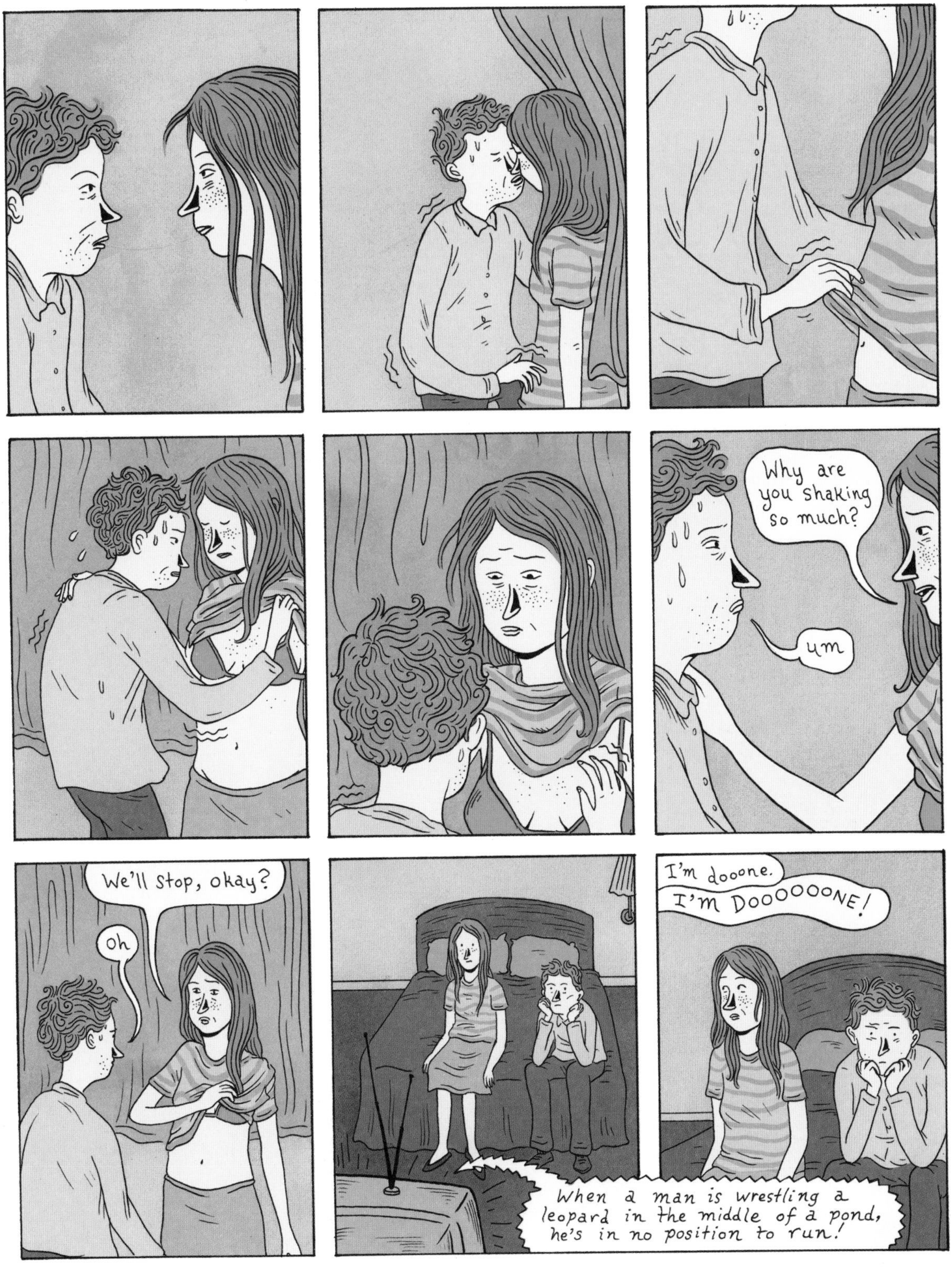
Why are you shaking so much?
um
We'll stop, okay?
Oh
When a man is wrestling a leopard in the middle of a pond, he's in no position to run!
I'm dooone.
I'M DOOOOOONE!

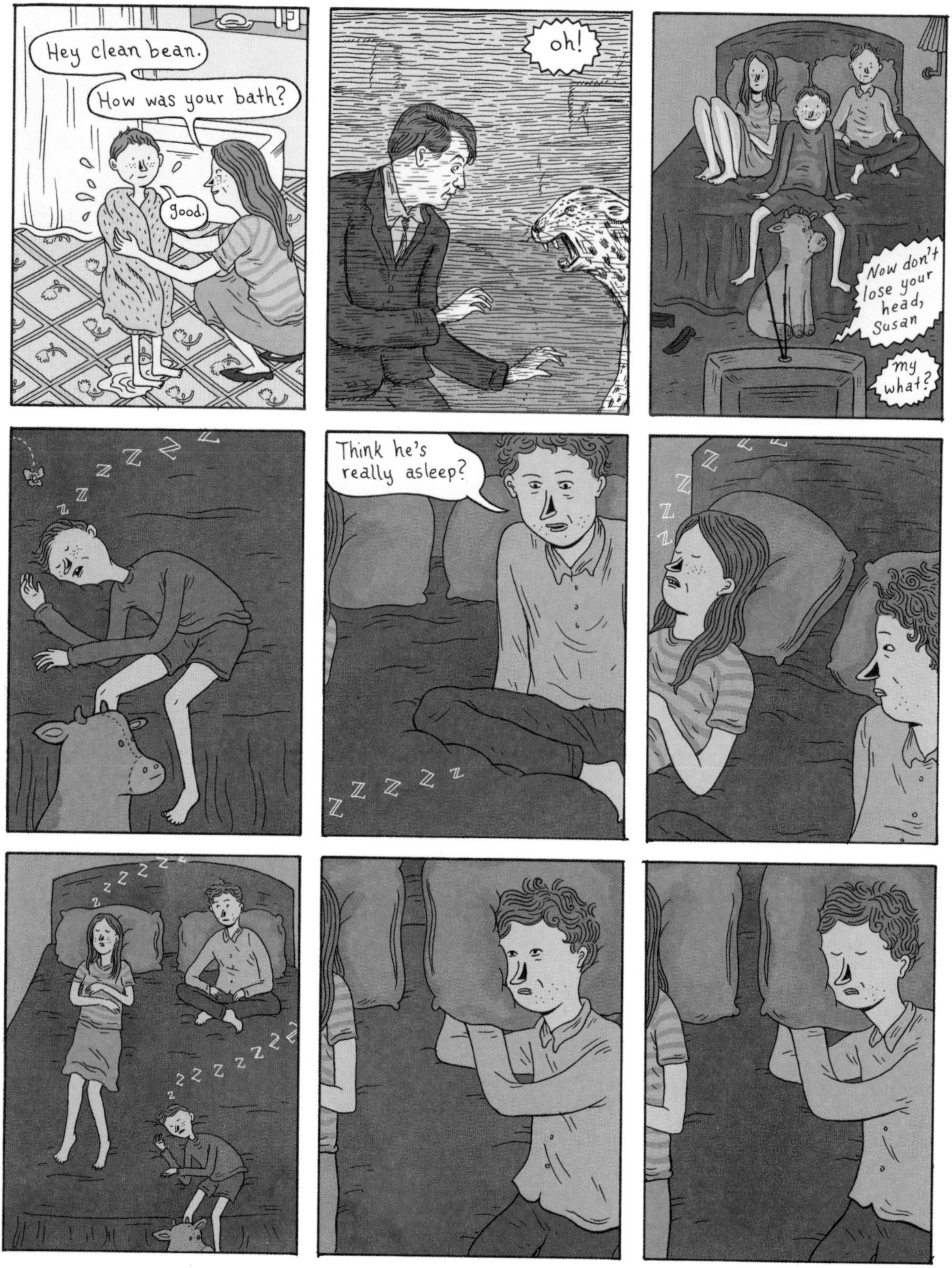
Hey clean bean.
How was your bath?
good.
oh!
Now don't lose your head, Susan
my what?
Think he's really asleep?

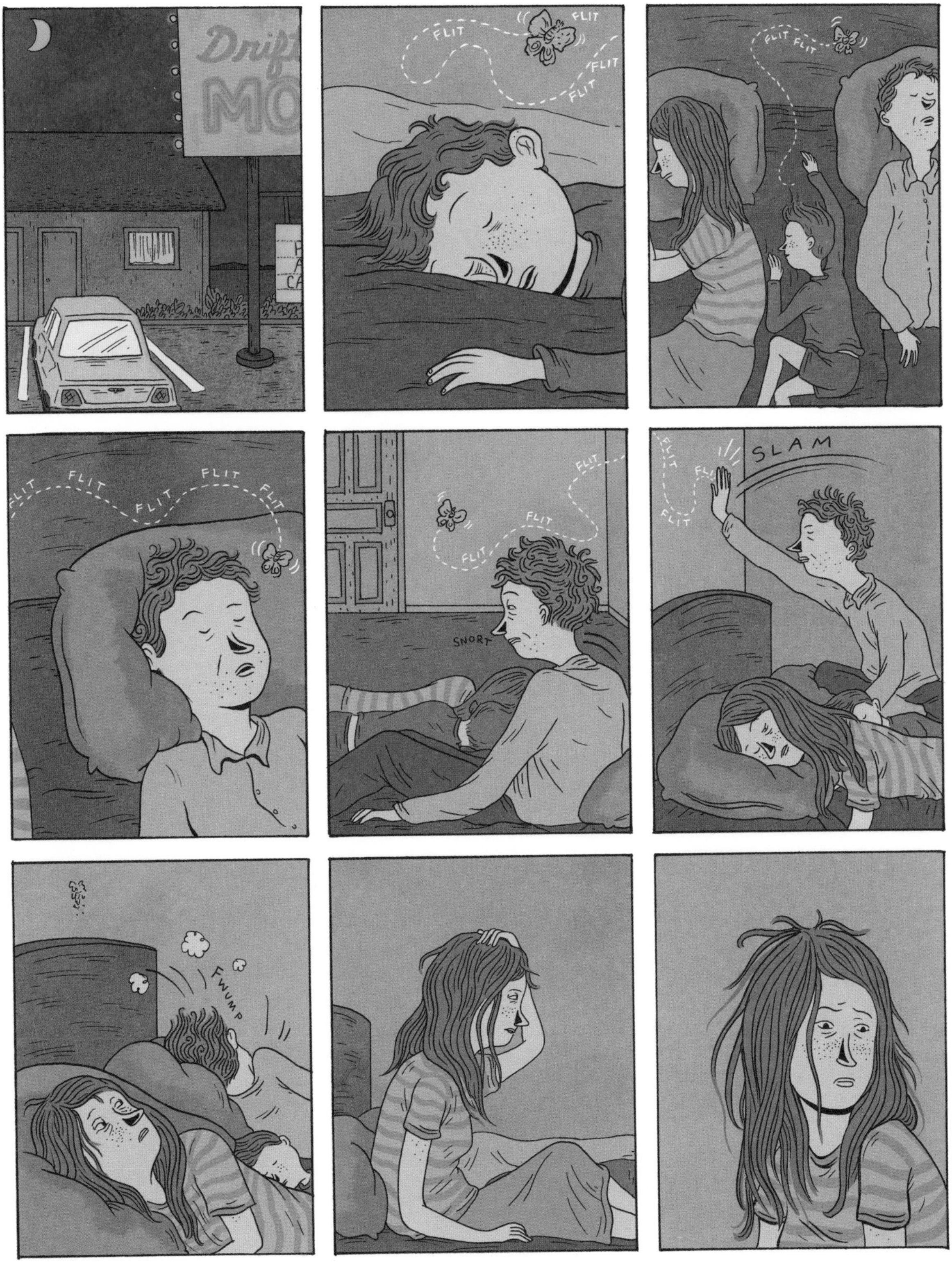
FLIT
FLIT
FLIT
FLIT
FLIT
FLIT
FLIT
FLIT
FLIT
FLIT
FLIT
FLIT
FLIT
FLIT
FLIT
SNORT
FLIT
FLI
FLIT
SLAM
FWUMP

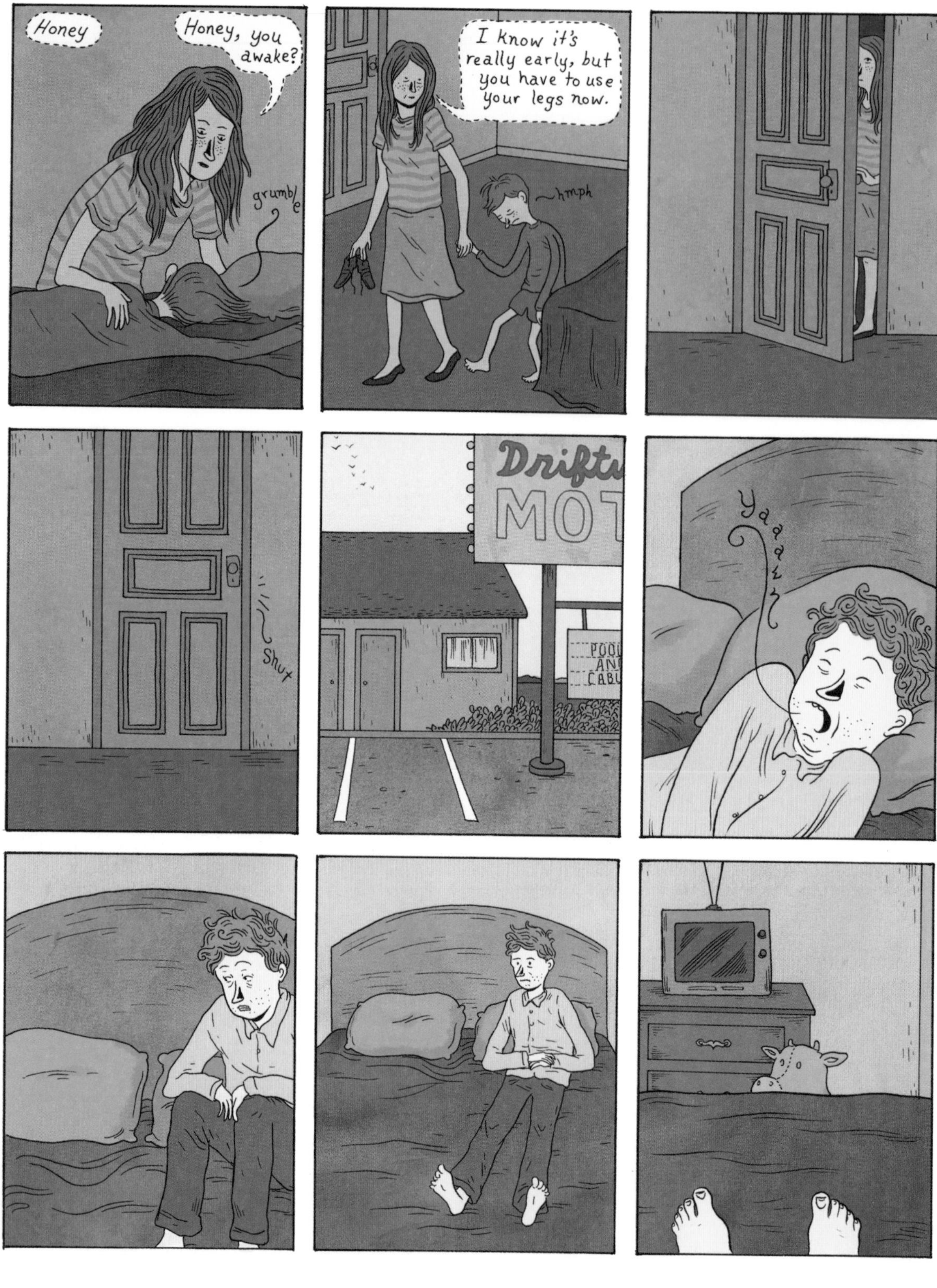
Honey
Honey, you awake?
grumble
I know it's really early, but you have to use your legs now.
~hmph
Shut
Yaaawn

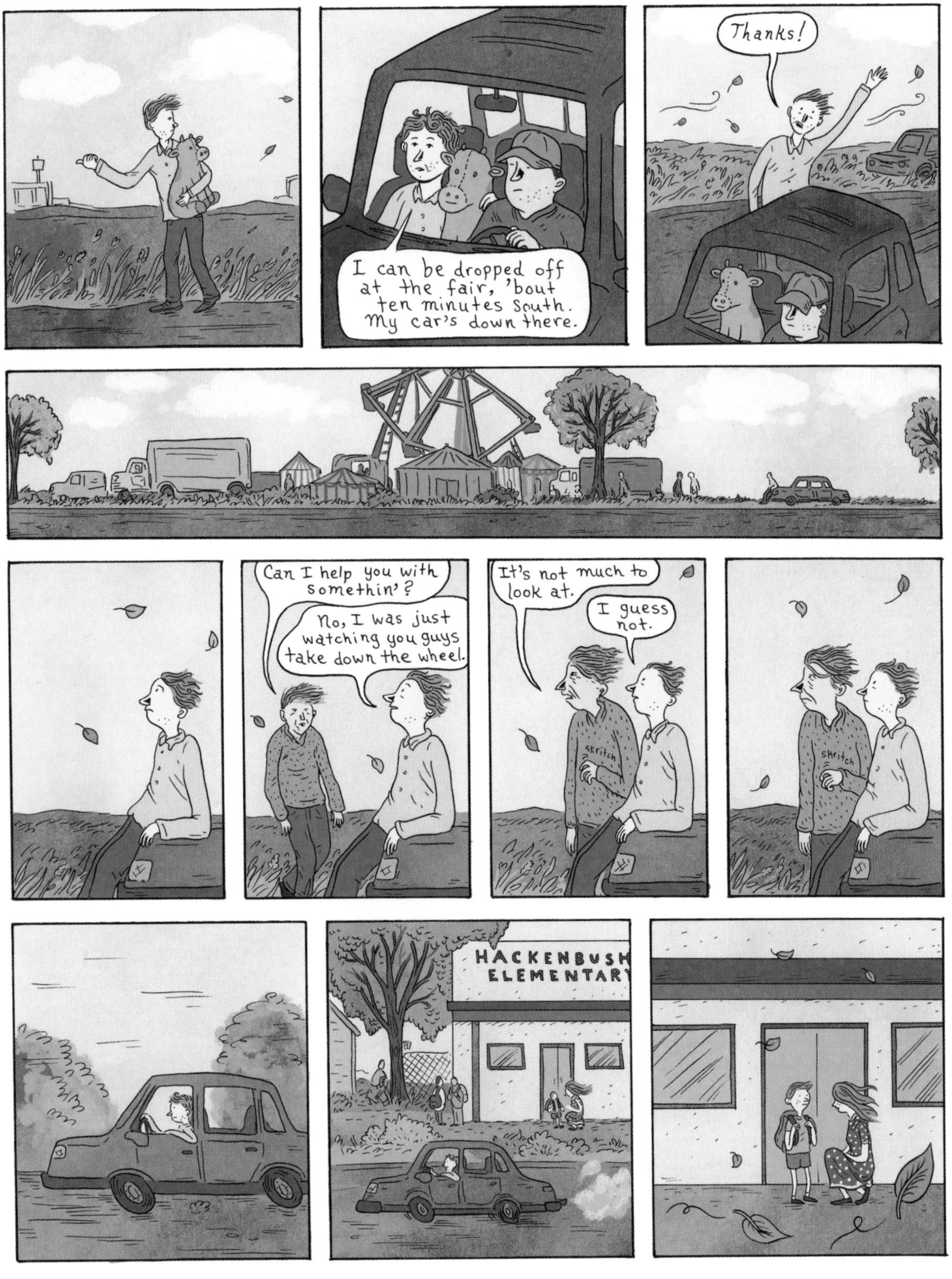

I can be dropped off at the fair, 'bout ten minutes south. My car's down there.
Thanks!
Can I help you with somethin'?
No, I was just watching you guys take down the wheel.
It's not much to look at.
I guess not.
skritch
skritch
HACKENBUSH ELEMENTARY

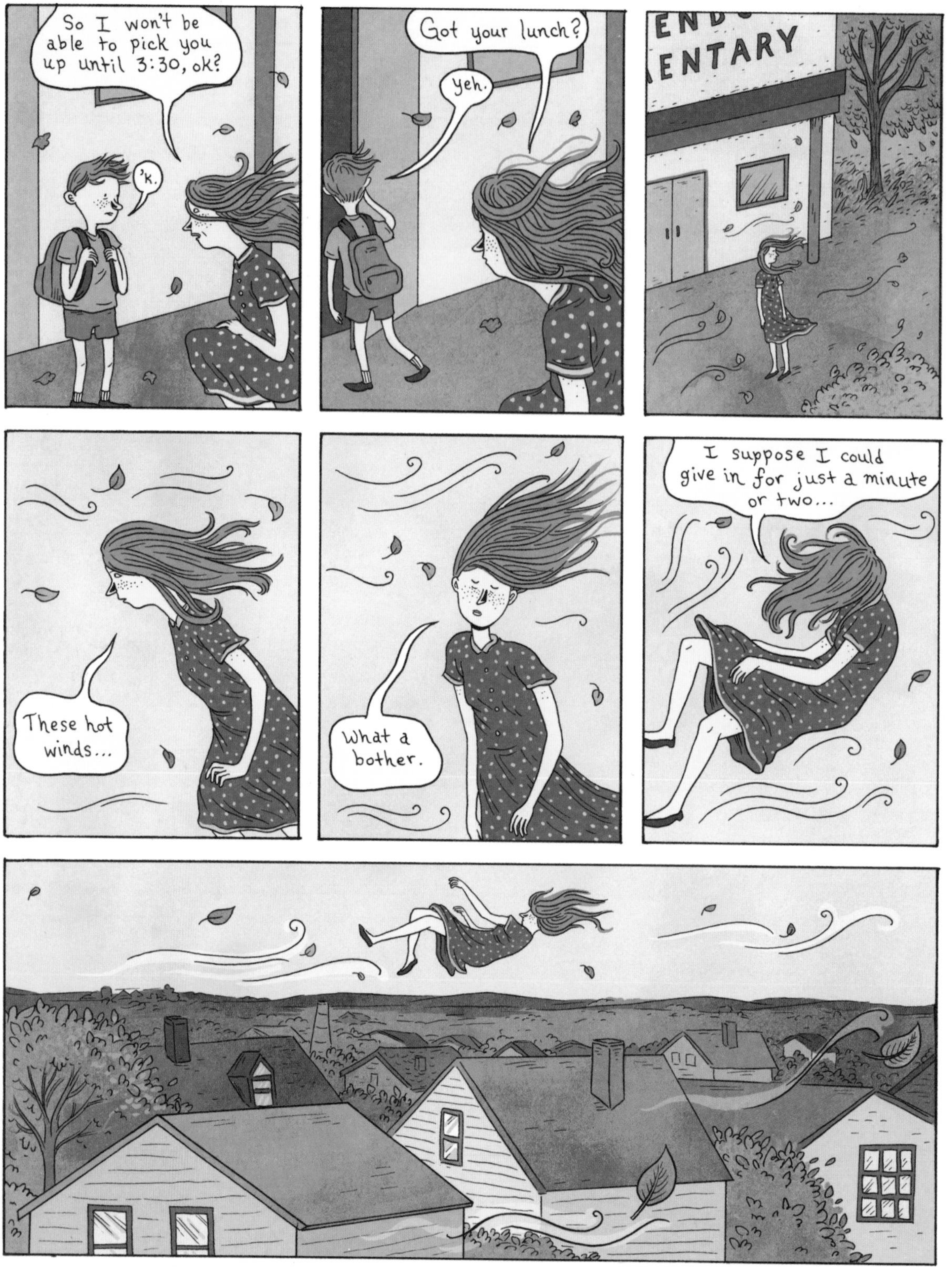
So I won't be able to pick you up until 3:30, ok?
'k.
Got your lunch?
Yeh.
ENDS
ENTARY
These hot winds...
What a bother.
I suppose I could give in for just a minute or two...

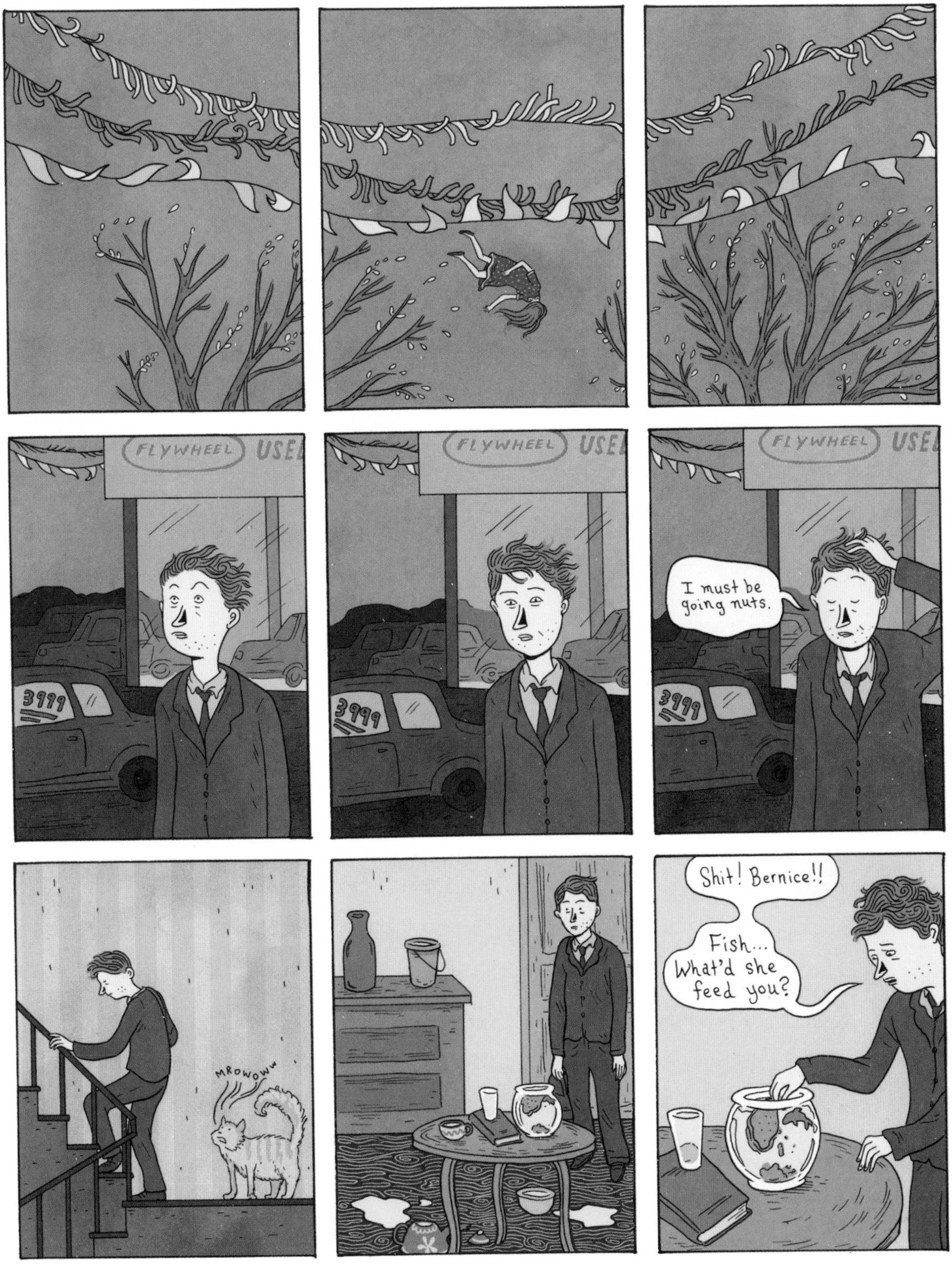
FLYWHEEL USED
3999
FLYWHEEL USED
3999
FLYWHEEL USED
I must be going nuts.
3999
MROWOWW
Shit! Bernice!!
Fish... What'd she feed you?

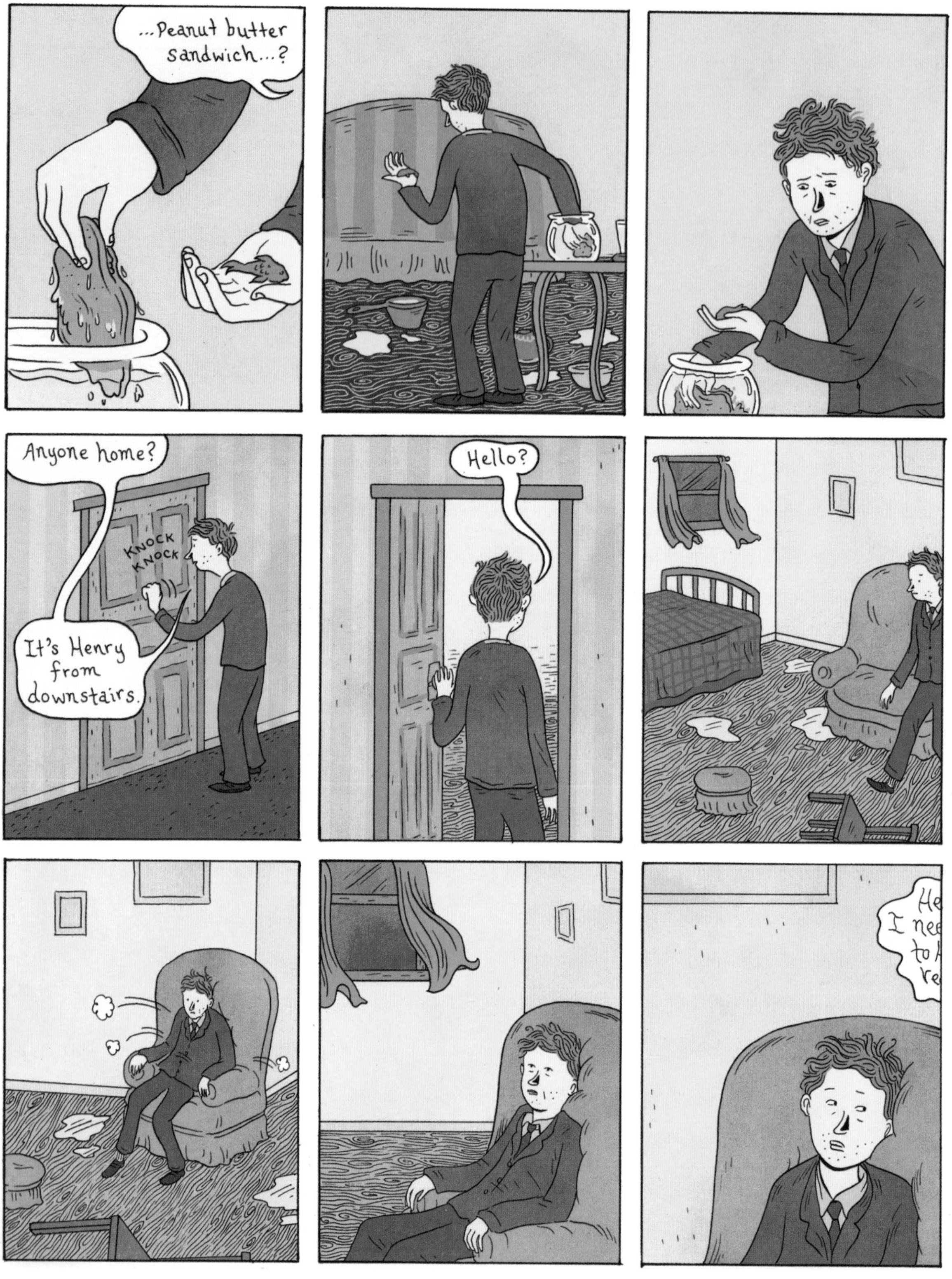
...Peanut butter sandwich...?
Anyone home?
KNOCK KNOCK
It's Henry from downstairs.
Hello?

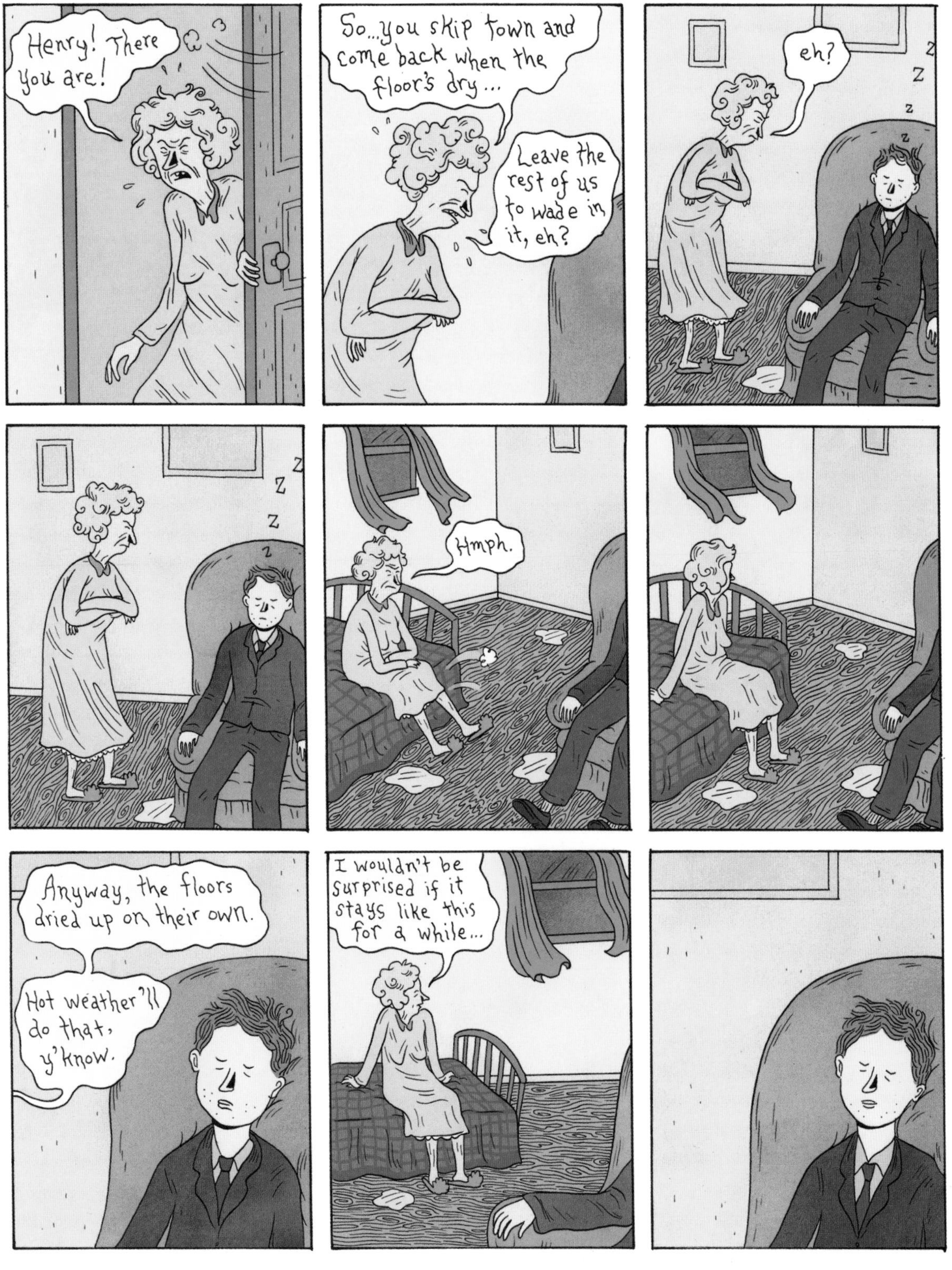
Henry! There you are!
So...you skip town and come back when the floor's dry...
Leave the rest of us to wade in it, eh?
eh?
Z Z Z Z
Z Z Z
Hmph.
Anyway, the floors dried up on their own.
Hot weather'll do that, y'know.
I wouldn't be surprised if it stays like this for a while...

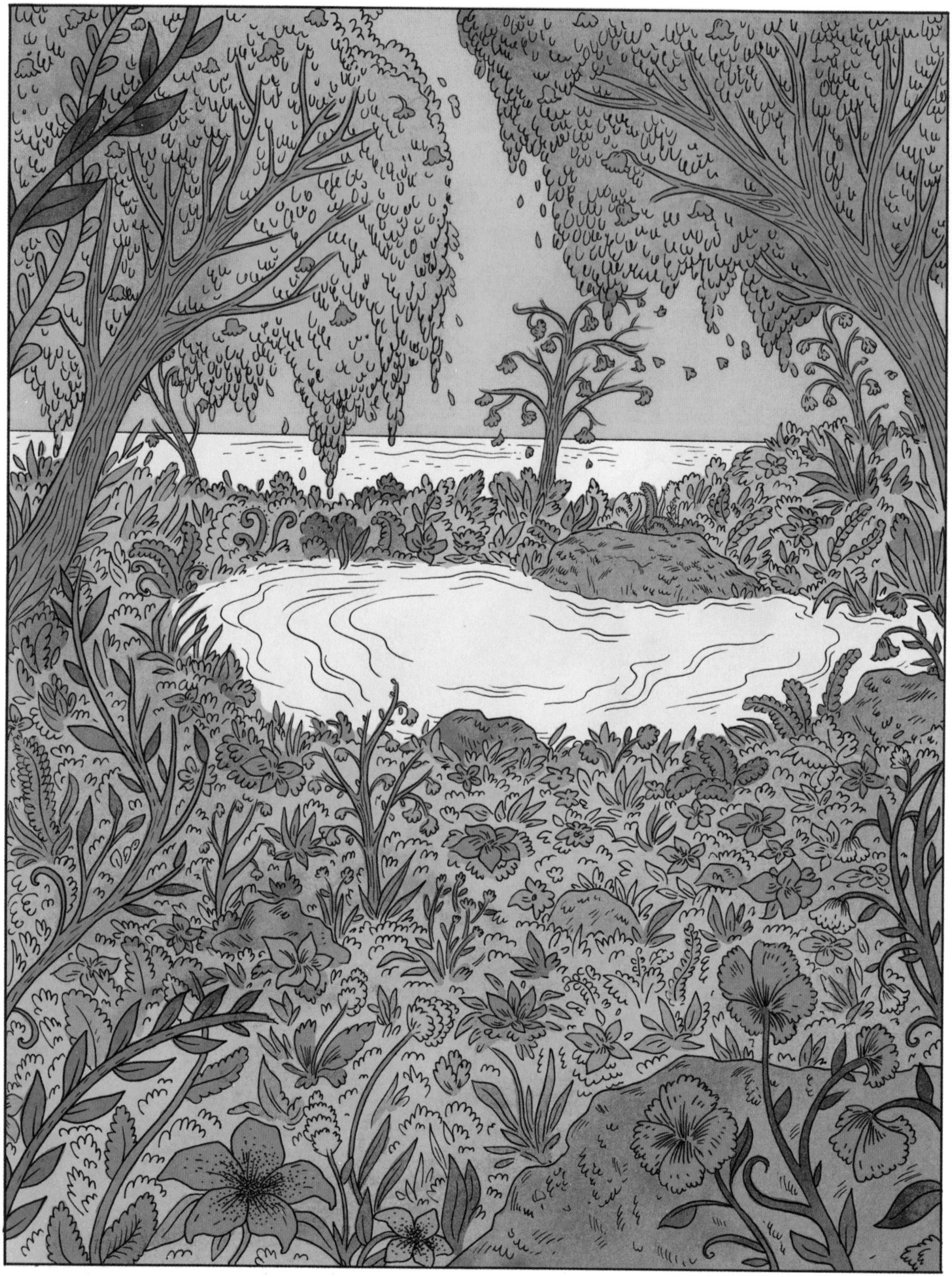

Too Hot
to Sleep

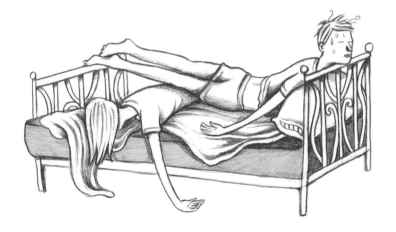

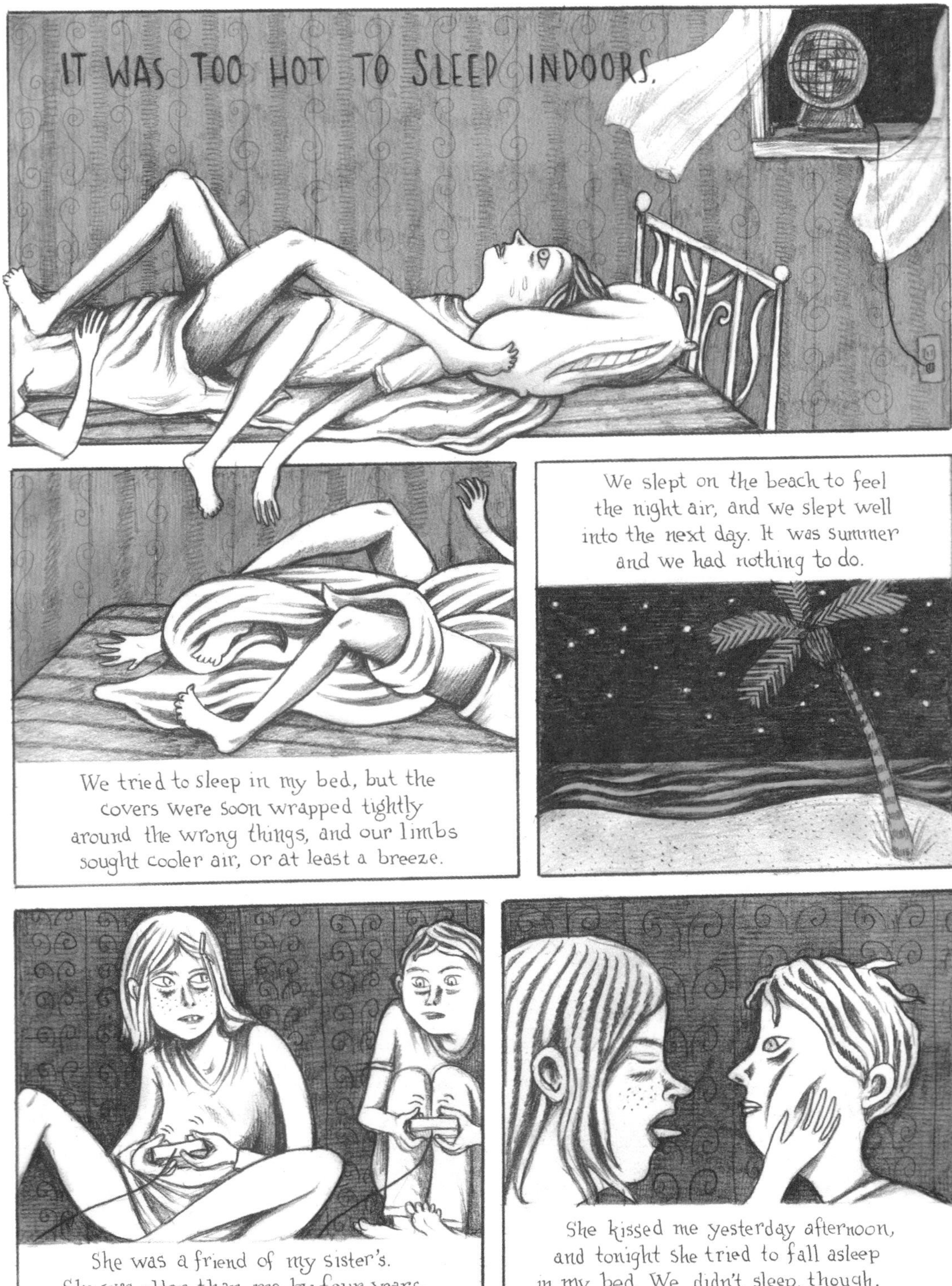
IT WAS TOO HOT TO SLEEP INDOORS.
We tried to sleep in my bed, but the covers were soon wrapped tightly around the wrong things, and our limbs sought cooler air, or at least a breeze.
We slept on the beach to feel the night air, and we slept well into the next day. It was summer and we had nothing to do.
She was a friend of my sister's. She was older than me by four years, and I had never seen legs like that.
She kissed me yesterday afternoon, and tonight she tried to fall asleep in my bed. We didn't sleep, though, we were only angry at the heat.

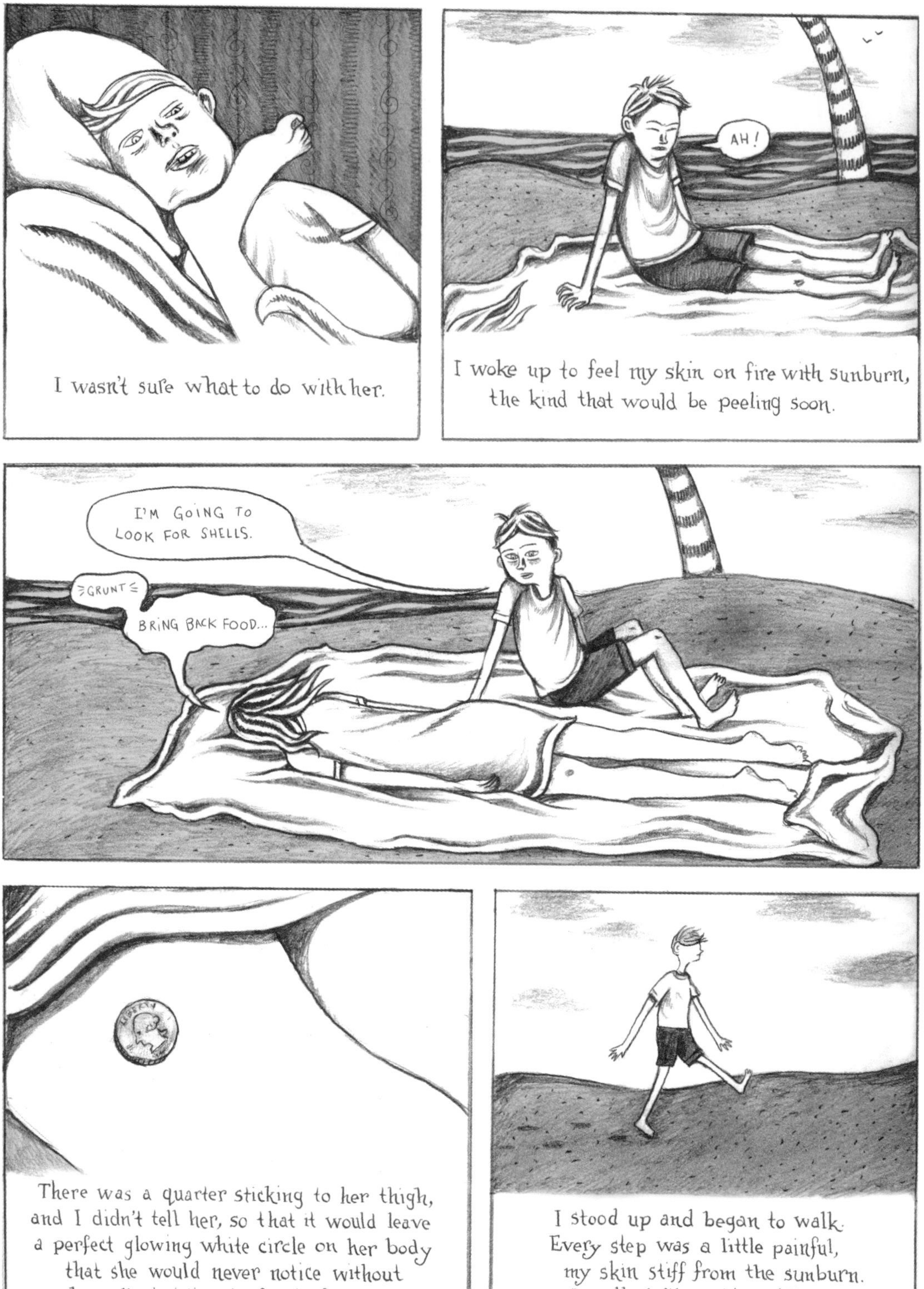
I wasn't sure what to do with her.
AH!
I woke up to feel my skin on fire with sunburn, the kind that would be peeling soon.
I'M GOING TO LOOK FOR SHELLS.
GRUNT
BRING BACK FOOD...
There was a quarter sticking to her thigh, and I didn't tell her, so that it would leave a perfect glowing white circle on her body that she would never notice without awkwardly twisting in front of a mirror.
I stood up and began to walk. Every step was a little painful, my skin stiff from the sunburn. I walked like a tin soldier.

I started to wander and look for things. At first I gathered some of your standard smooth rocks, sea glass and muscle shells.

Then I found a good scattering of sea anemones, dried-out crab bodies, and other delicate little skeletons.

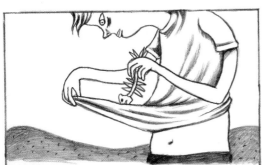

I cradled these in my shirt and brought them back to our resting spot, where she was laying face-down, red as a strawberry, a quarter on her skin.

I'M BACK.

GRUNT

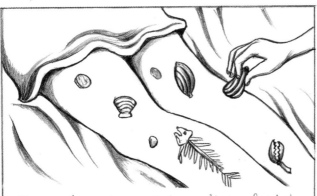

She soon began to snore again, making up for lost sleep. I gingerly placed my finds-of-the-day on her legs, and arranged them in a pattern that would hopefully leave its shadow behind on her skin.

I headed out again to scavenge.

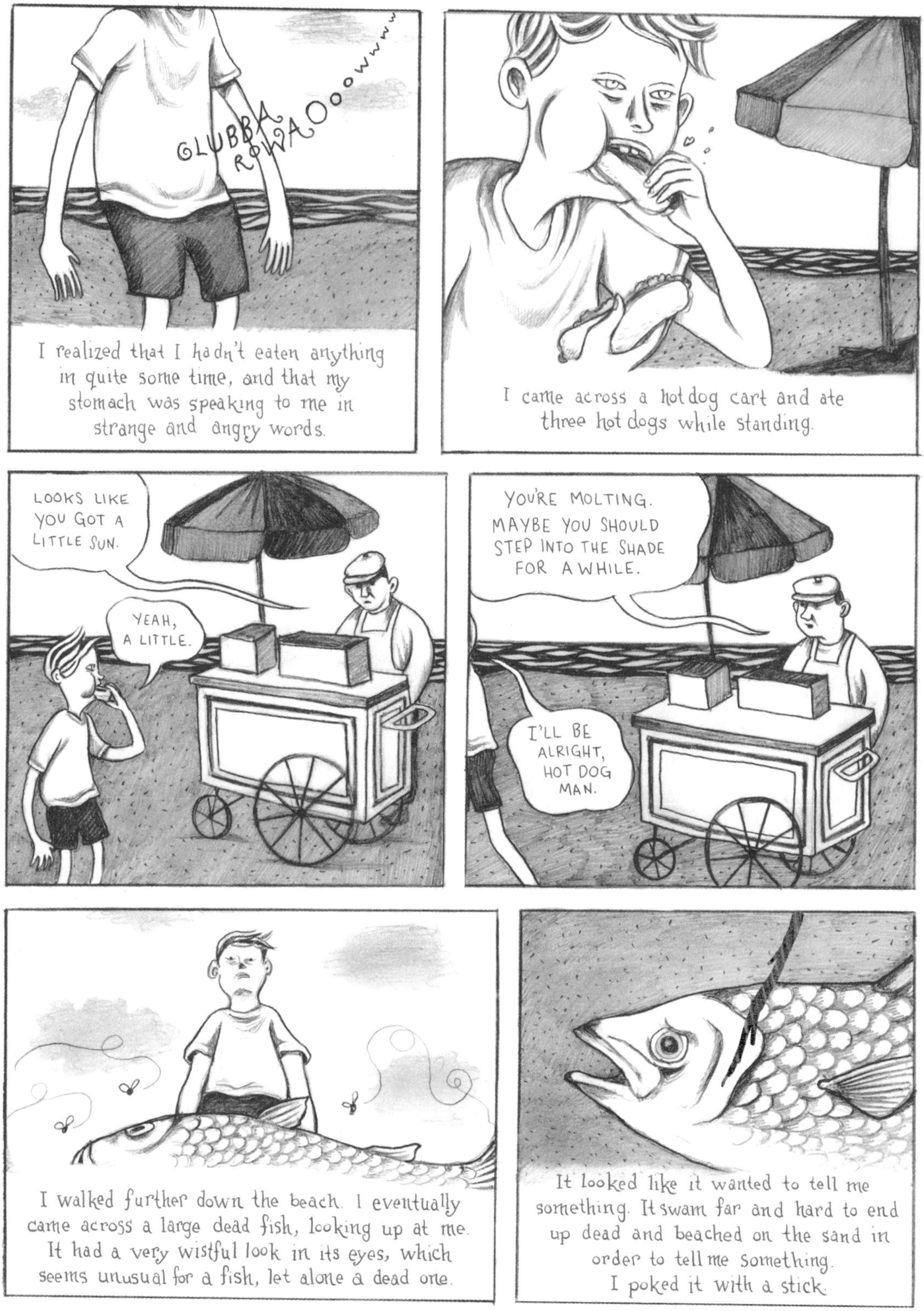
GLUBBA ROWAOooowww
I realized that I hadn't eaten anything in quite some time, and that my stomach was speaking to me in strange and angry words.
I came across a hot dog cart and ate three hot dogs while standing.
LOOKS LIKE YOU GOT A LITTLE SUN.
YEAH, A LITTLE.
YOU'RE MOLTING. MAYBE YOU SHOULD STEP INTO THE SHADE FOR A WHILE.
I'LL BE ALRIGHT, HOT DOG MAN.
I walked further down the beach. I eventually came across a large dead fish, looking up at me. It had a very wistful look in its eyes, which seems unusual for a fish, let alone a dead one.
It looked like it wanted to tell me something. It swam far and hard to end up dead and beached on the sand in order to tell me something.
I poked it with a stick.

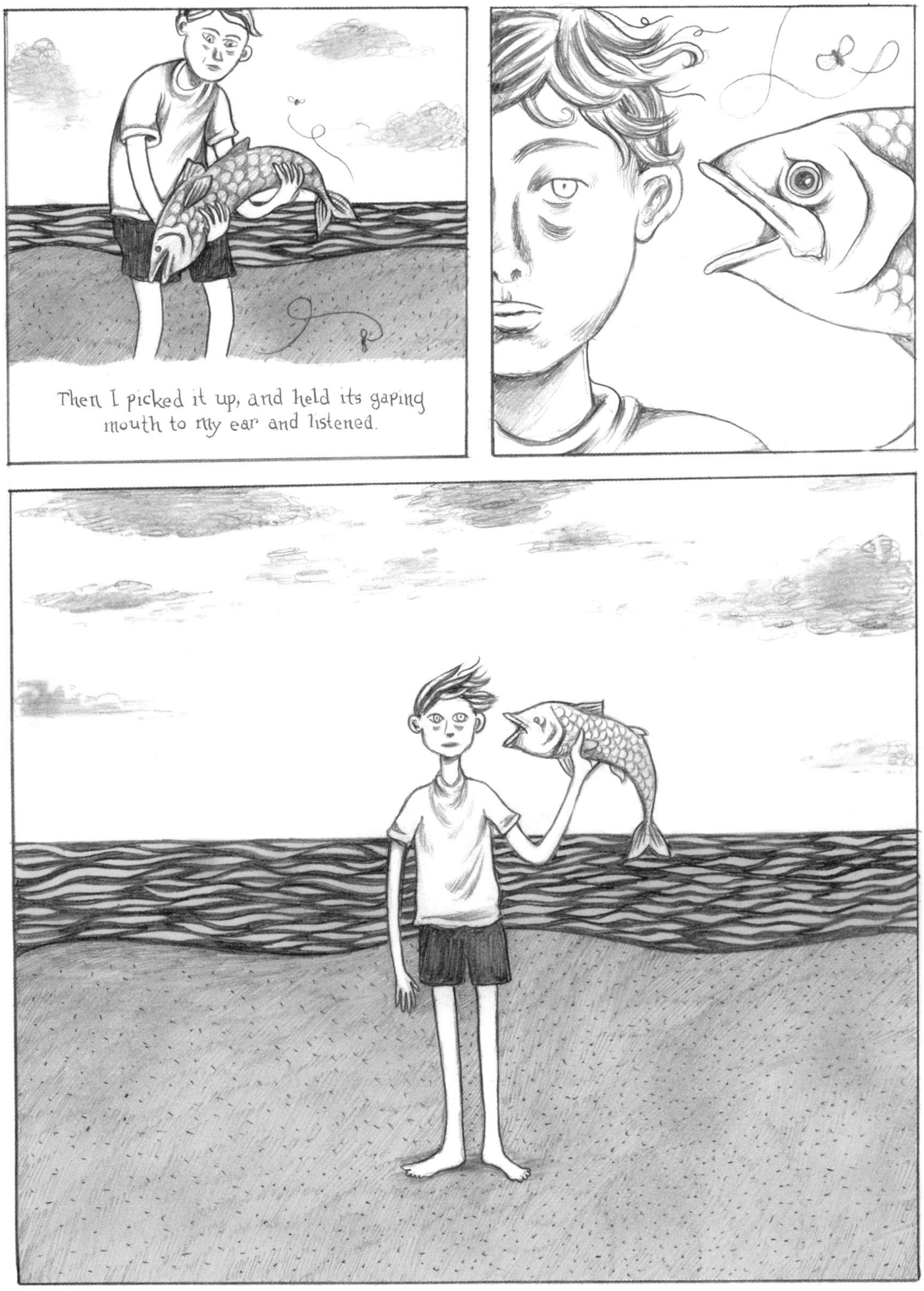
Then I picked it up, and held its gaping mouth to my ear and listened.

I guess it didn't have much to say, just the sort of hollow hum from the mouth of a dead fish.

I brought it back with me anyway, to show her.

She was gone, however. My collected shells and anemones and things were scattered around the blanket.

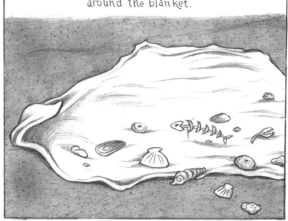

I waited with the fish, eager for her to get back. The sun was setting now.

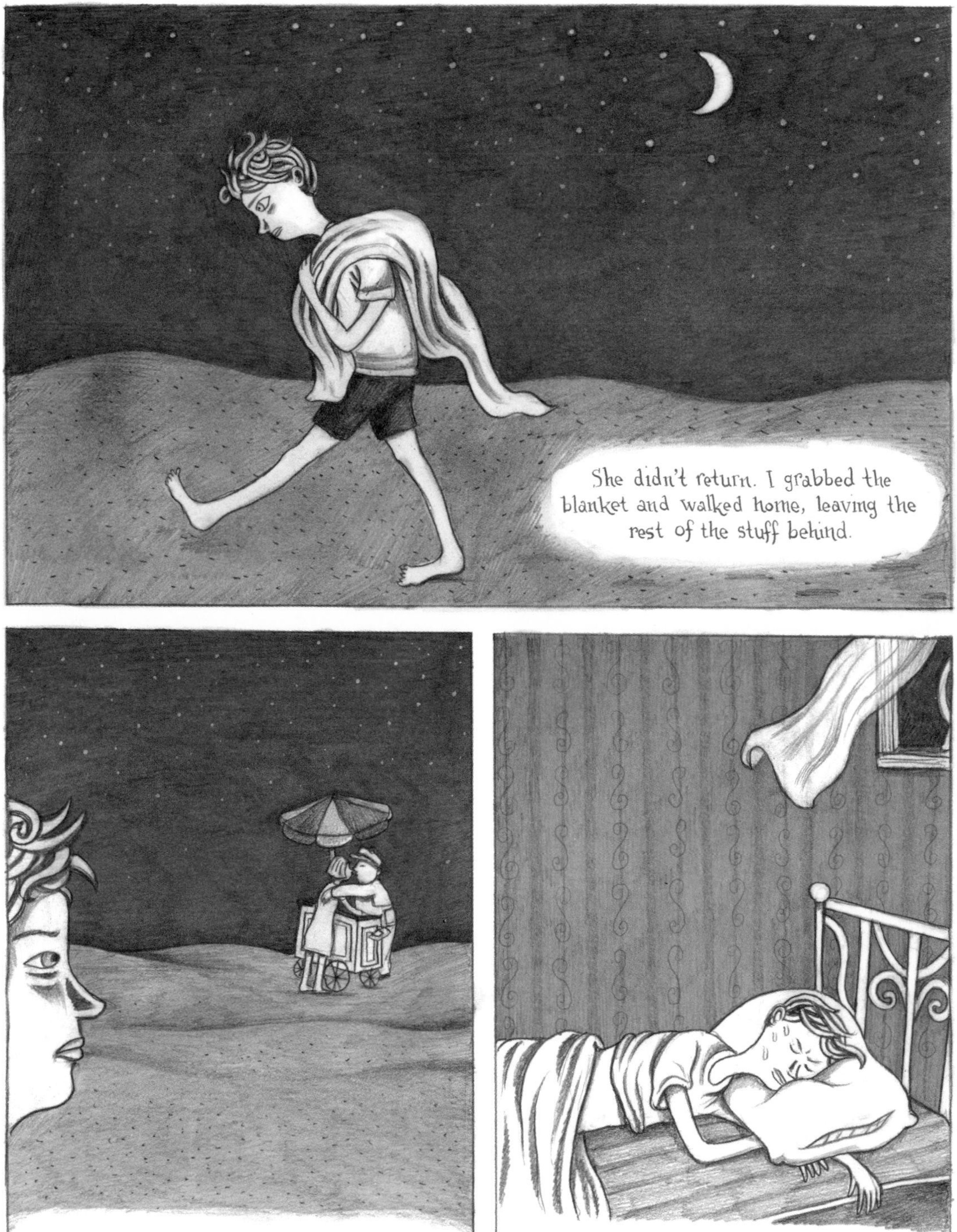
She didn't return. I grabbed the blanket and walked home, leaving the rest of the stuff behind.
I saw a girl a little ways down the beach, frenching a hot dog vendor.
I fell into my bed and slept deeply, my skin like it was on fire.

Rainbow

Moment

fig 21

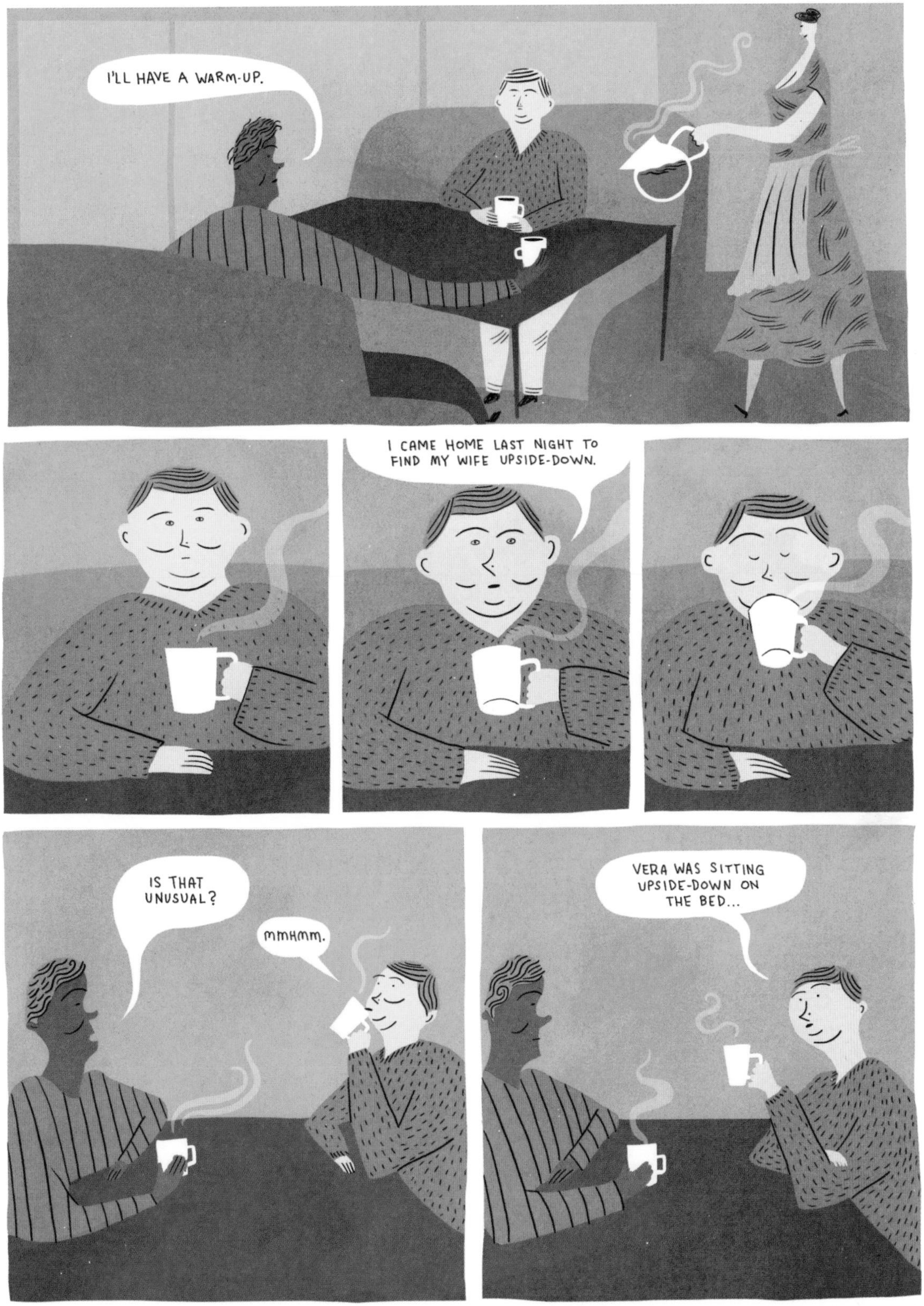

I'LL HAVE A WARM-UP.
I CAME HOME LAST NIGHT TO FIND MY WIFE UPSIDE-DOWN.
IS THAT UNUSUAL?
MMHMM.
VERA WAS SITTING UPSIDE-DOWN ON THE BED...

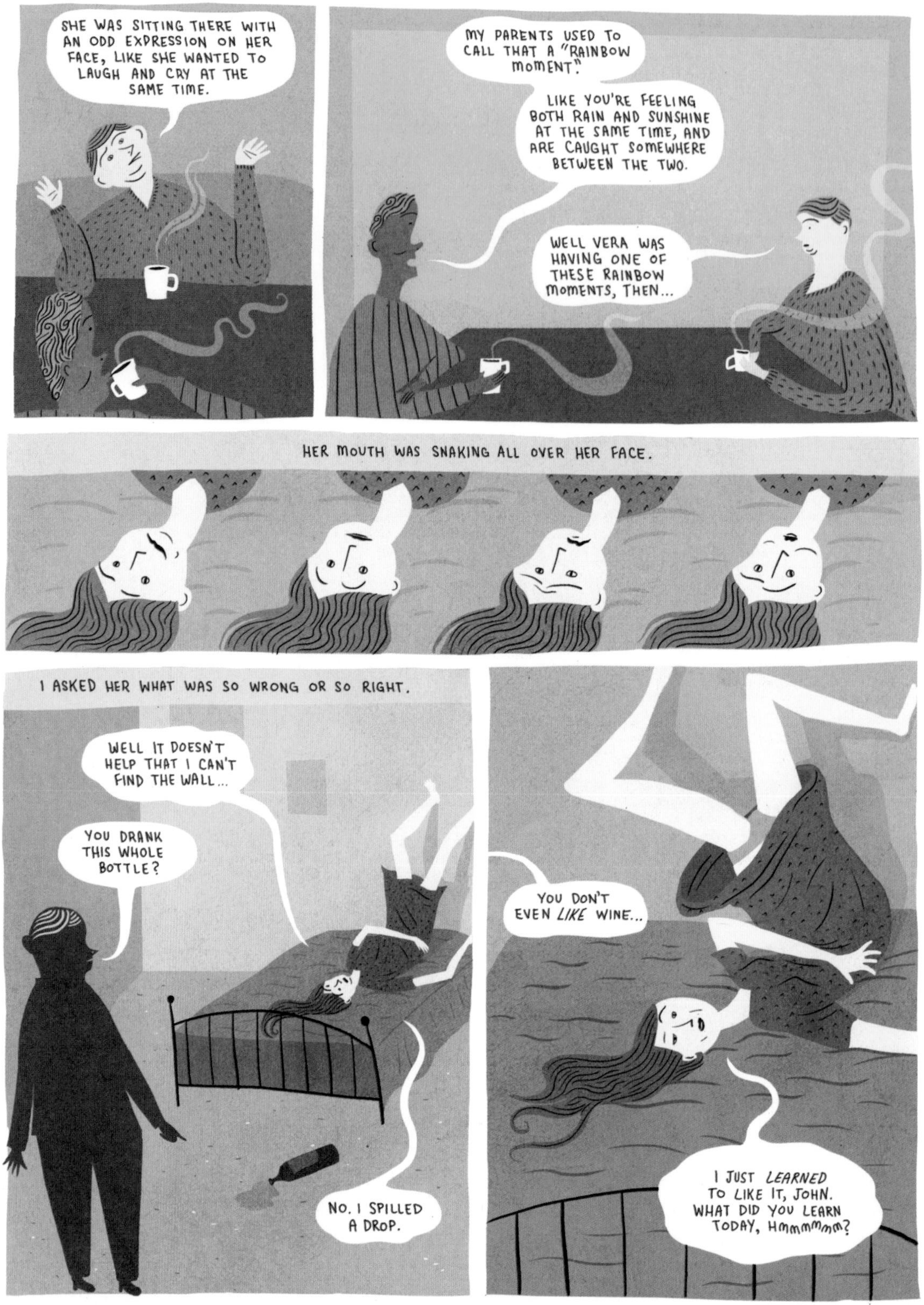
SHE WAS SITTING THERE WITH AN ODD EXPRESSION ON HER FACE, LIKE SHE WANTED TO LAUGH AND CRY AT THE SAME TIME.
MY PARENTS USED TO CALL THAT A "RAINBOW MOMENT."
LIKE YOU'RE FEELING BOTH RAIN AND SUNSHINE AT THE SAME TIME, AND ARE CAUGHT SOMEWHERE BETWEEN THE TWO.
WELL VERA WAS HAVING ONE OF THESE RAINBOW MOMENTS, THEN...
HER MOUTH WAS SNAKING ALL OVER HER FACE.
I ASKED HER WHAT WAS SO WRONG OR SO RIGHT.
WELL IT DOESN'T HELP THAT I CAN'T FIND THE WALL...
YOU DRANK THIS WHOLE BOTTLE?
NO. I SPILLED A DROP.
YOU DON'T EVEN *LIKE* WINE...
I JUST *LEARNED* TO LIKE IT, JOHN. WHAT DID YOU LEARN TODAY, Hmmmmmm?

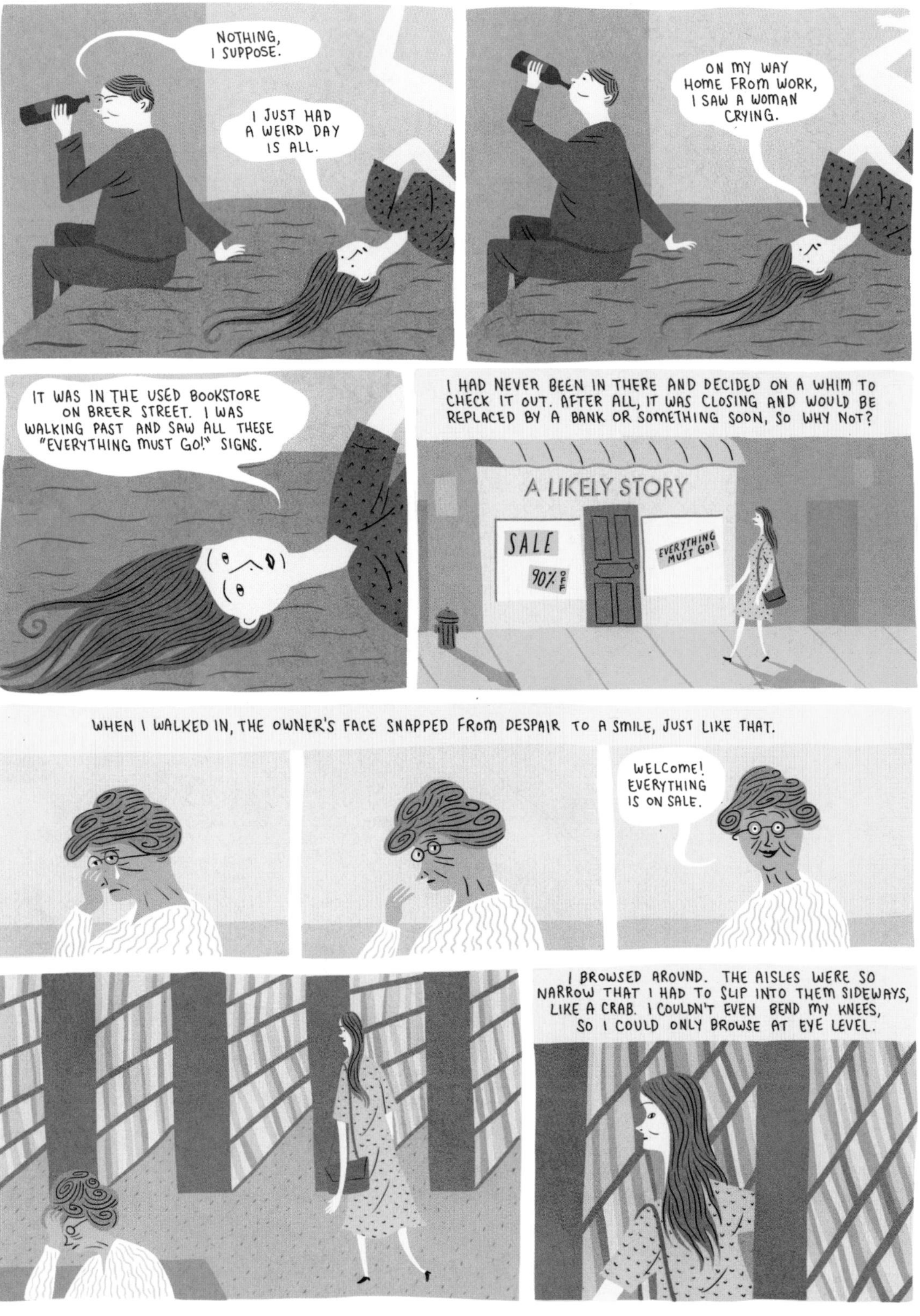
NOTHING, I SUPPOSE.
I JUST HAD A WEIRD DAY IS ALL.
ON MY WAY HOME FROM WORK, I SAW A WOMAN CRYING.
IT WAS IN THE USED BOOKSTORE ON BREER STREET. I WAS WALKING PAST AND SAW ALL THESE "EVERYTHING MUST GO!" SIGNS.
I HAD NEVER BEEN IN THERE AND DECIDED ON A WHIM TO CHECK IT OUT. AFTER ALL, IT WAS CLOSING AND WOULD BE REPLACED BY A BANK OR SOMETHING SOON, SO WHY NOT?
A LIKELY STORY
SALE
90% OFF
EVERYTHING MUST GO!
WHEN I WALKED IN, THE OWNER'S FACE SNAPPED FROM DESPAIR TO A SMILE, JUST LIKE THAT.
WELCOME! EVERYTHING IS ON SALE.
I BROWSED AROUND. THE AISLES WERE SO NARROW THAT I HAD TO SLIP INTO THEM SIDEWAYS, LIKE A CRAB. I COULDN'T EVEN BEND MY KNEES, SO I COULD ONLY BROWSE AT EYE LEVEL.

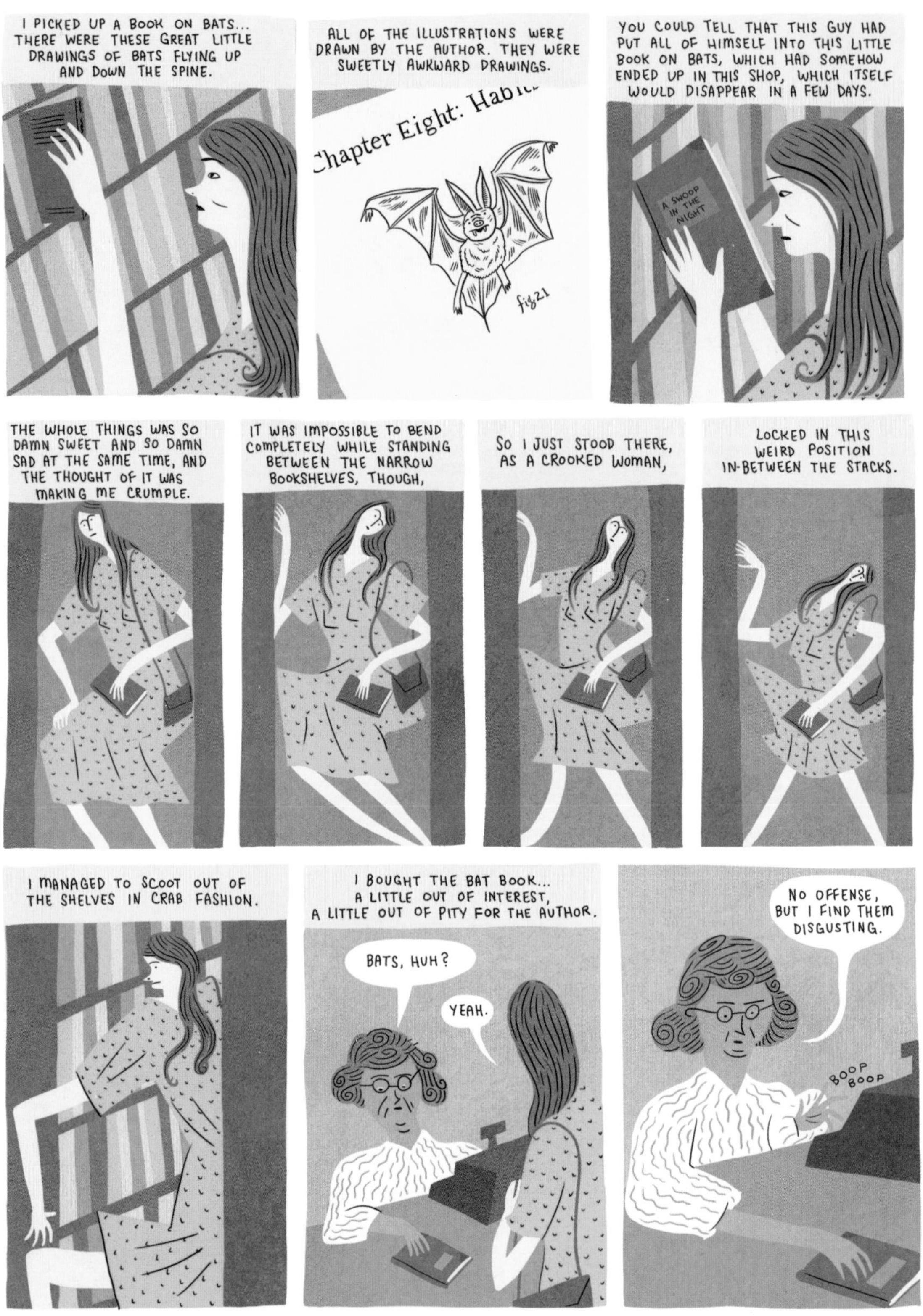
I PICKED UP A BOOK ON BATS... THERE WERE THESE GREAT LITTLE DRAWINGS OF BATS FLYING UP AND DOWN THE SPINE.
ALL OF THE ILLUSTRATIONS WERE DRAWN BY THE AUTHOR. THEY WERE SWEETLY AWKWARD DRAWINGS.
Chapter Eight: Habit
fig.21
YOU COULD TELL THAT THIS GUY HAD PUT ALL OF HIMSELF INTO THIS LITTLE BOOK ON BATS, WHICH HAD SOMEHOW ENDED UP IN THIS SHOP, WHICH ITSELF WOULD DISAPPEAR IN A FEW DAYS.
A SWOOP IN THE NIGHT
THE WHOLE THINGS WAS SO DAMN SWEET AND SO DAMN SAD AT THE SAME TIME, AND THE THOUGHT OF IT WAS MAKING ME CRUMPLE.
IT WAS IMPOSSIBLE TO BEND COMPLETELY WHILE STANDING BETWEEN THE NARROW BOOKSHELVES, THOUGH,
SO I JUST STOOD THERE, AS A CROOKED WOMAN,
LOCKED IN THIS WEIRD POSITION IN-BETWEEN THE STACKS.
I MANAGED TO SCOOT OUT OF THE SHELVES IN CRAB FASHION.
I BOUGHT THE BAT BOOK... A LITTLE OUT OF INTEREST, A LITTLE OUT OF PITY FOR THE AUTHOR.
BATS, HUH?
YEAH.
NO OFFENSE, BUT I FIND THEM DISGUSTING.
BOOP BOOP

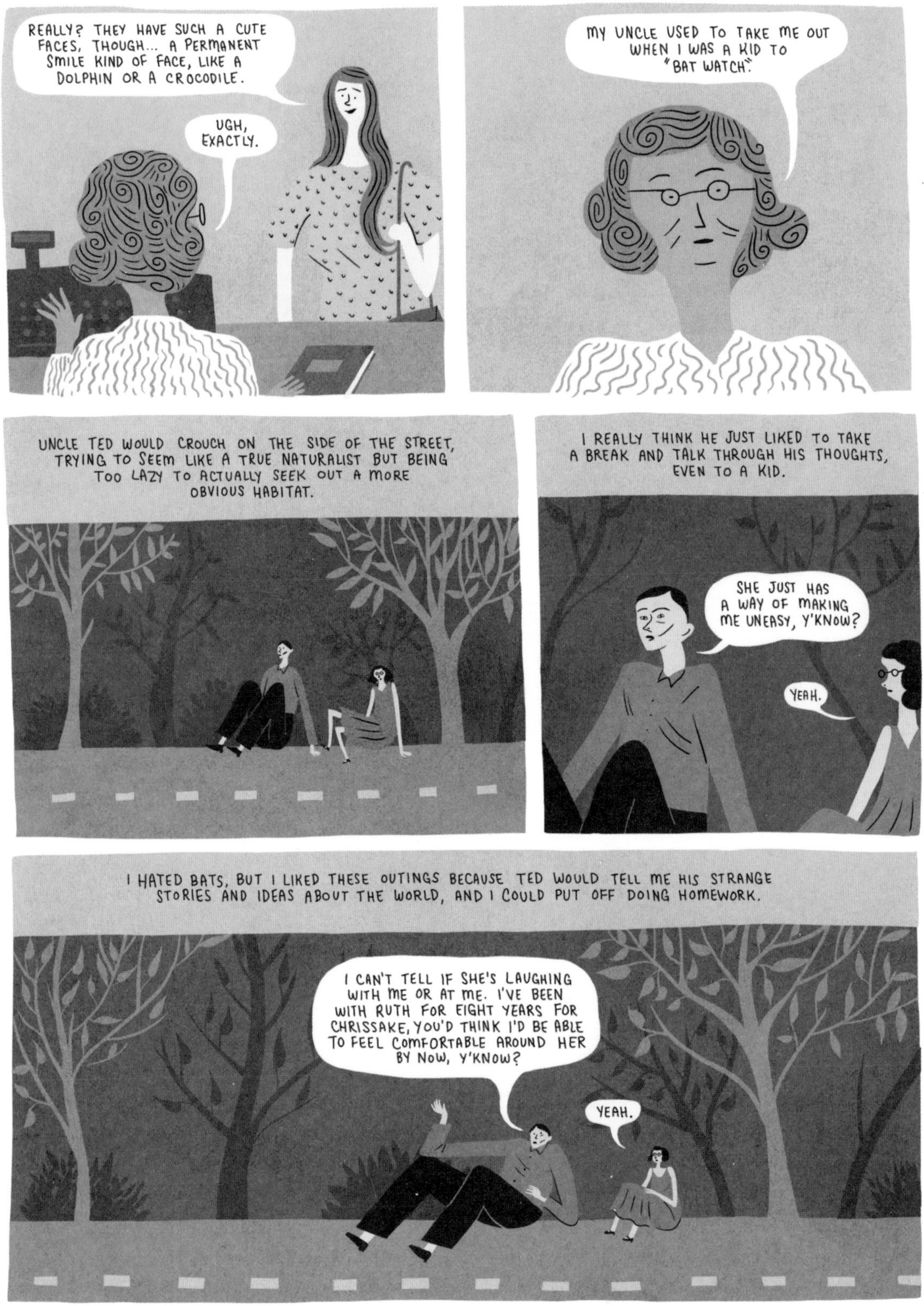
REALLY? THEY HAVE SUCH A CUTE FACES, THOUGH... A PERMANENT SMILE KIND OF FACE, LIKE A DOLPHIN OR A CROCODILE.
UGH, EXACTLY.
MY UNCLE USED TO TAKE ME OUT WHEN I WAS A KID TO "BAT WATCH."
UNCLE TED WOULD CROUCH ON THE SIDE OF THE STREET, TRYING TO SEEM LIKE A TRUE NATURALIST BUT BEING TOO LAZY TO ACTUALLY SEEK OUT A MORE OBVIOUS HABITAT.
I REALLY THINK HE JUST LIKED TO TAKE A BREAK AND TALK THROUGH HIS THOUGHTS, EVEN TO A KID.
SHE JUST HAS A WAY OF MAKING ME UNEASY, Y'KNOW?
YEAH.
I HATED BATS, BUT I LIKED THESE OUTINGS BECAUSE TED WOULD TELL ME HIS STRANGE STORIES AND IDEAS ABOUT THE WORLD, AND I COULD PUT OFF DOING HOMEWORK.
I CAN'T TELL IF SHE'S LAUGHING WITH ME OR AT ME. I'VE BEEN WITH RUTH FOR EIGHT YEARS FOR CHRISSAKE, YOU'D THINK I'D BE ABLE TO FEEL COMFORTABLE AROUND HER BY NOW, Y'KNOW?
YEAH.

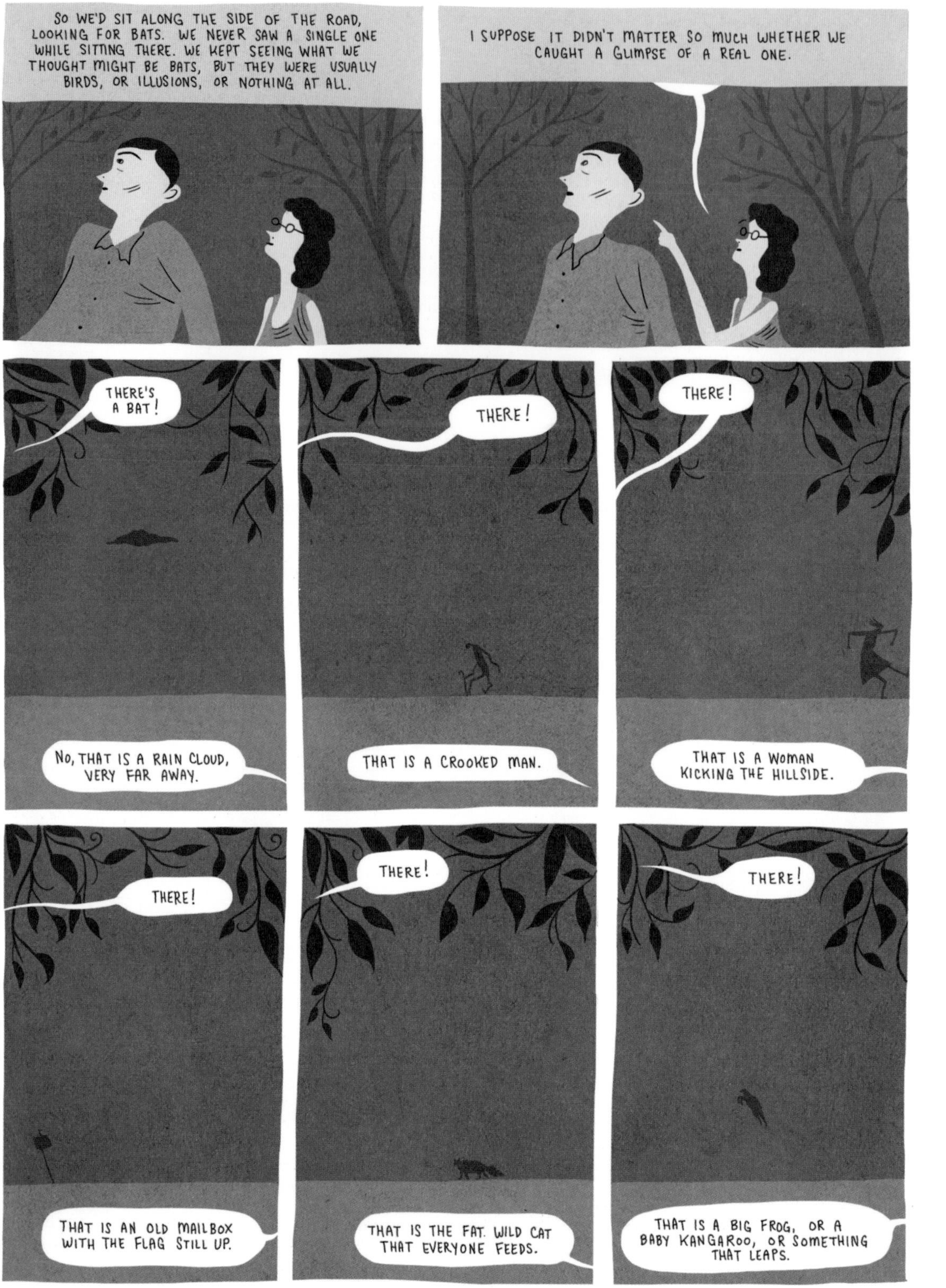
SO WE'D SIT ALONG THE SIDE OF THE ROAD, LOOKING FOR BATS. WE NEVER SAW A SINGLE ONE WHILE SITTING THERE. WE KEPT SEEING WHAT WE THOUGHT MIGHT BE BATS, BUT THEY WERE USUALLY BIRDS, OR ILLUSIONS, OR NOTHING AT ALL.
I SUPPOSE IT DIDN'T MATTER SO MUCH WHETHER WE CAUGHT A GLIMPSE OF A REAL ONE.
THERE'S A BAT!
NO, THAT IS A RAIN CLOUD, VERY FAR AWAY.
THERE!
THAT IS A CROOKED MAN.
THERE!
THAT IS A WOMAN KICKING THE HILLSIDE.
THERE!
THAT IS AN OLD MAILBOX WITH THE FLAG STILL UP.
THERE!
THAT IS THE FAT, WILD CAT THAT EVERYONE FEEDS.
THERE!
THAT IS A BIG FROG, OR A BABY KANGAROO, OR SOMETHING THAT LEAPS.

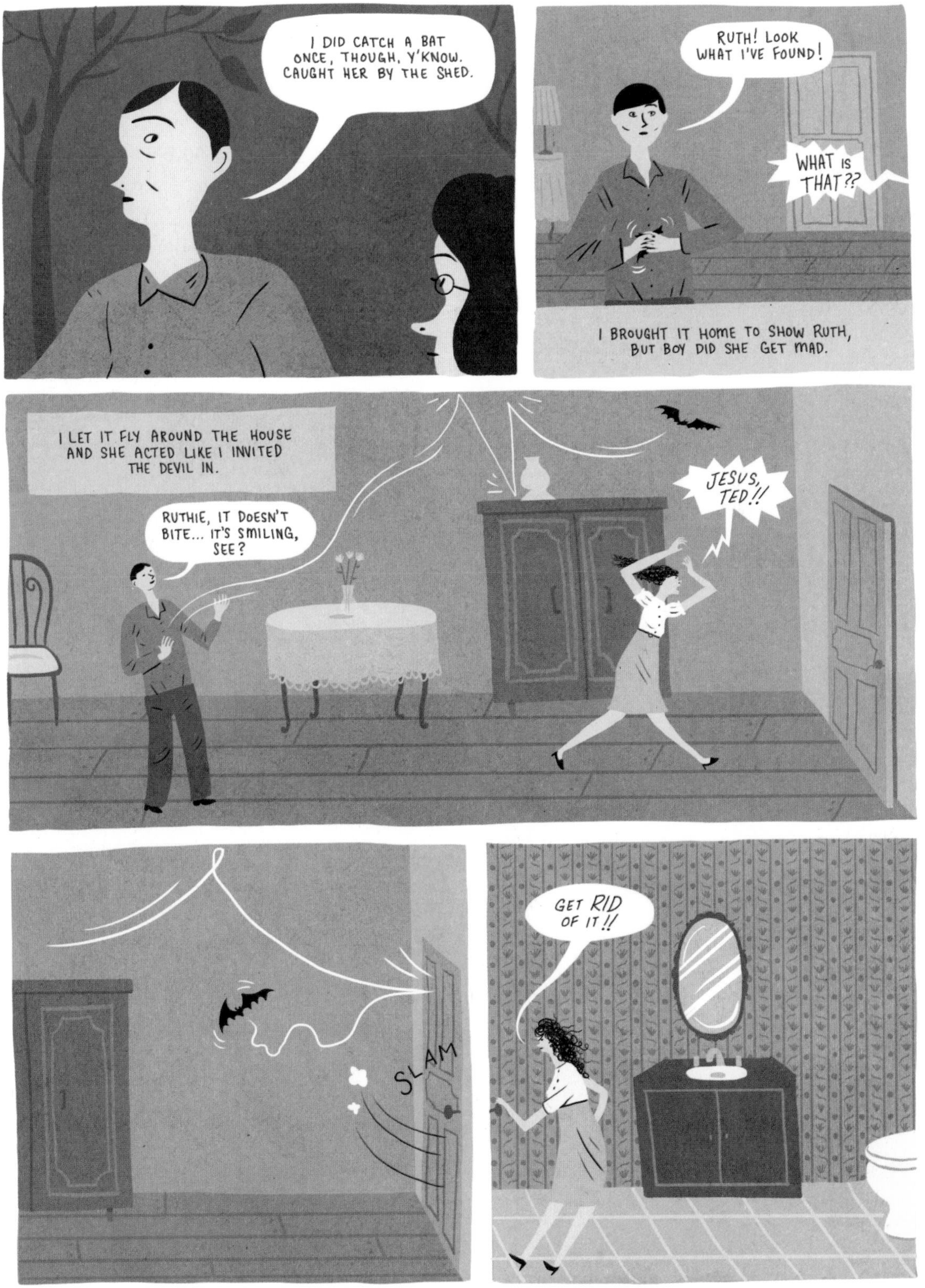
I DID CATCH A BAT ONCE, THOUGH, Y'KNOW. CAUGHT HER BY THE SHED.
RUTH! LOOK WHAT I'VE FOUND!
WHAT IS THAT??
I BROUGHT IT HOME TO SHOW RUTH, BUT BOY DID SHE GET MAD.
I LET IT FLY AROUND THE HOUSE AND SHE ACTED LIKE I INVITED THE DEVIL IN.
RUTHIE, IT DOESN'T BITE... IT'S SMILING, SEE?
JESUS, TED!!
SLAM
GET RID OF IT!!

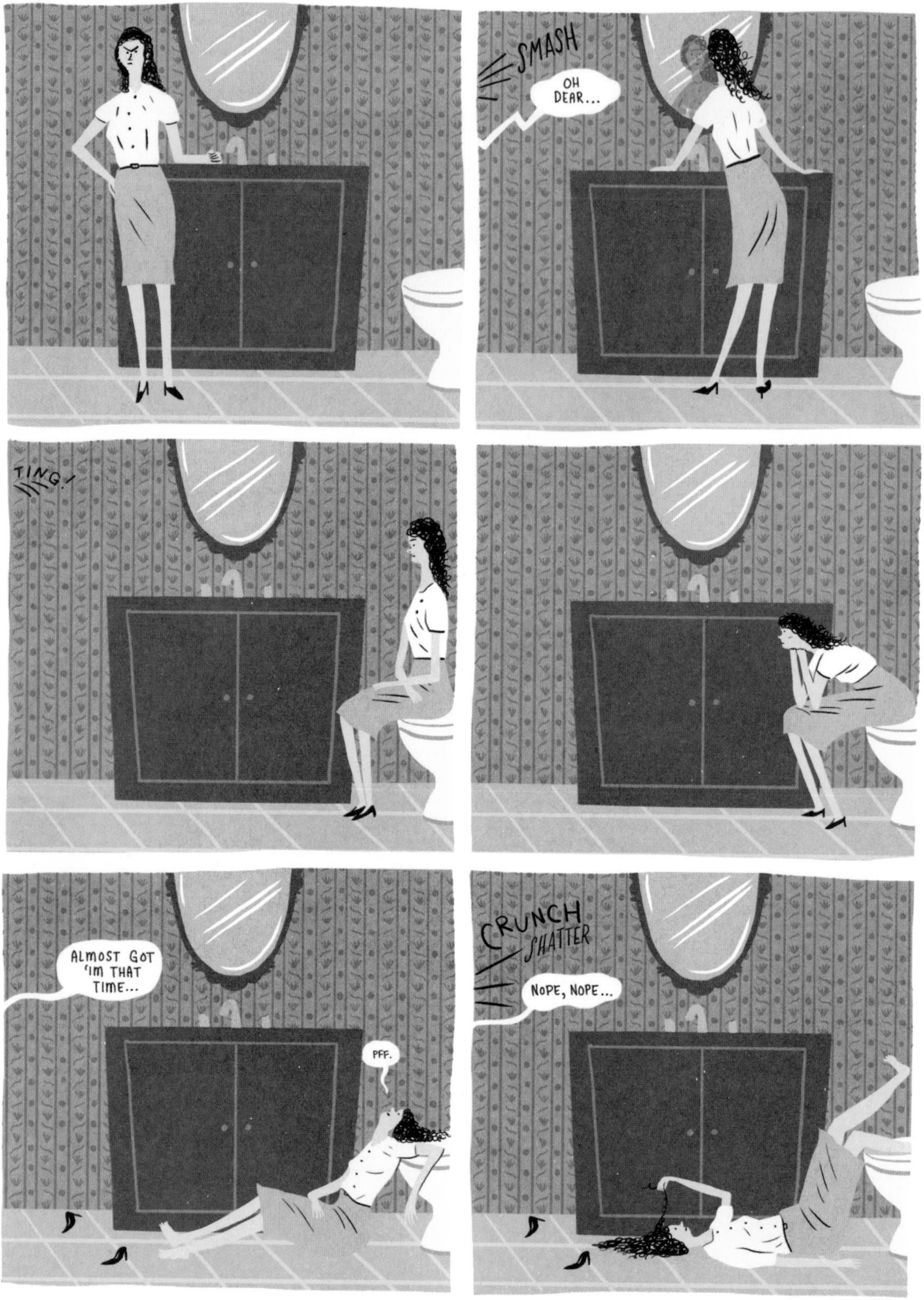
SMASH
OH DEAR...
TING!
ALMOST GOT 'IM THAT TIME...
PFF.
CRUNCH
SHATTER
NOPE, NOPE...

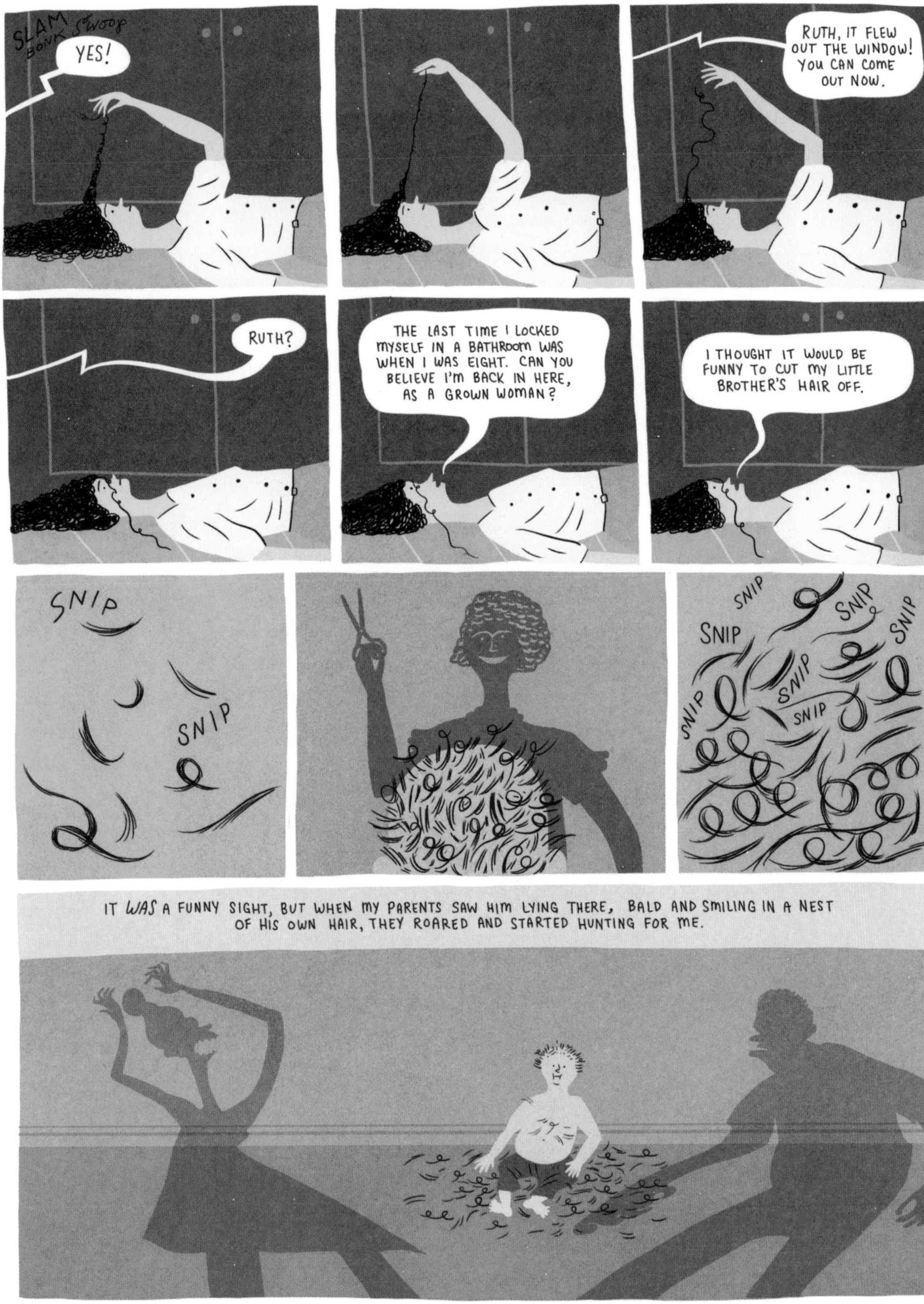
SLAM
BONK
SWOOP
YES!
RUTH, IT FLEW OUT THE WINDOW! YOU CAN COME OUT NOW.
RUTH?
THE LAST TIME I LOCKED MYSELF IN A BATHROOM WAS WHEN I WAS EIGHT. CAN YOU BELIEVE I'M BACK IN HERE, AS A GROWN WOMAN?
I THOUGHT IT WOULD BE FUNNY TO CUT MY LITTLE BROTHER'S HAIR OFF.
SNIP
SNIP
SNIP
SNIP
SNIP
SNIP
SNIP
SNIP
SNIP
IT *WAS* A FUNNY SIGHT, BUT WHEN MY PARENTS SAW HIM LYING THERE, BALD AND SMILING IN A NEST OF HIS OWN HAIR, THEY ROARED AND STARTED HUNTING FOR ME.

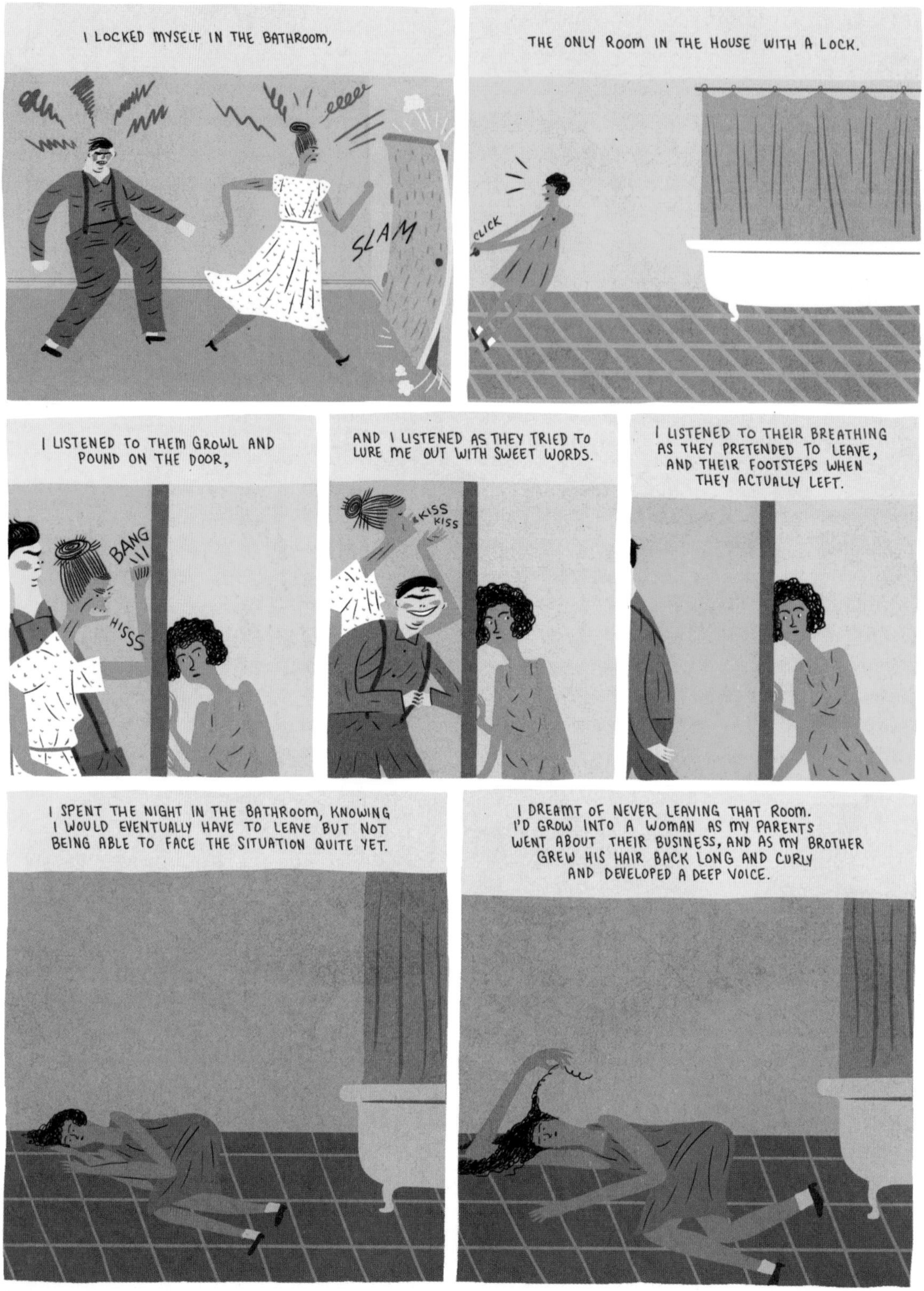
I LOCKED MYSELF IN THE BATHROOM,
SLAM
THE ONLY ROOM IN THE HOUSE WITH A LOCK.
CLICK
I LISTENED TO THEM GROWL AND POUND ON THE DOOR,
BANG
HISSS
AND I LISTENED AS THEY TRIED TO LURE ME OUT WITH SWEET WORDS.
KISS KISS
I LISTENED TO THEIR BREATHING AS THEY PRETENDED TO LEAVE, AND THEIR FOOTSTEPS WHEN THEY ACTUALLY LEFT.
I SPENT THE NIGHT IN THE BATHROOM, KNOWING I WOULD EVENTUALLY HAVE TO LEAVE BUT NOT BEING ABLE TO FACE THE SITUATION QUITE YET.
I DREAMT OF NEVER LEAVING THAT ROOM. I'D GROW INTO A WOMAN AS MY PARENTS WENT ABOUT THEIR BUSINESS, AND AS MY BROTHER GREW HIS HAIR BACK LONG AND CURLY AND DEVELOPED A DEEP VOICE.

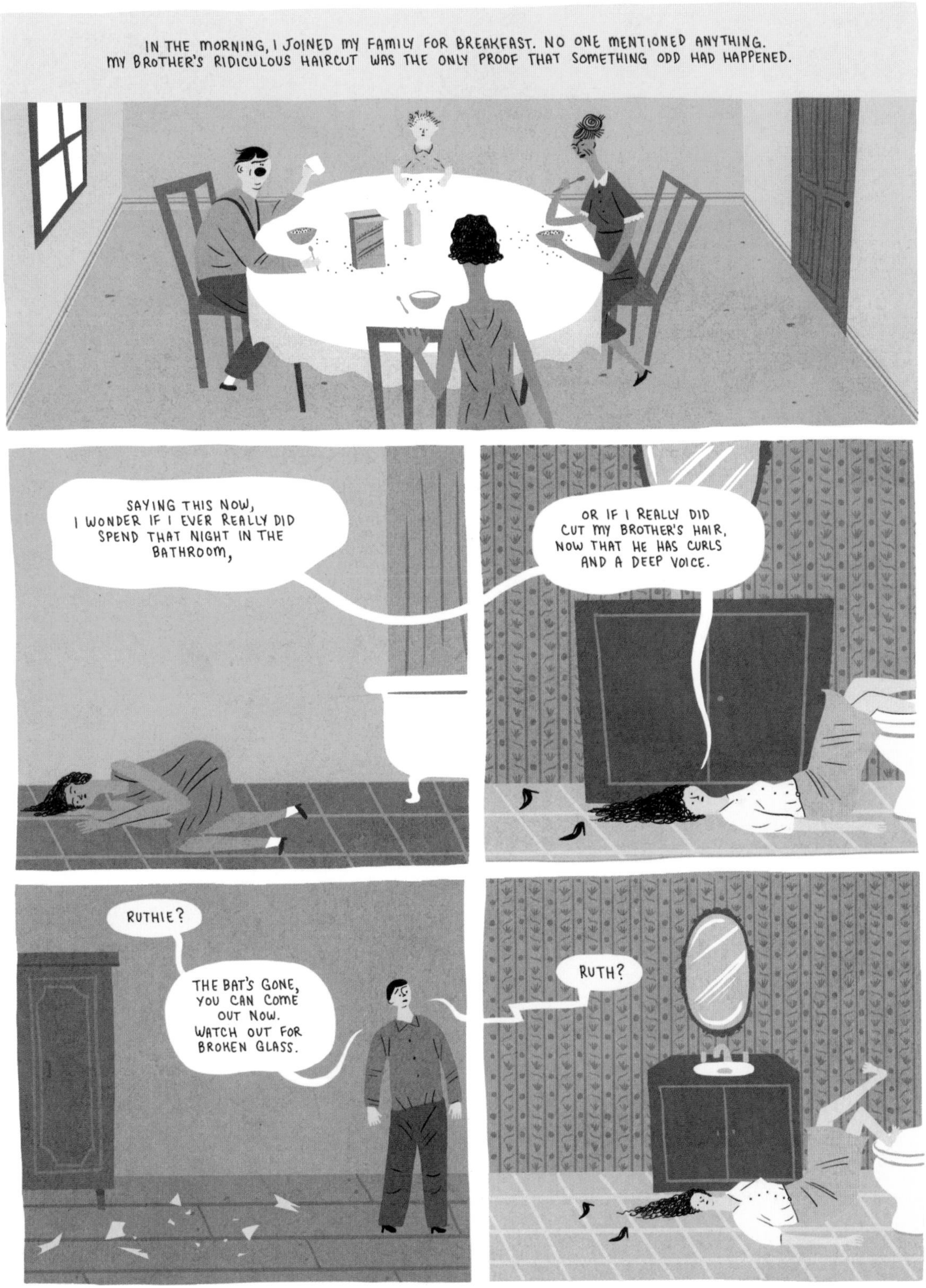
IN THE MORNING, I JOINED MY FAMILY FOR BREAKFAST. NO ONE MENTIONED ANYTHING. MY BROTHER'S RIDICULOUS HAIRCUT WAS THE ONLY PROOF THAT SOMETHING ODD HAD HAPPENED.
SAYING THIS NOW, I WONDER IF I EVER REALLY DID SPEND THAT NIGHT IN THE BATHROOM,
OR IF I REALLY DID CUT MY BROTHER'S HAIR, NOW THAT HE HAS CURLS AND A DEEP VOICE.
RUTHIE?
THE BAT'S GONE, YOU CAN COME OUT NOW. WATCH OUT FOR BROKEN GLASS.
RUTH?

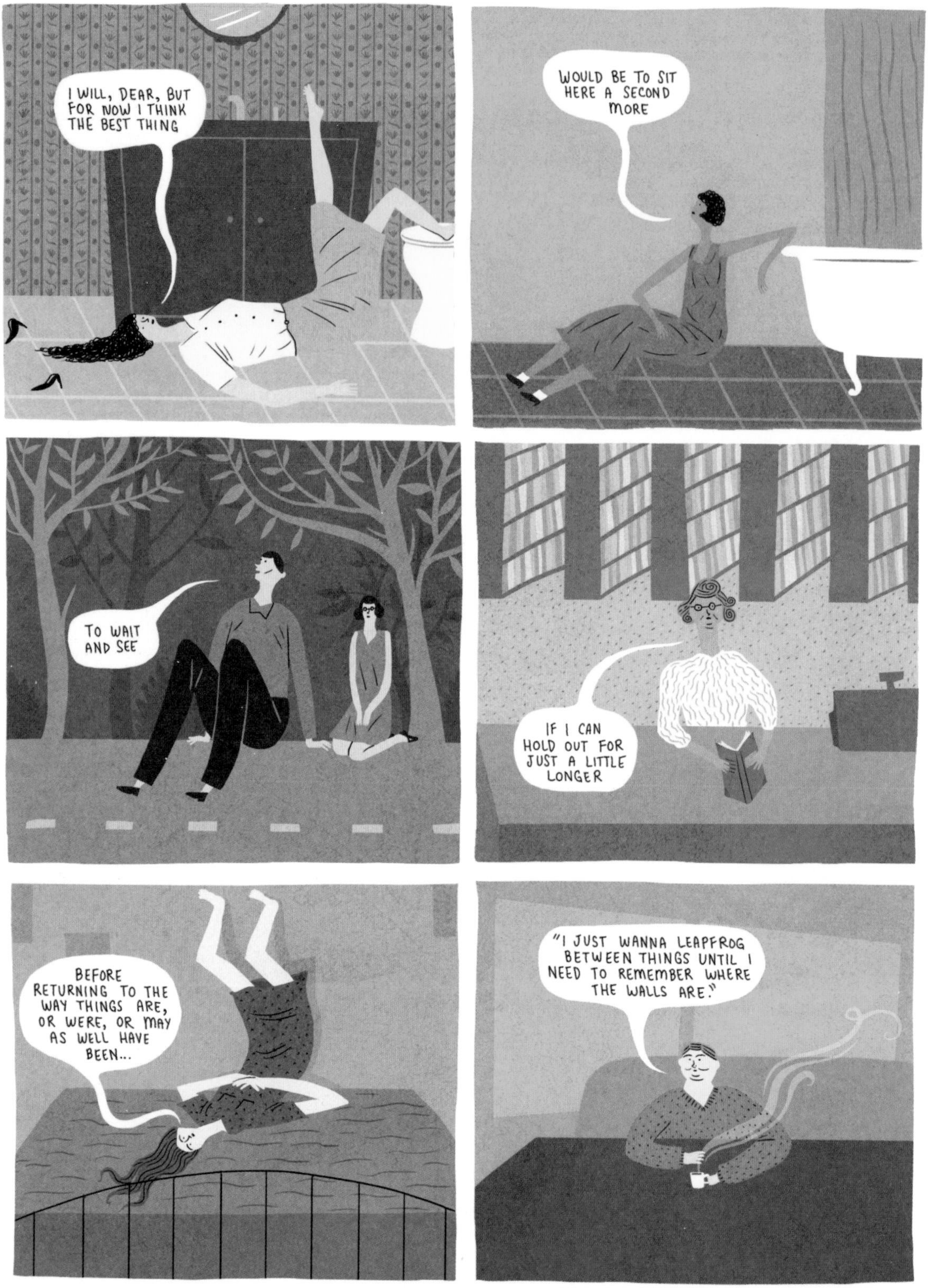
I WILL, DEAR, BUT FOR NOW I THINK THE BEST THING
WOULD BE TO SIT HERE A SECOND MORE
TO WAIT AND SEE
IF I CAN HOLD OUT FOR JUST A LITTLE LONGER
BEFORE RETURNING TO THE WAY THINGS ARE, OR WERE, OR MAY AS WELL HAVE BEEN...
"I JUST WANNA LEAPFROG BETWEEN THINGS UNTIL I NEED TO REMEMBER WHERE THE WALLS ARE."

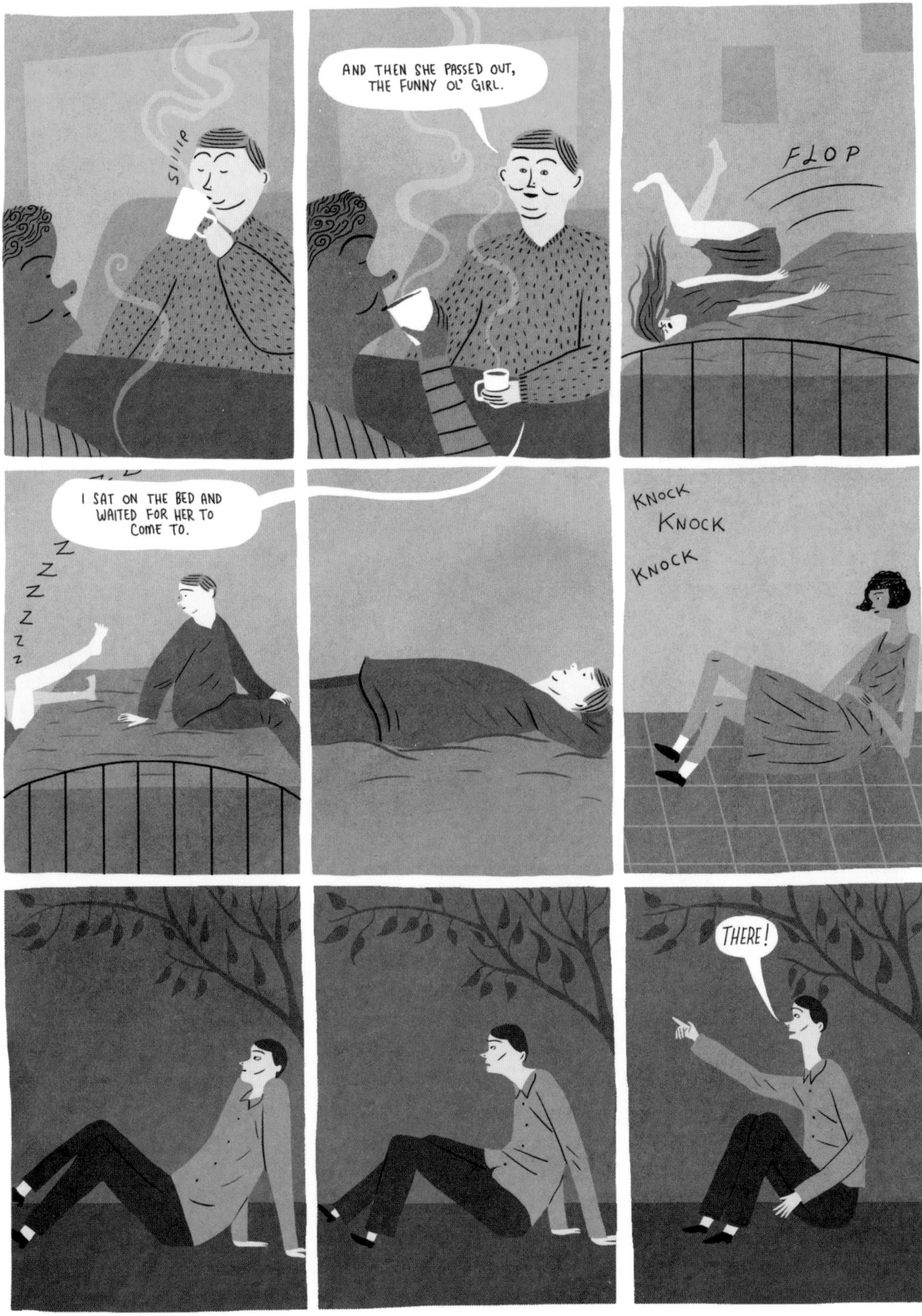
SLIIIP
AND THEN SHE PASSED OUT, THE FUNNY OL' GIRL.
FLOP
I SAT ON THE BED AND WAITED FOR HER TO COME TO.
Z Z Z Z Z Z
KNOCK
KNOCK
KNOCK
THERE!

The Flip

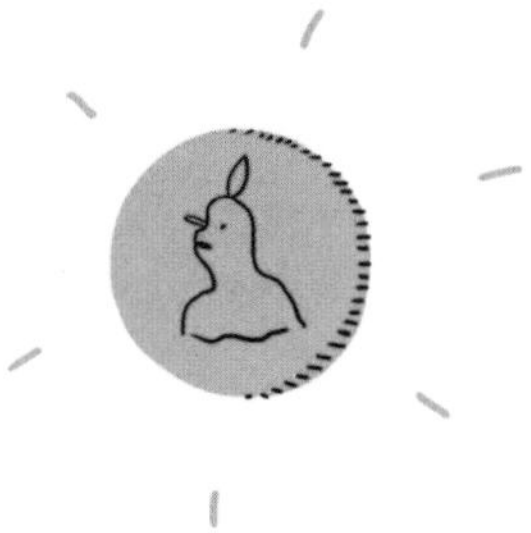

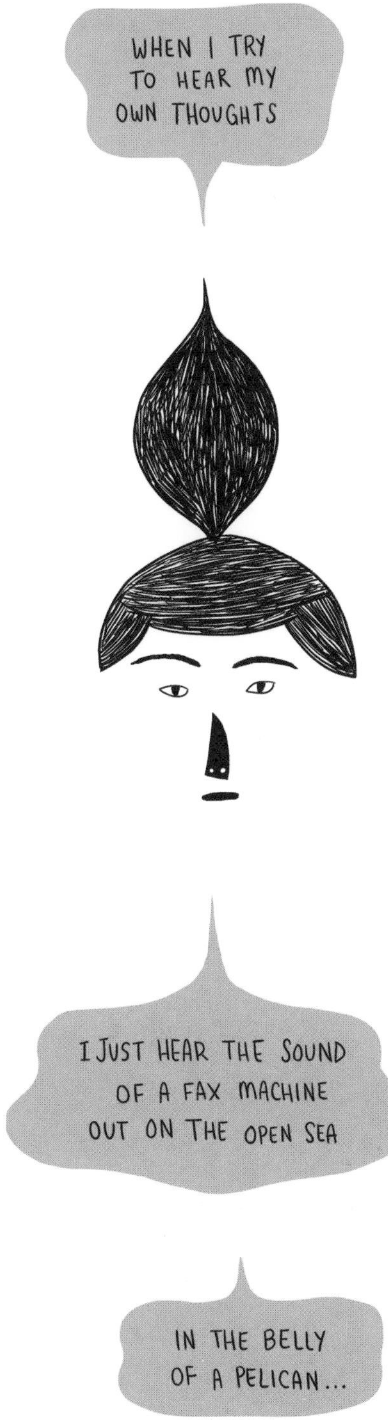
WHEN I TRY TO HEAR MY OWN THOUGHTS
I JUST HEAR THE SOUND OF A FAX MACHINE OUT ON THE OPEN SEA
IN THE BELLY OF A PELICAN...

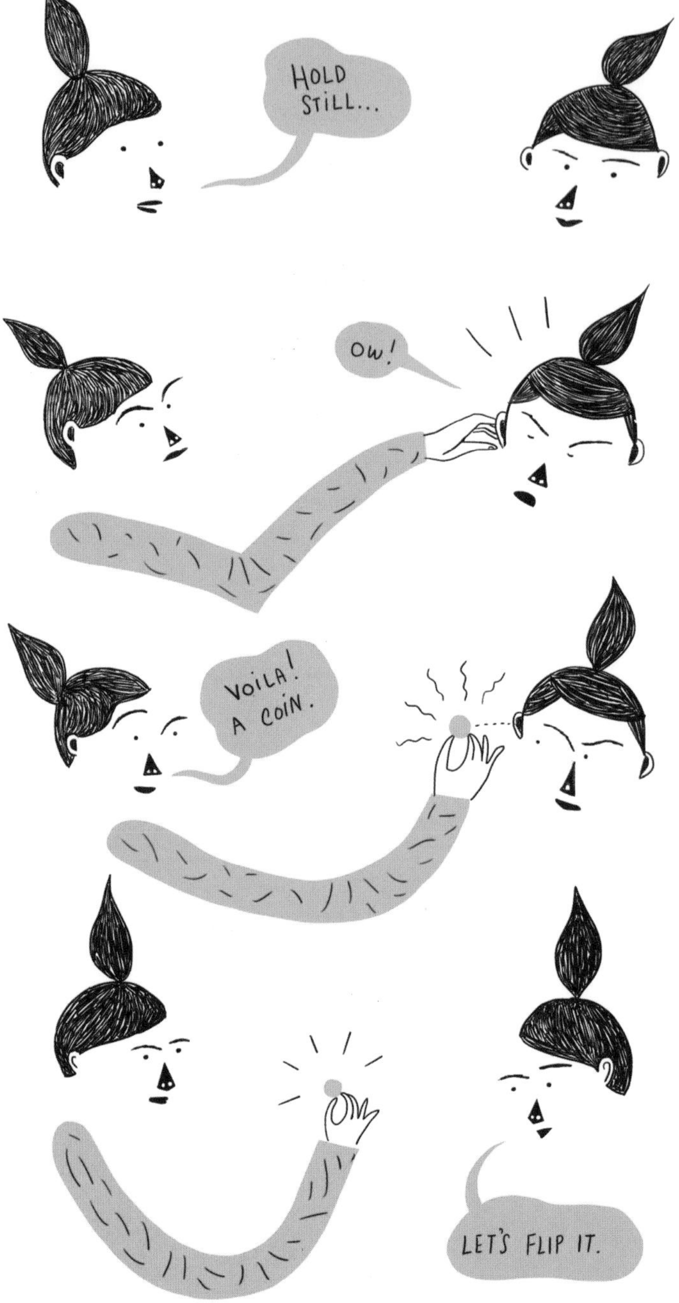
HOLD STILL...
OW!
VOILA! A COIN.
LET'S FLIP IT.

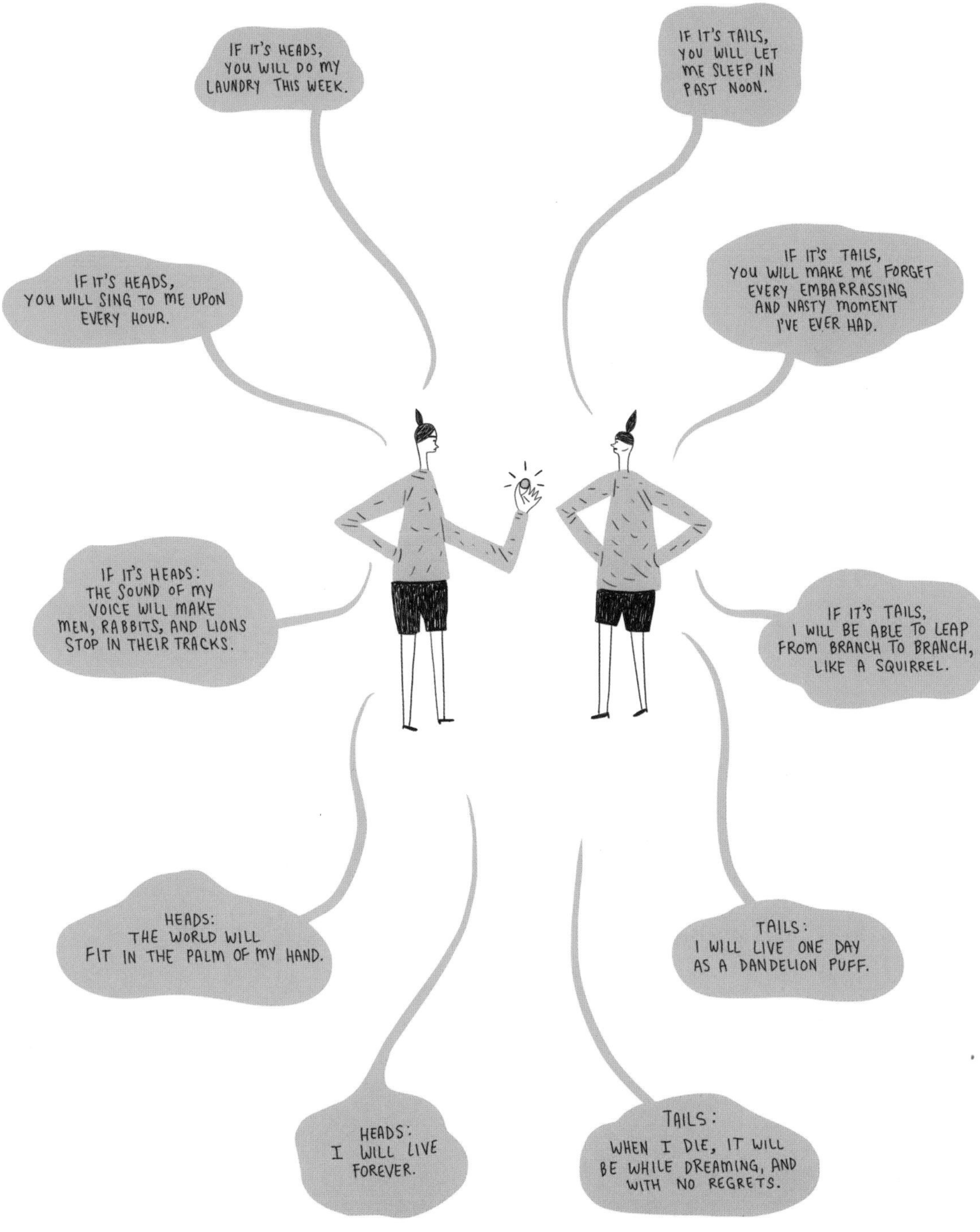
IF IT'S HEADS, YOU WILL DO MY LAUNDRY THIS WEEK.
IF IT'S TAILS, YOU WILL LET ME SLEEP IN PAST NOON.
IF IT'S HEADS, YOU WILL SING TO ME UPON EVERY HOUR.
IF IT'S TAILS, YOU WILL MAKE ME FORGET EVERY EMBARRASSING AND NASTY MOMENT I'VE EVER HAD.
IF IT'S HEADS: THE SOUND OF MY VOICE WILL MAKE MEN, RABBITS, AND LIONS STOP IN THEIR TRACKS.
IF IT'S TAILS, I WILL BE ABLE TO LEAP FROM BRANCH TO BRANCH, LIKE A SQUIRREL.
HEADS: THE WORLD WILL FIT IN THE PALM OF MY HAND.
TAILS: I WILL LIVE ONE DAY AS A DANDELION PUFF.
HEADS: I WILL LIVE FOREVER.
TAILS: WHEN I DIE, IT WILL BE WHILE DREAMING, AND WITH NO REGRETS.

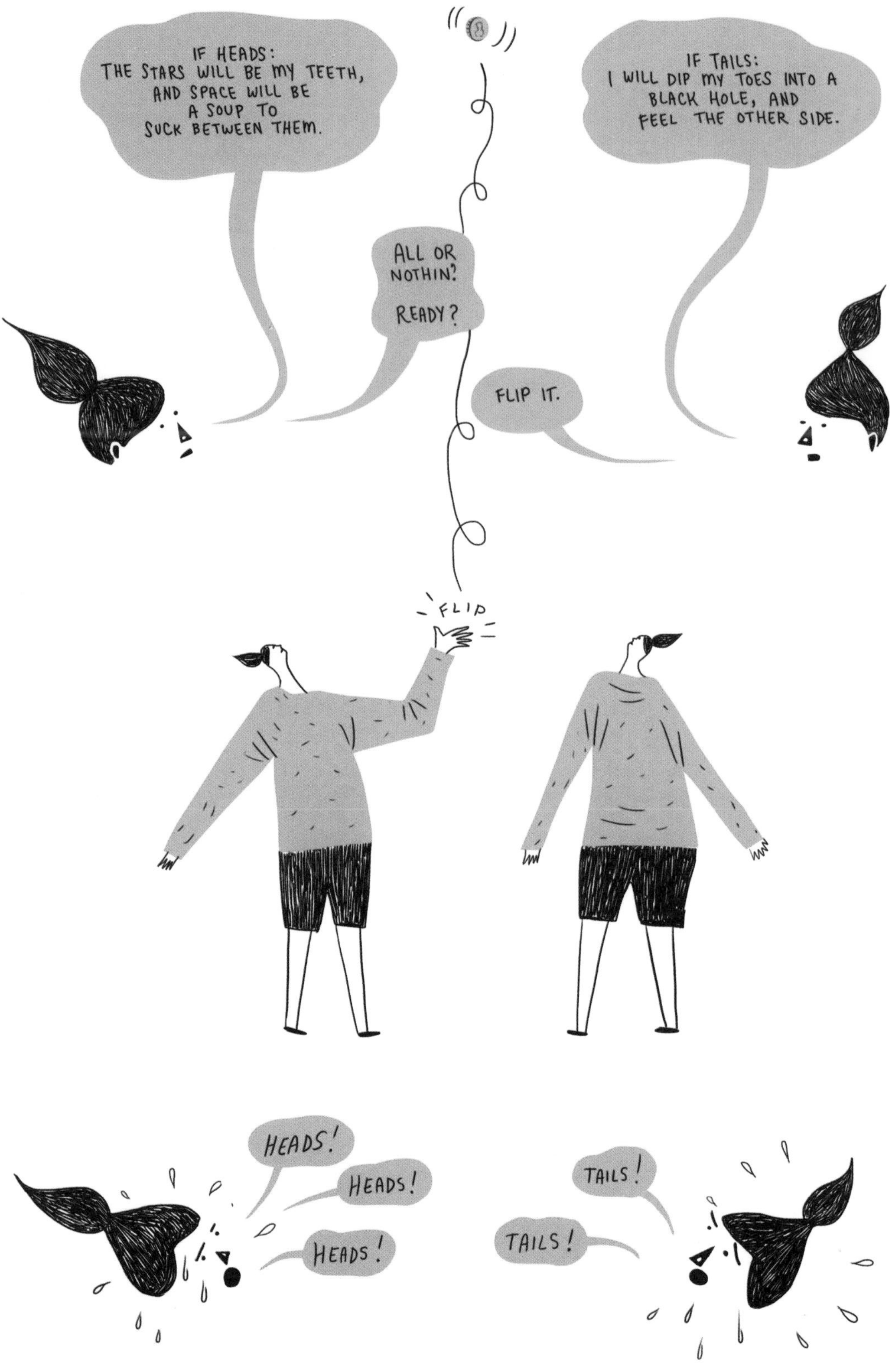
IF HEADS: THE STARS WILL BE MY TEETH, AND SPACE WILL BE A SOUP TO SUCK BETWEEN THEM.
IF TAILS: I WILL DIP MY TOES INTO A BLACK HOLE, AND FEEL THE OTHER SIDE.
ALL OR NOTHIN? READY?
FLIP IT.
FLIP
HEADS!
HEADS!
HEADS!
TAILS!
TAILS!

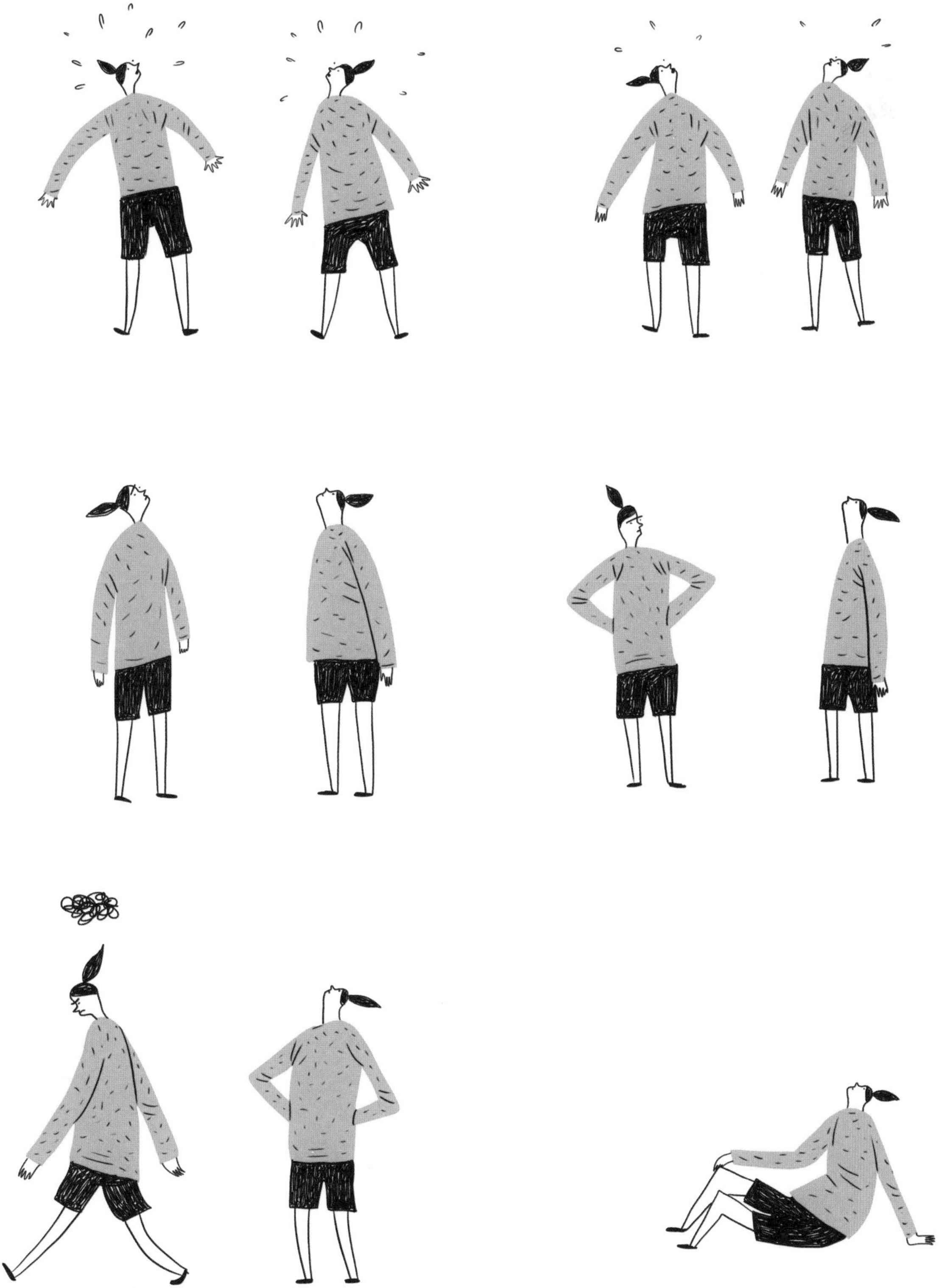

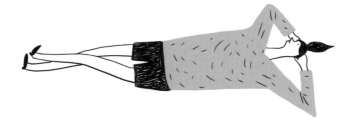

Short Bits

A Collection of Shorter Pieces

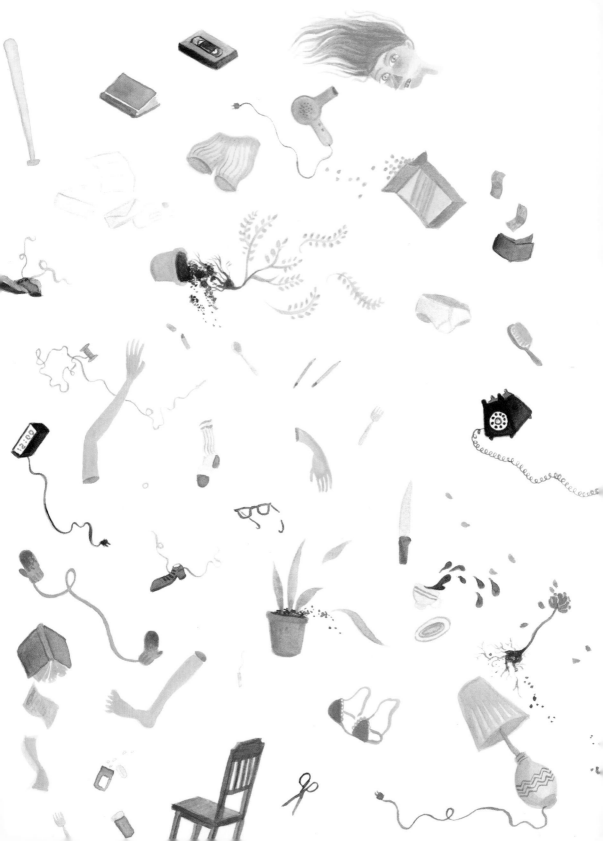

JUST GOTTA LET THE CARROTS SOAK OVERNI...

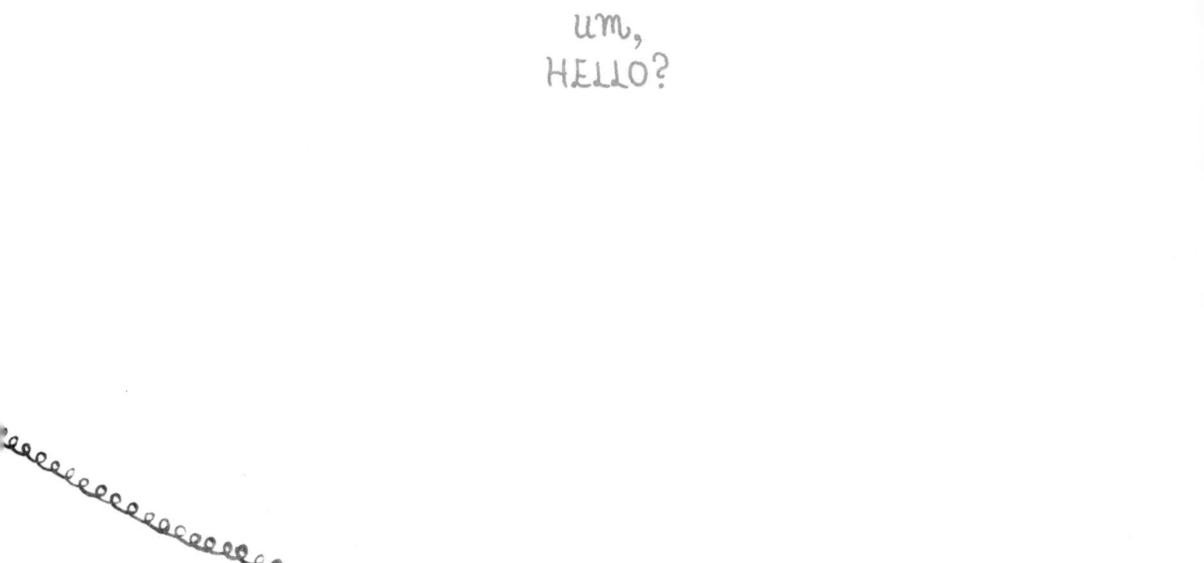
um,
HELLO?

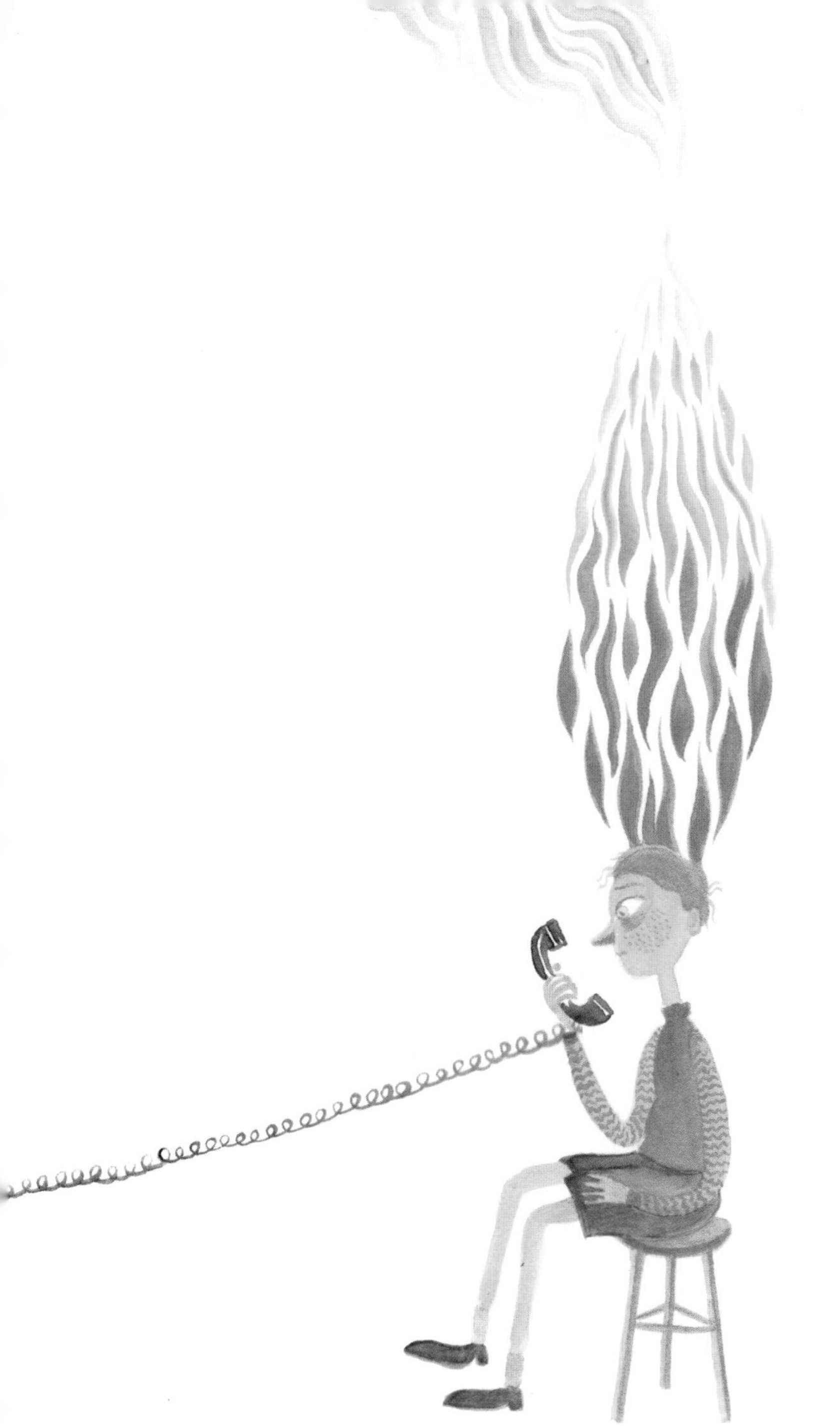

ALL IN A DAY'S WORK

by LILLI CARRÉ

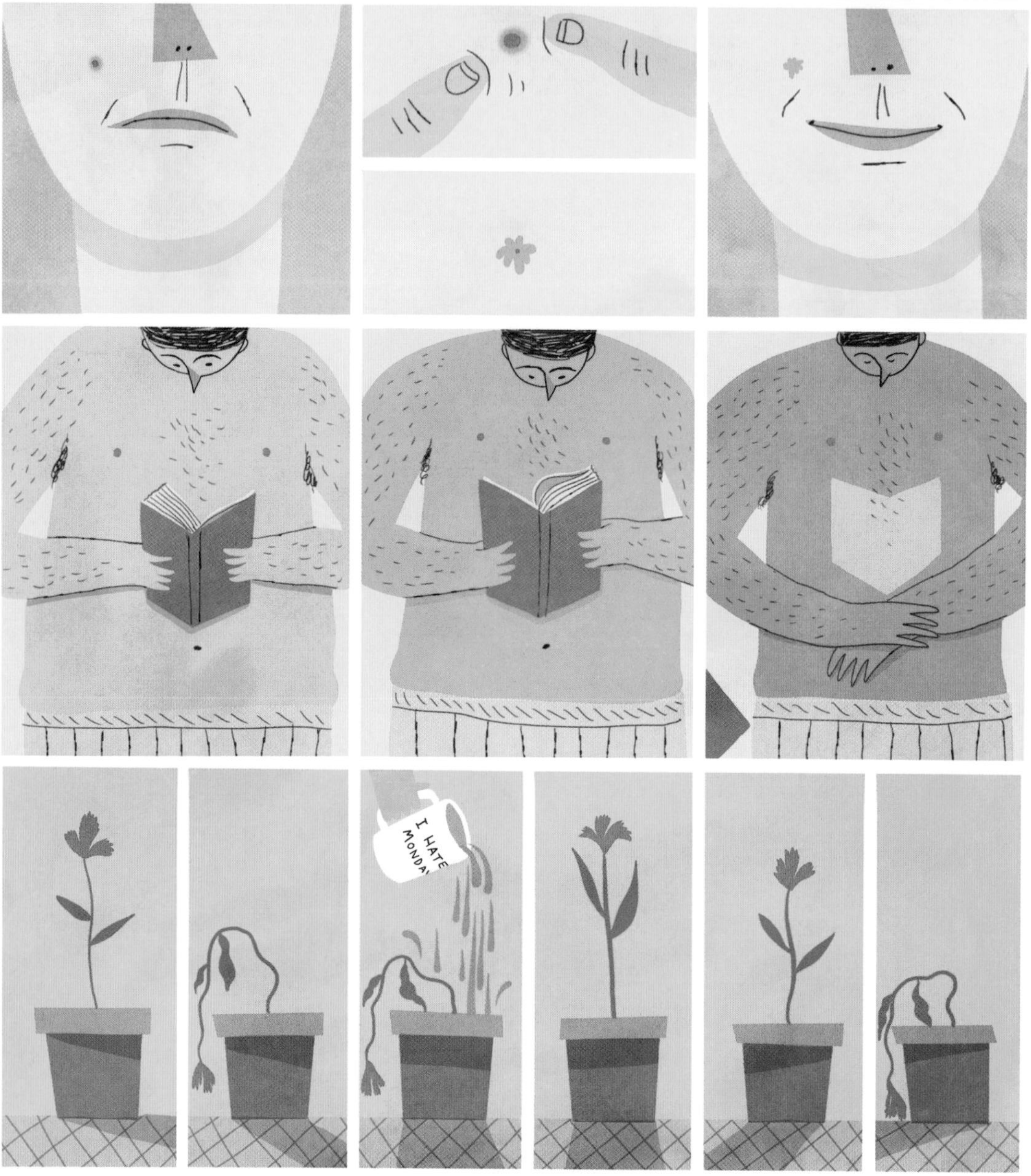
I HATE
MONDA

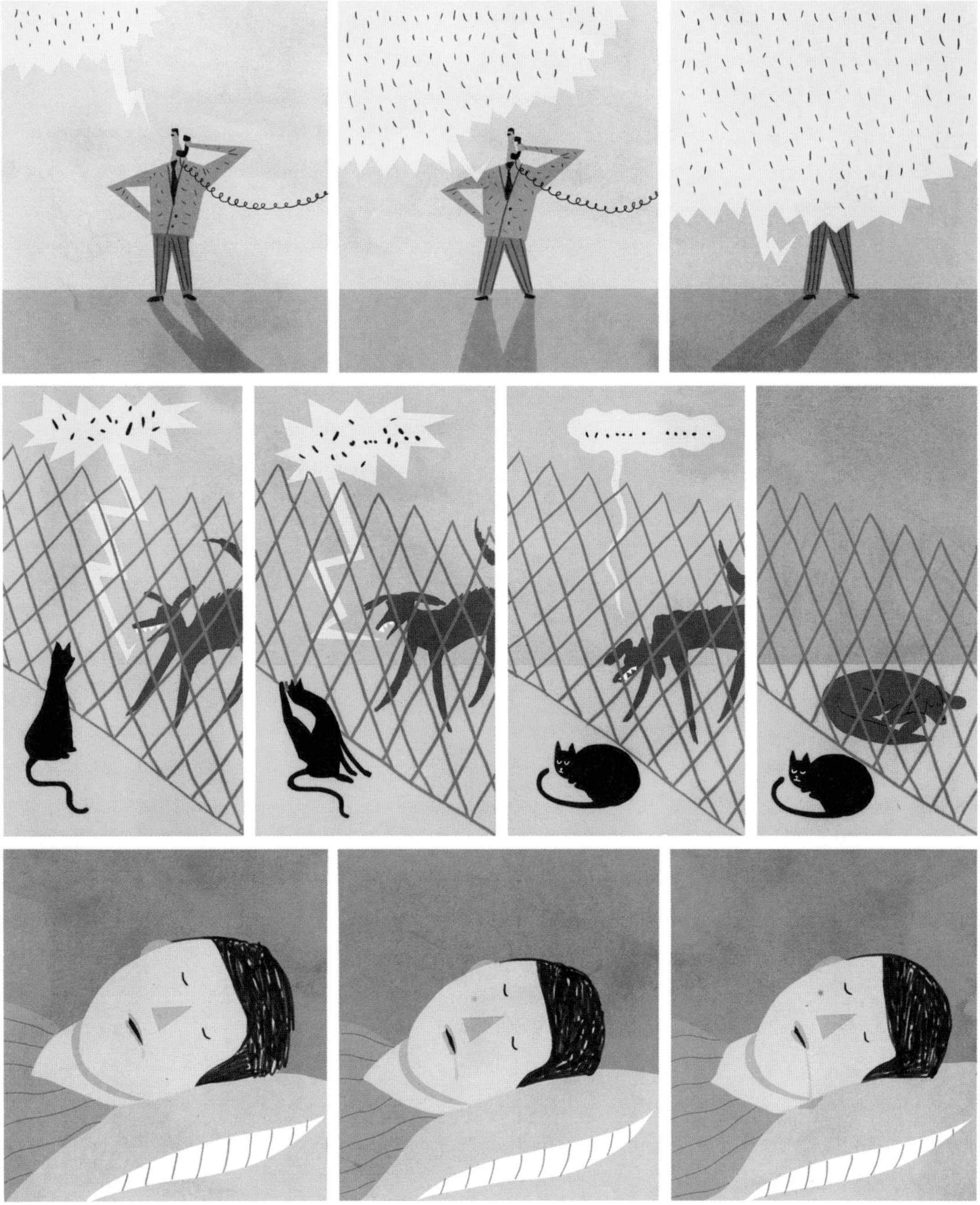

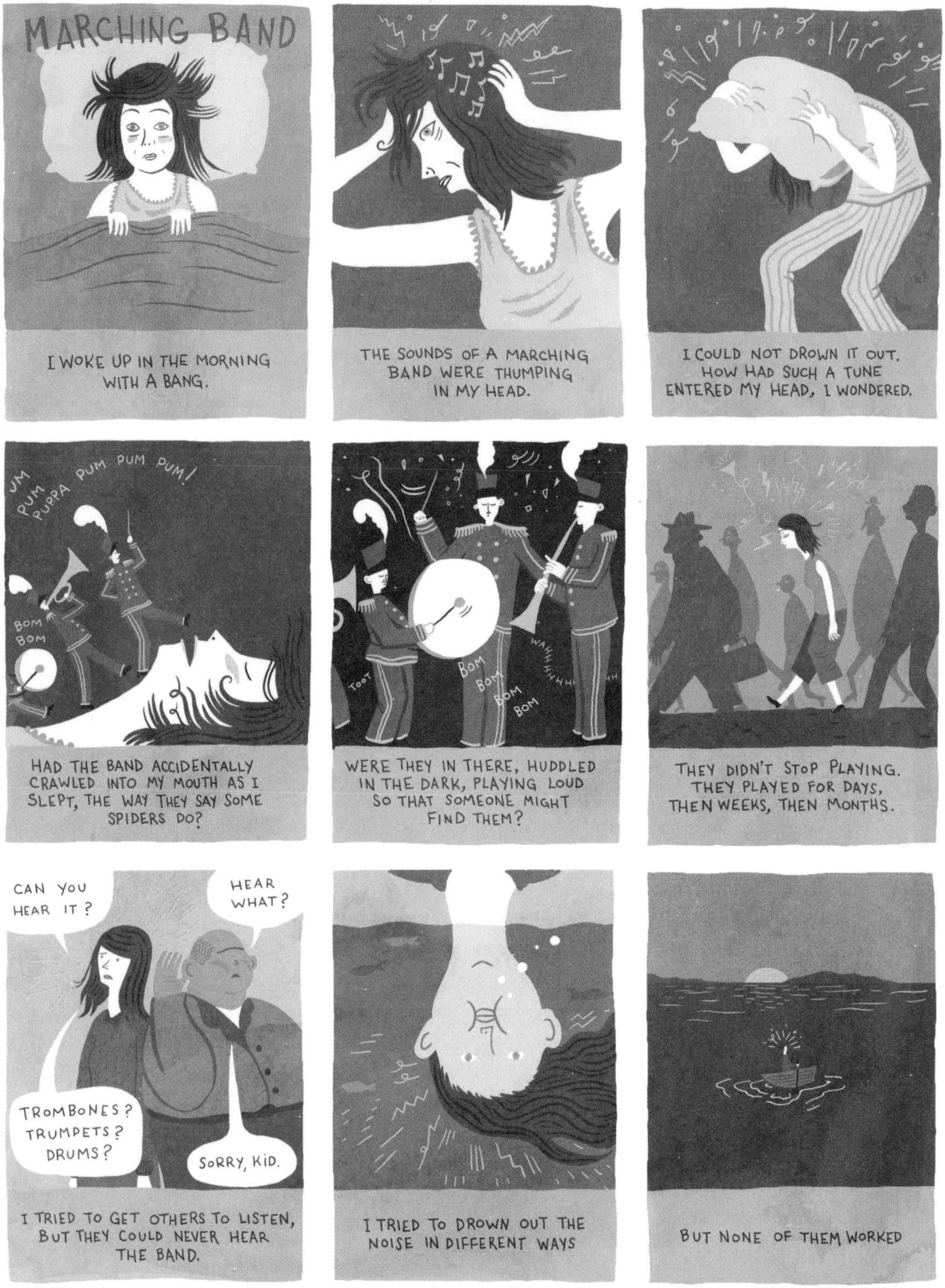
MARCHING BAND
I WOKE UP IN THE MORNING WITH A BANG.
THE SOUNDS OF A MARCHING BAND WERE THUMPING IN MY HEAD.
I COULD NOT DROWN IT OUT. HOW HAD SUCH A TUNE ENTERED MY HEAD, I WONDERED.
PUM PUPPA PUM PUM PUM!
BOM BOM
HAD THE BAND ACCIDENTALLY CRAWLED INTO MY MOUTH AS I SLEPT, THE WAY THEY SAY SOME SPIDERS DO?
TOOT
BOM BOM BOM BOM
WERE THEY IN THERE, HUDDLED IN THE DARK, PLAYING LOUD SO THAT SOMEONE MIGHT FIND THEM?
THEY DIDN'T STOP PLAYING. THEY PLAYED FOR DAYS, THEN WEEKS, THEN MONTHS.
CAN YOU HEAR IT?
HEAR WHAT?
TROMBONES? TRUMPETS? DRUMS?
SORRY, KID.
I TRIED TO GET OTHERS TO LISTEN, BUT THEY COULD NEVER HEAR THE BAND.
I TRIED TO DROWN OUT THE NOISE IN DIFFERENT WAYS
BUT NONE OF THEM WORKED

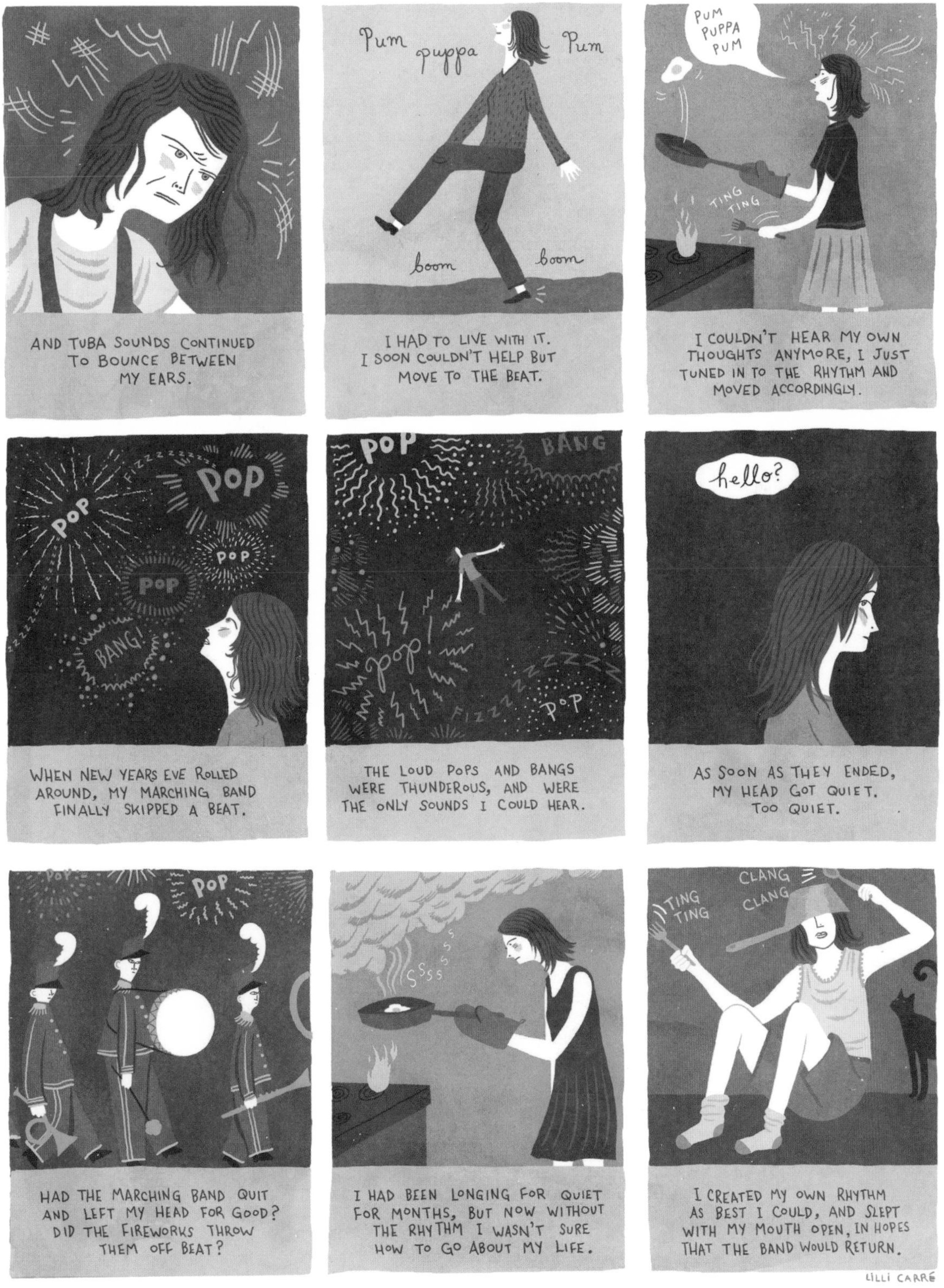
AND TUBA SOUNDS CONTINUED TO BOUNCE BETWEEN MY EARS.
Pum puppa Pum
boom boom
I HAD TO LIVE WITH IT. I SOON COULDN'T HELP BUT MOVE TO THE BEAT.
PUM PUPPA PUM
TING TING
I COULDN'T HEAR MY OWN THOUGHTS ANYMORE, I JUST TUNED IN TO THE RHYTHM AND MOVED ACCORDINGLY.
FIZZZZZZZZ
POP
POP
POP
POP
BANG!
WHEN NEW YEARS EVE ROLLED AROUND, MY MARCHING BAND FINALLY SKIPPED A BEAT.
POP
BANG
pop!
FIZZZ
POP
THE LOUD POPS AND BANGS WERE THUNDEROUS, AND WERE THE ONLY SOUNDS I COULD HEAR.
hello?
AS SOON AS THEY ENDED, MY HEAD GOT QUIET. TOO QUIET.
POP
POP
HAD THE MARCHING BAND QUIT AND LEFT MY HEAD FOR GOOD? DID THE FIREWORKS THROW THEM OFF BEAT?
SSSSS
I HAD BEEN LONGING FOR QUIET FOR MONTHS, BUT NOW WITHOUT THE RHYTHM I WASN'T SURE HOW TO GO ABOUT MY LIFE.
TING TING
CLANG CLANG
I CREATED MY OWN RHYTHM AS BEST I COULD, AND SLEPT WITH MY MOUTH OPEN, IN HOPES THAT THE BAND WOULD RETURN.
LILLI CARRÉ

Moss

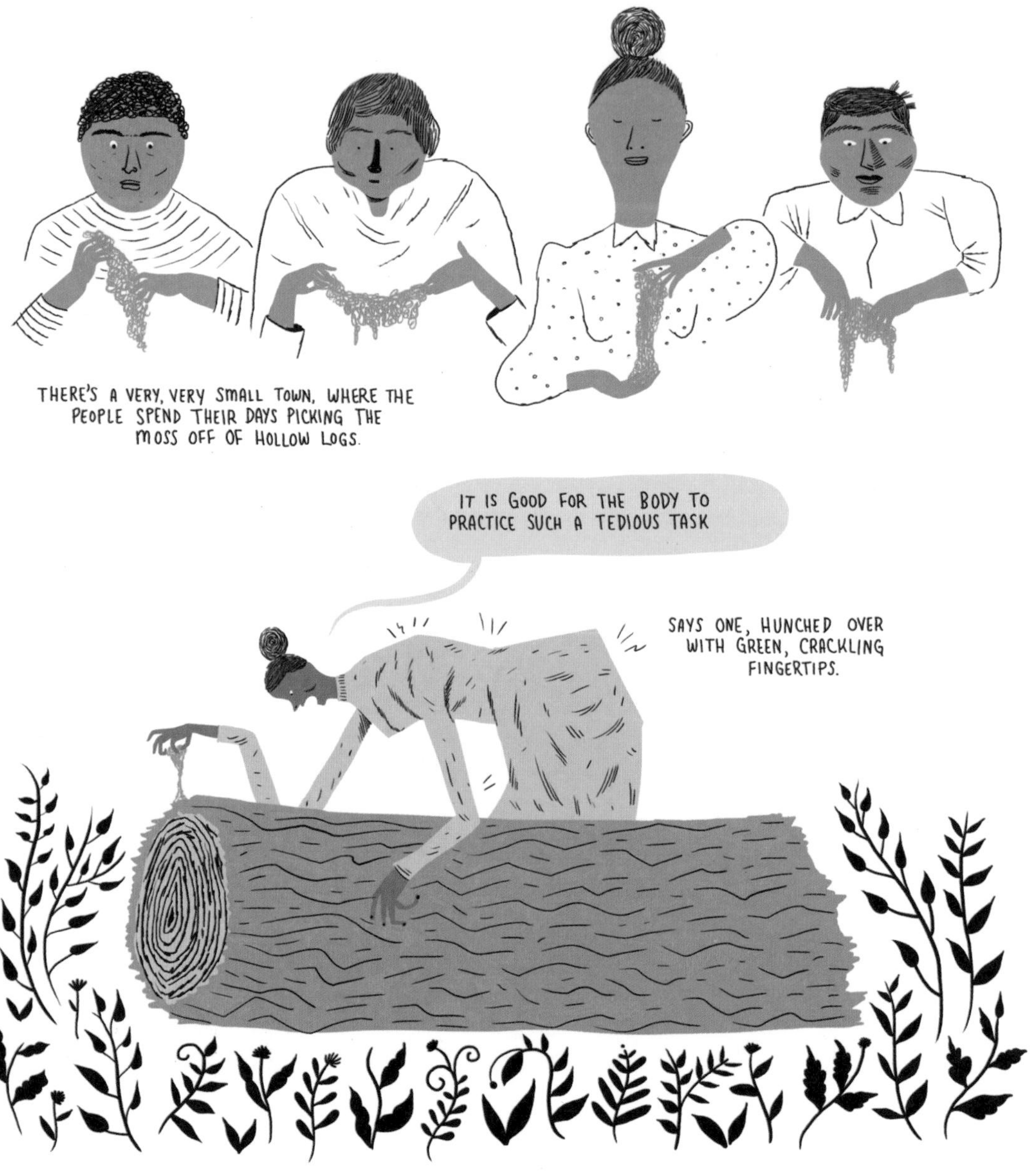

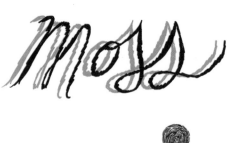

THERE'S A VERY, VERY SMALL TOWN, WHERE THE PEOPLE SPEND THEIR DAYS PICKING THE MOSS OFF OF HOLLOW LOGS.
IT IS GOOD FOR THE BODY TO PRACTICE SUCH A TEDIOUS TASK
SAYS ONE, HUNCHED OVER WITH GREEN, CRACKLING FINGERTIPS.

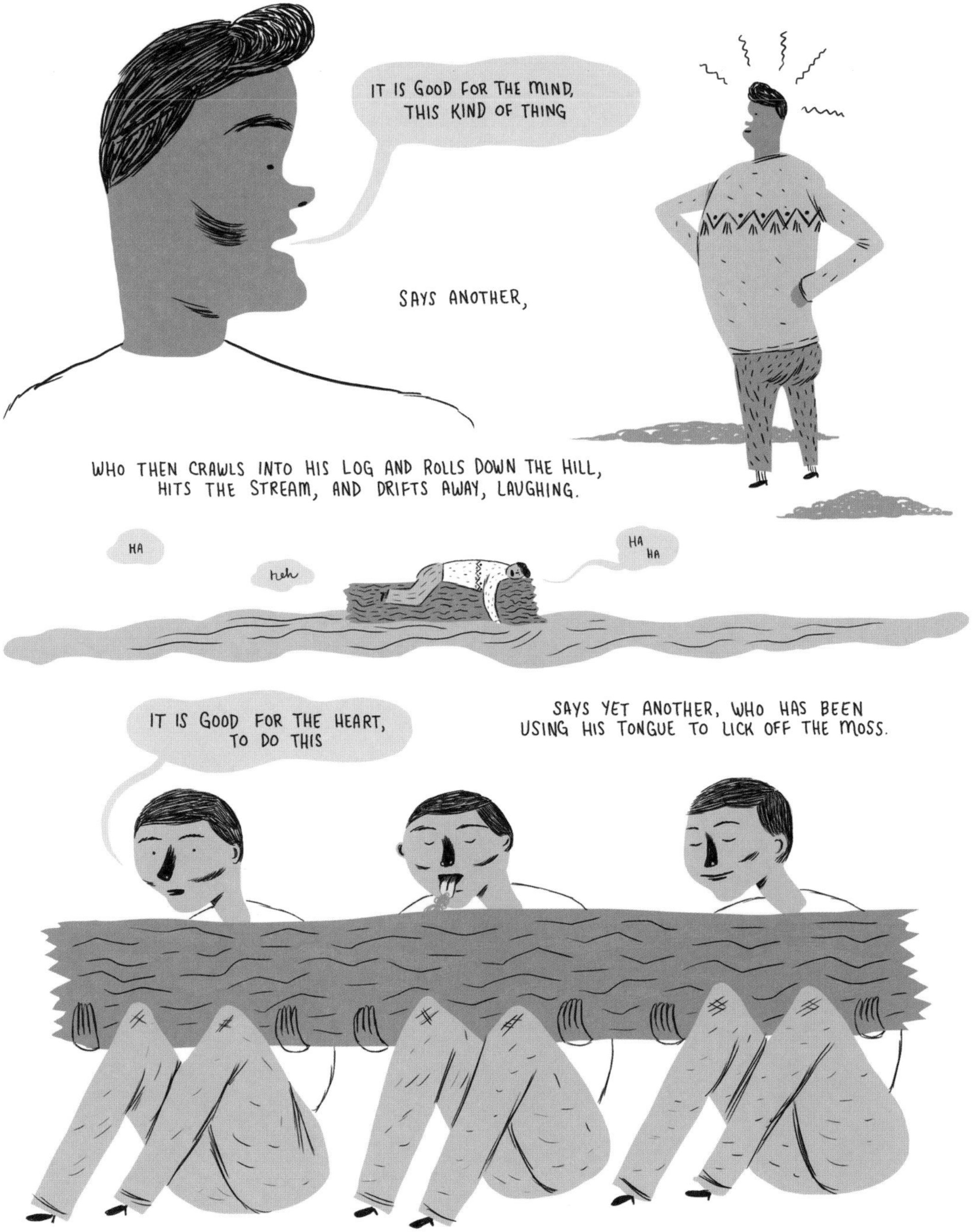
IT IS GOOD FOR THE MIND, THIS KIND OF THING
SAYS ANOTHER,
WHO THEN CRAWLS INTO HIS LOG AND ROLLS DOWN THE HILL, HITS THE STREAM, AND DRIFTS AWAY, LAUGHING.
HA
heh
HA HA
IT IS GOOD FOR THE HEART, TO DO THIS
SAYS YET ANOTHER, WHO HAS BEEN USING HIS TONGUE TO LICK OFF THE MOSS.

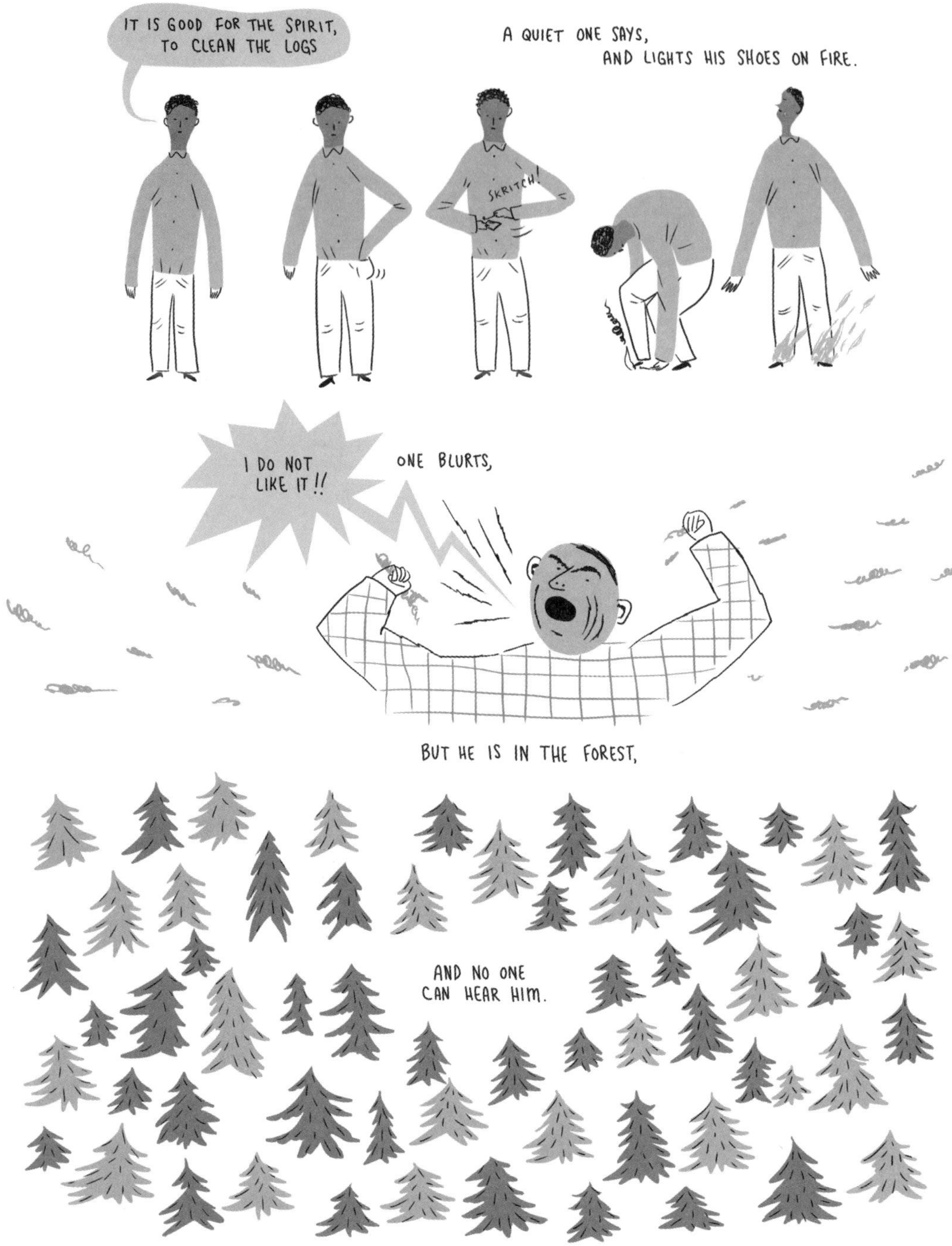
IT IS GOOD FOR THE SPIRIT, TO CLEAN THE LOGS
A QUIET ONE SAYS, AND LIGHTS HIS SHOES ON FIRE.
SKRITCH!
I DO NOT LIKE IT!!
ONE BLURTS,
BUT HE IS IN THE FOREST,
AND NO ONE CAN HEAR HIM.

IT IS GOOD FOR THE TOWN, TO HAVE CLEAN LOGS LIKE THESE

ONE SAYS, STANDING BACK AND ADMIRING HER WORK.

THE LOGS REALLY ARE SOMETHING TO SEE. CLEAN AND POLISHED, AS IF UNTOUCHED BY TIME.

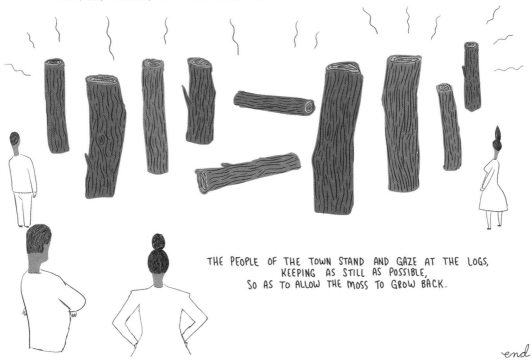

THE PEOPLE OF THE TOWN STAND AND GAZE AT THE LOGS, KEEPING AS STILL AS POSSIBLE, SO AS TO ALLOW THE MOSS TO GROW BACK.

end

MUCH BETTER

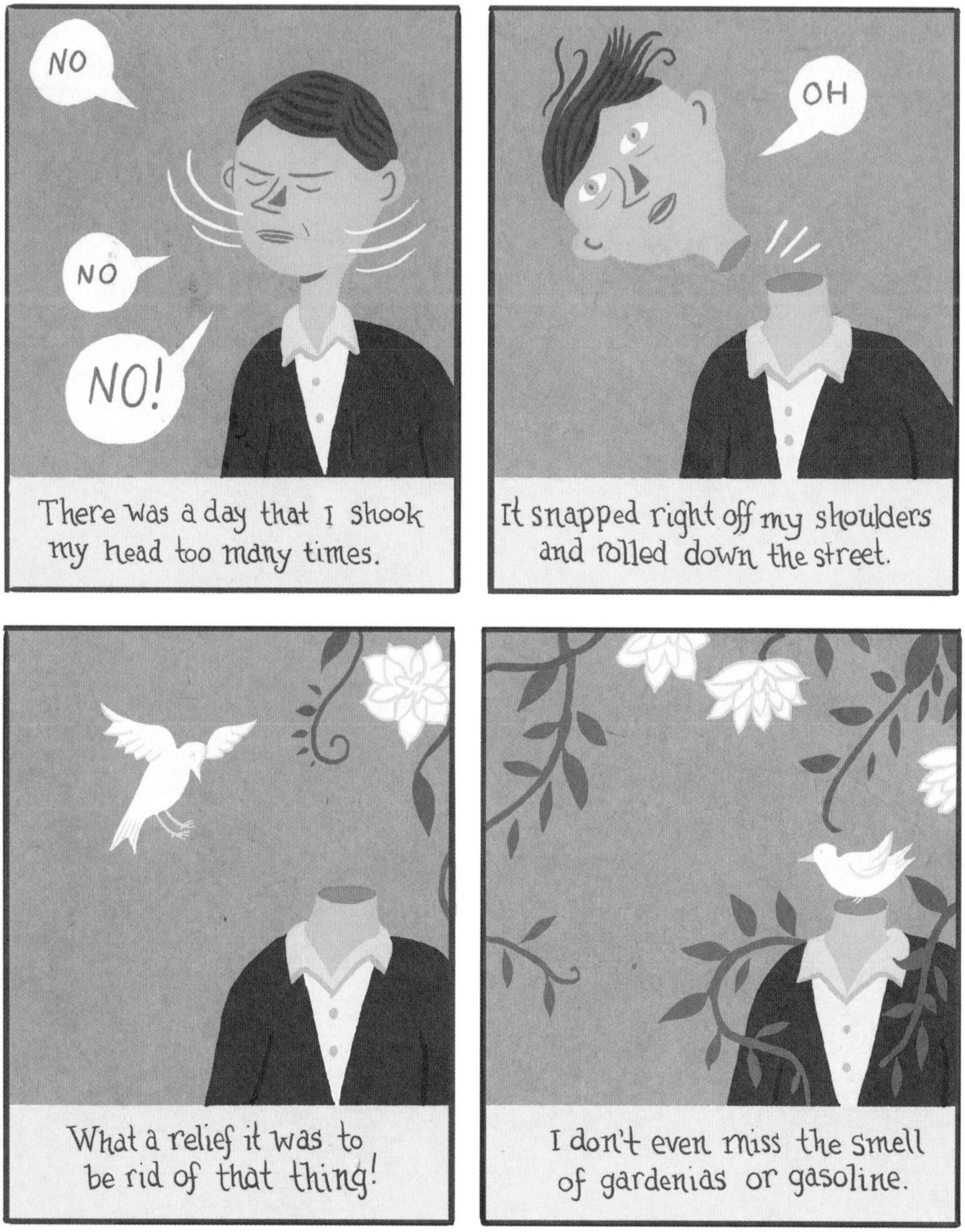

NO
NO
NO!
There was a day that I shook my head too many times.
OH
It snapped right off my shoulders and rolled down the street.
What a relief it was to be rid of that thing!
I don't even miss the smell of gardenias or gasoline.

PAINT

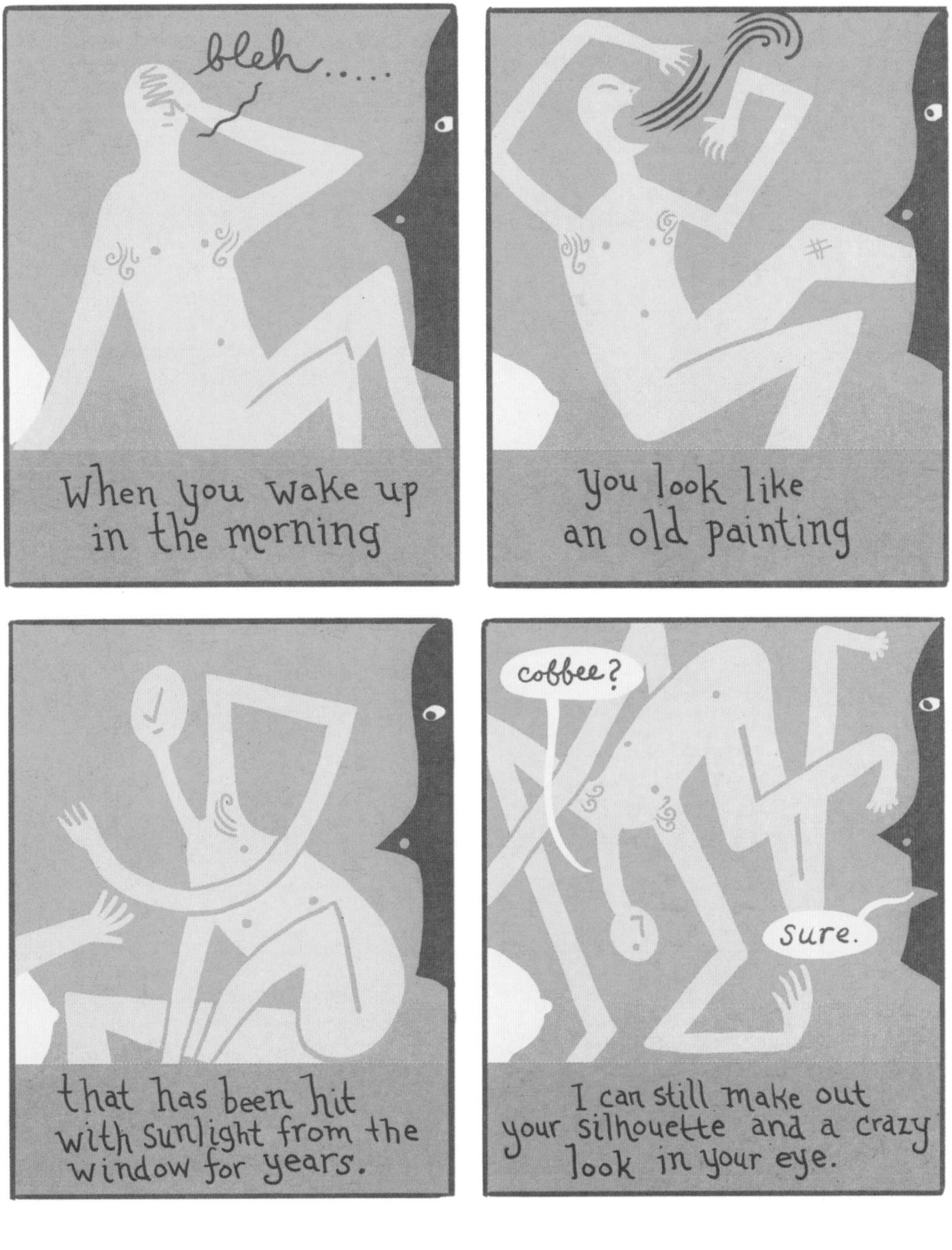
bleh.....
When you wake up in the morning
You look like an old painting
that has been hit with sunlight from the window for years.
cobbee?
sure.
I can still make out your silhouette and a crazy look in your eye.

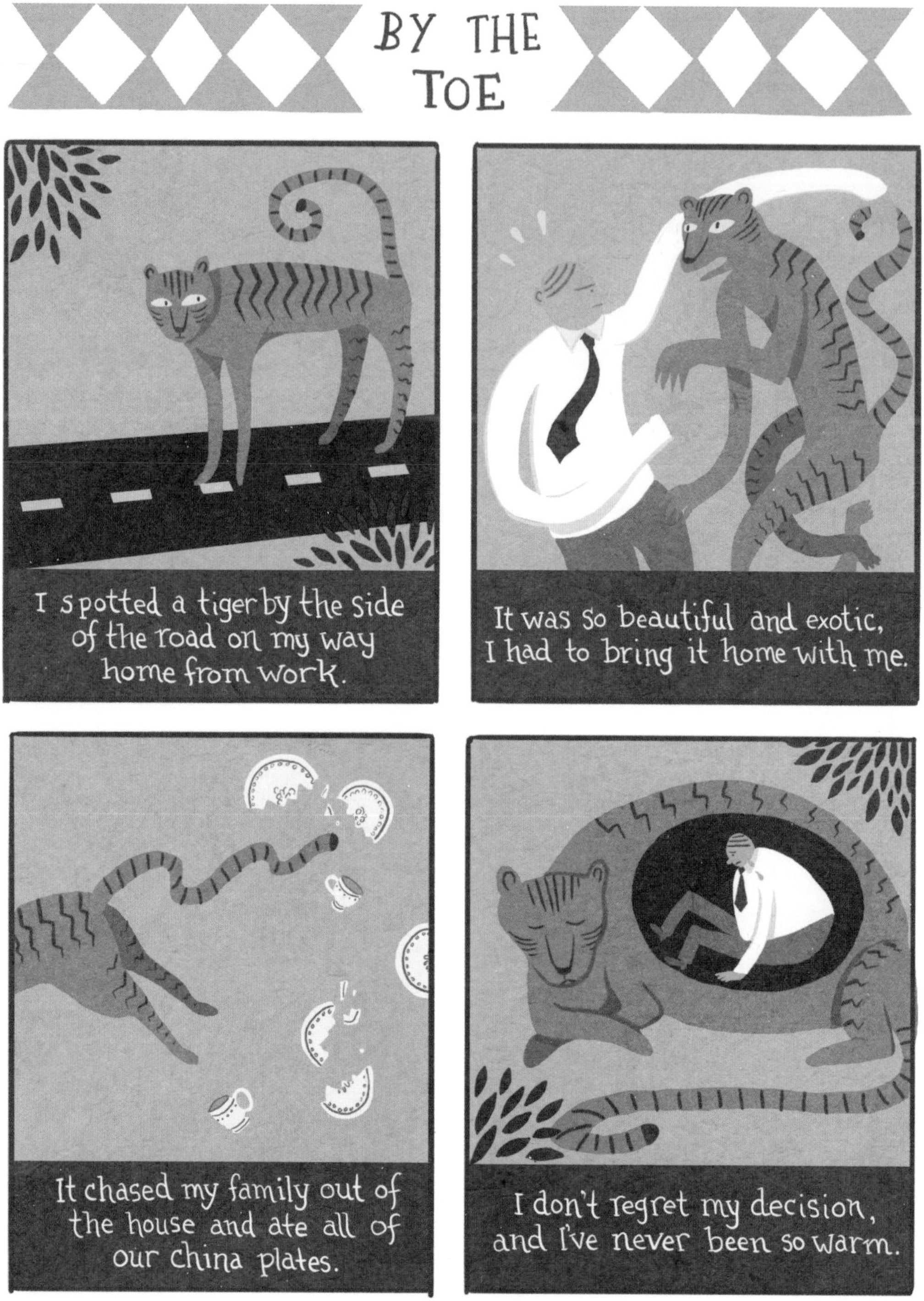
BY THE TOE
I spotted a tiger by the side of the road on my way home from work.
It was so beautiful and exotic, I had to bring it home with me.
It chased my family out of the house and ate all of our china plates.
I don't regret my decision, and I've never been so warm.

SPOTLESS

I used to be spotless

until my first lover.

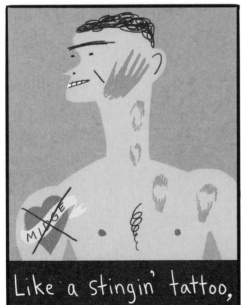

Like a stingin' tattoo,

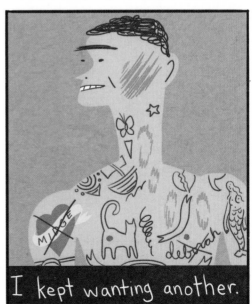

I kept wanting another.

MY NIGHT DANCE

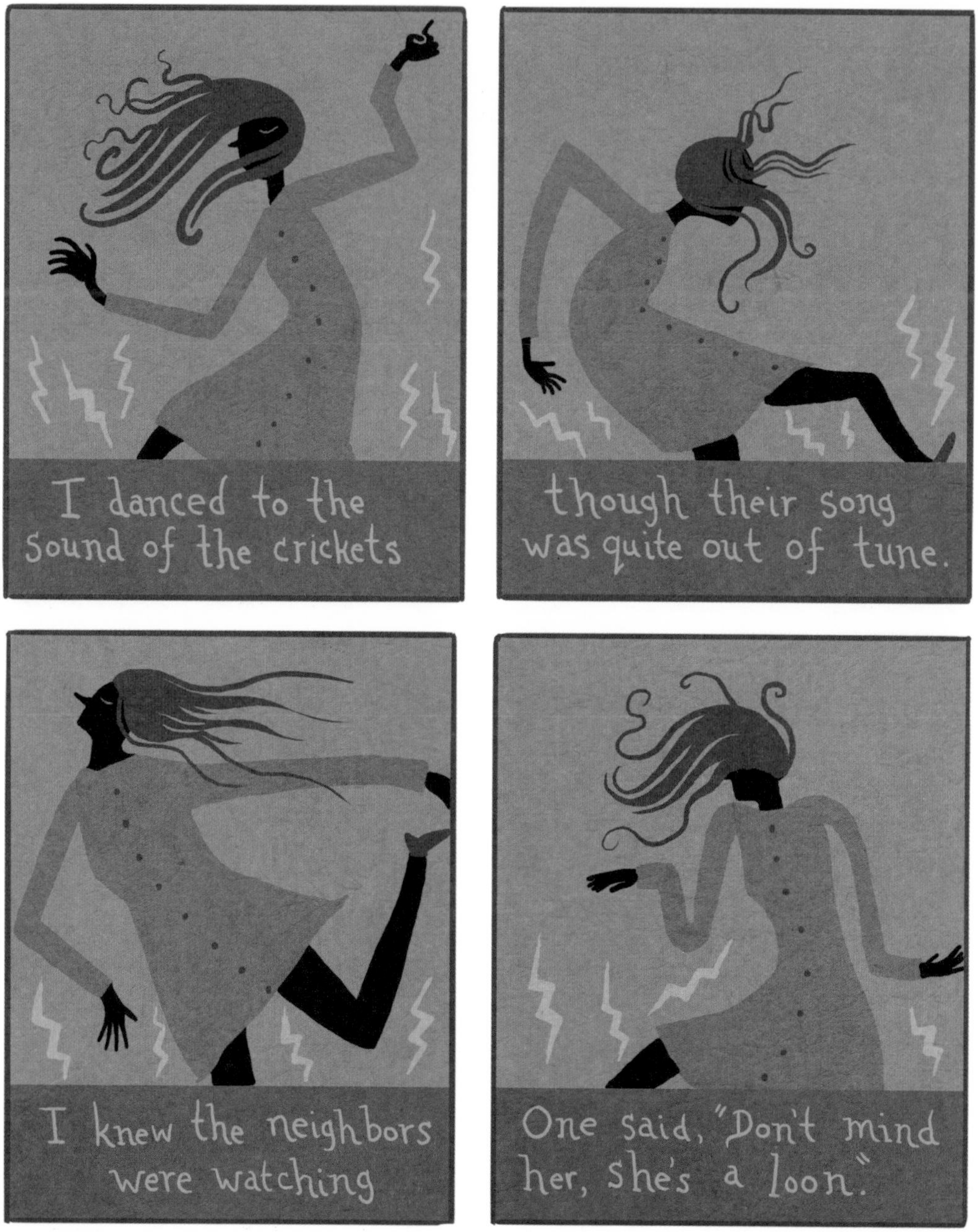
I danced to the sound of the crickets
though their song was quite out of tune.
I knew the neighbors were watching
One said, "Don't mind her, she's a loon."

MY DAY DANCE

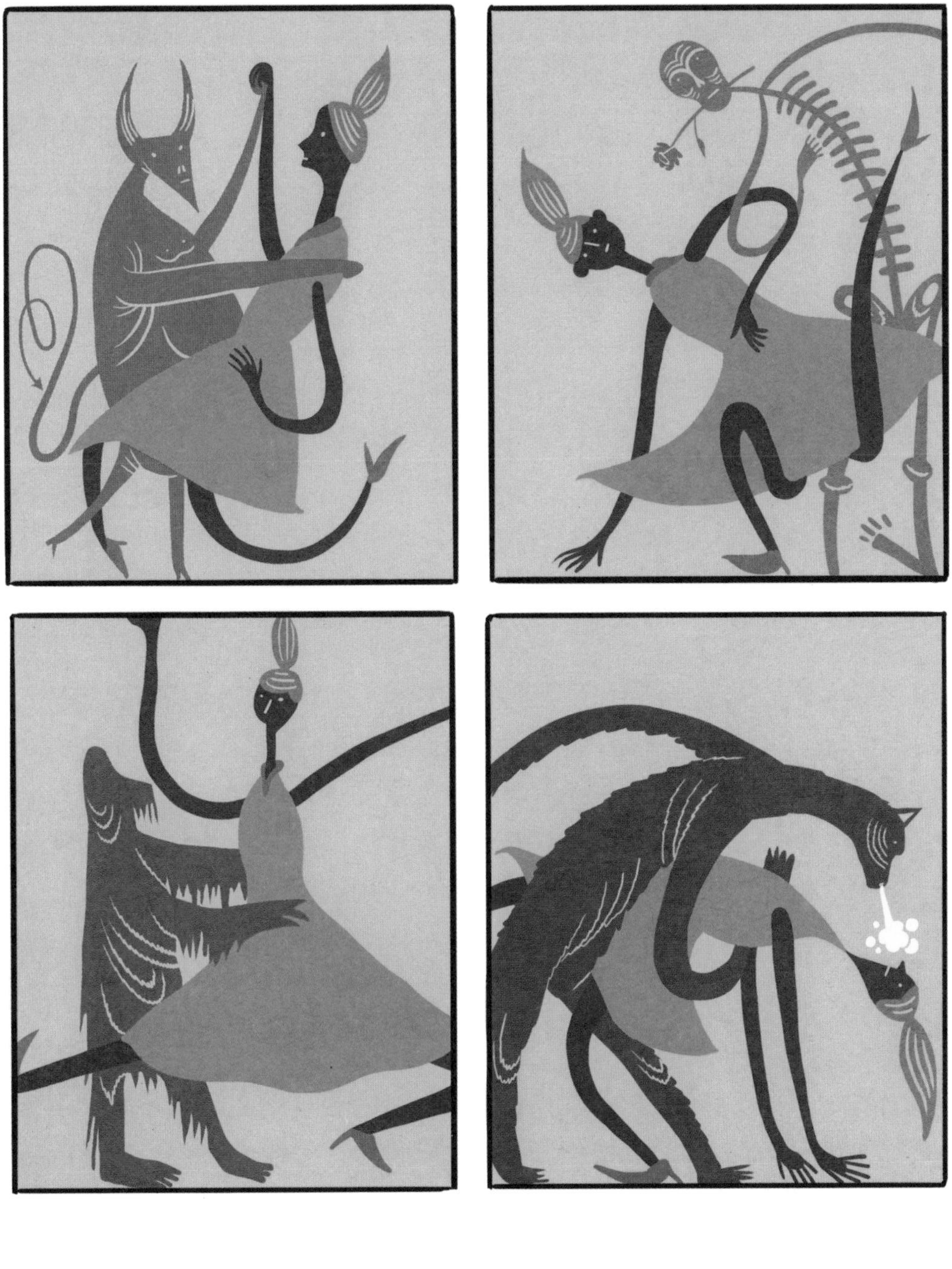

THE TWIST

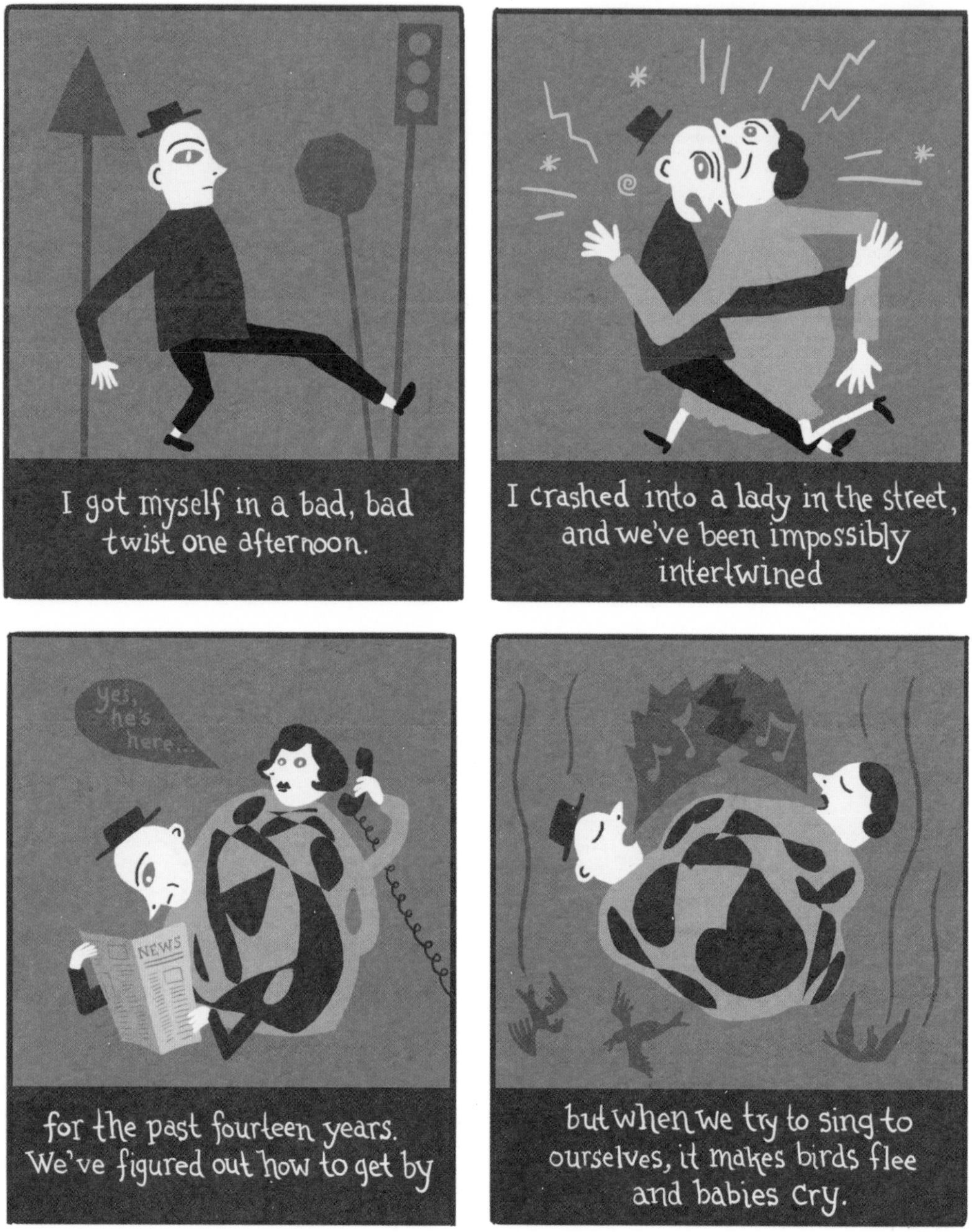
I got myself in a bad, bad twist one afternoon.
I crashed into a lady in the street, and we've been impossibly intertwined
yes, he's here...
NEWS
for the past fourteen years. We've figured out how to get by
but when we try to sing to ourselves, it makes birds flee and babies cry.

STRESS ORCHESTRA

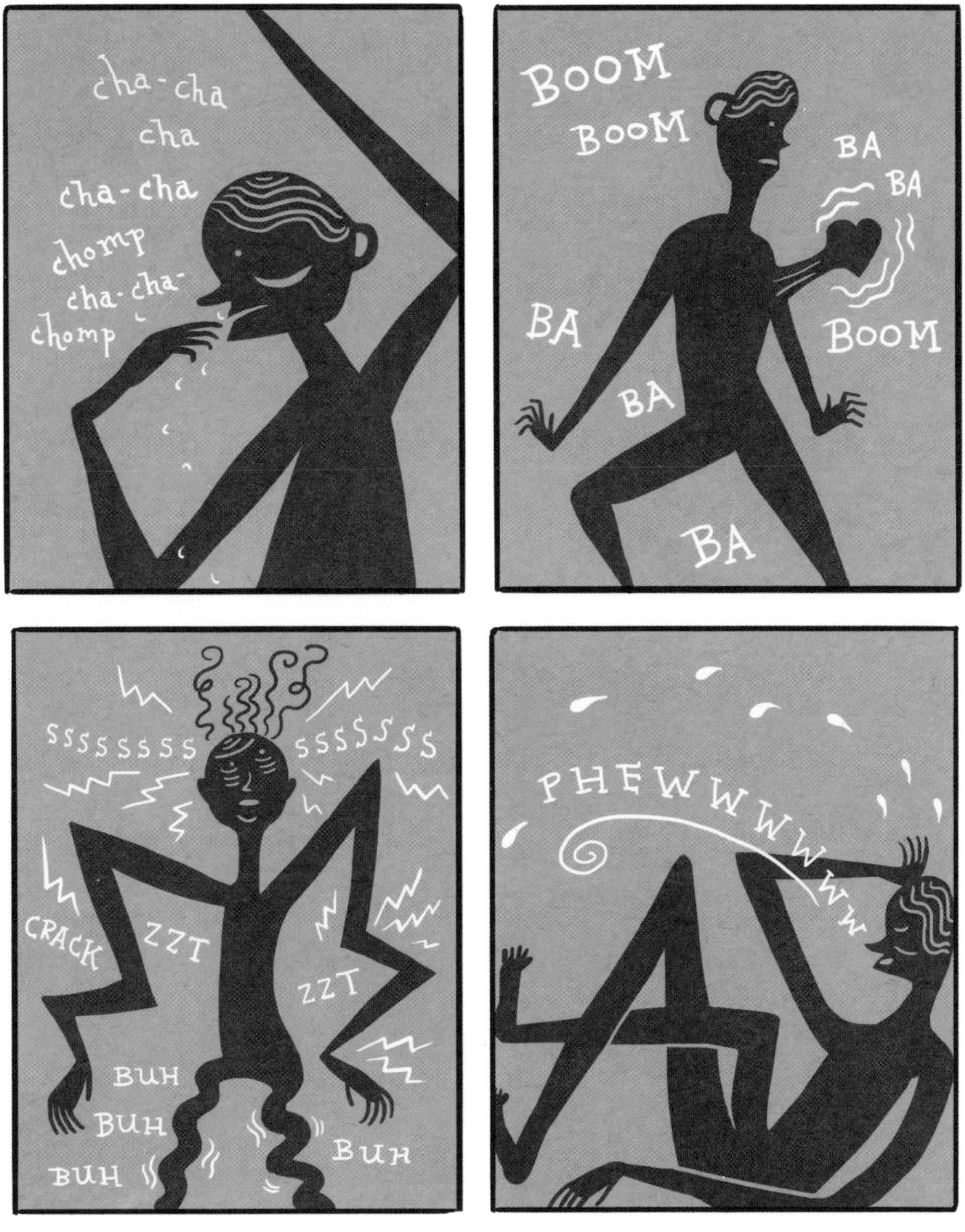
cha-cha
cha
cha-cha
chomp
cha-cha-
chomp
BOOM
BOOM
BA
BA
BA
BA
BA
BOOM
SSSSSSSS
SSSSSSSS
CRACK
ZZT
ZZT
BUH
BUH
BUH
BUH
PHEWWWWWWW

MY NEW LOOK

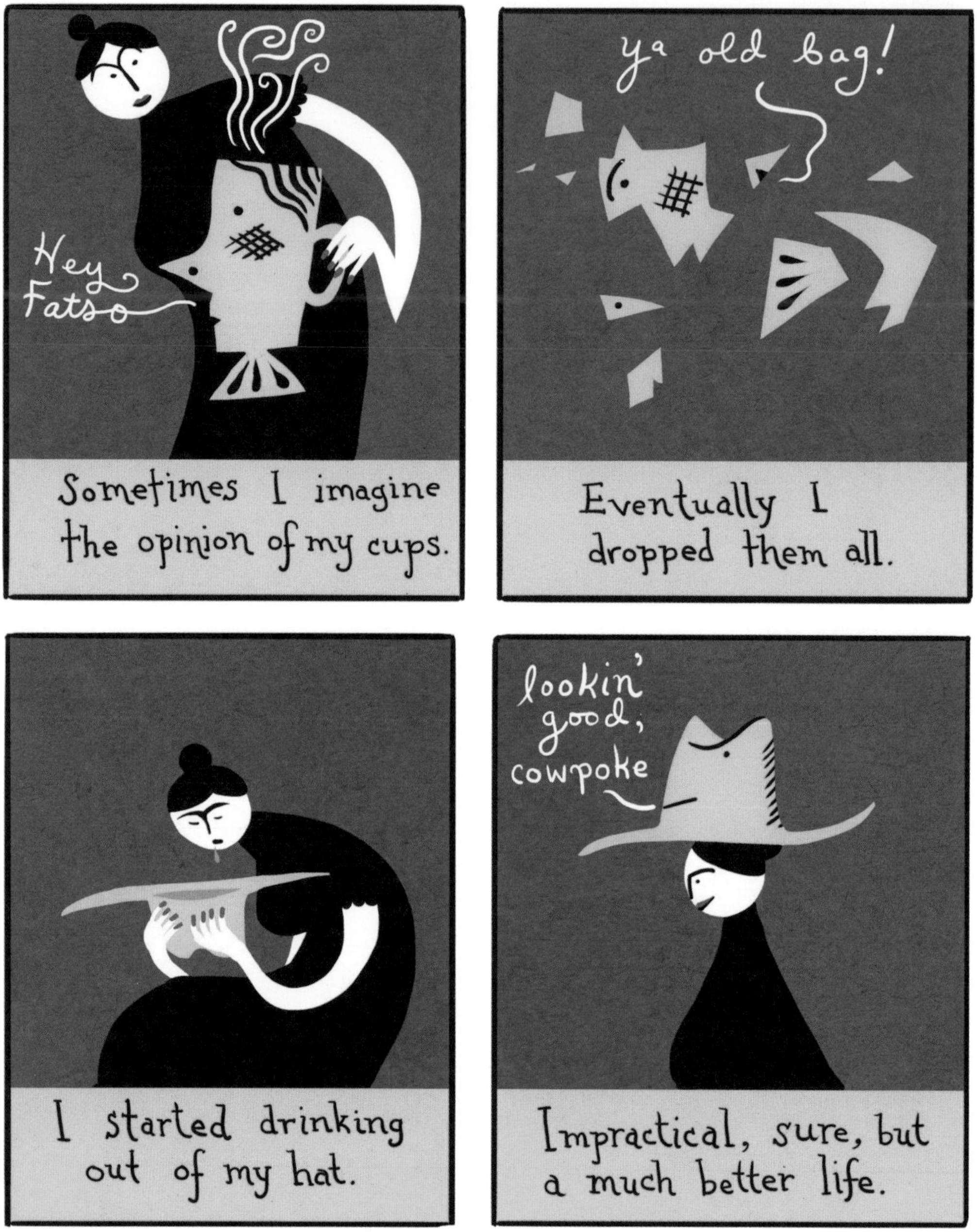
Hey Fatso
Sometimes I imagine the opinion of my cups.
ya old bag!
Eventually I dropped them all.
I started drinking out of my hat.
lookin' good, cowpoke
Impractical, sure, but a much better life.

HARD-HEADED BEAUTY

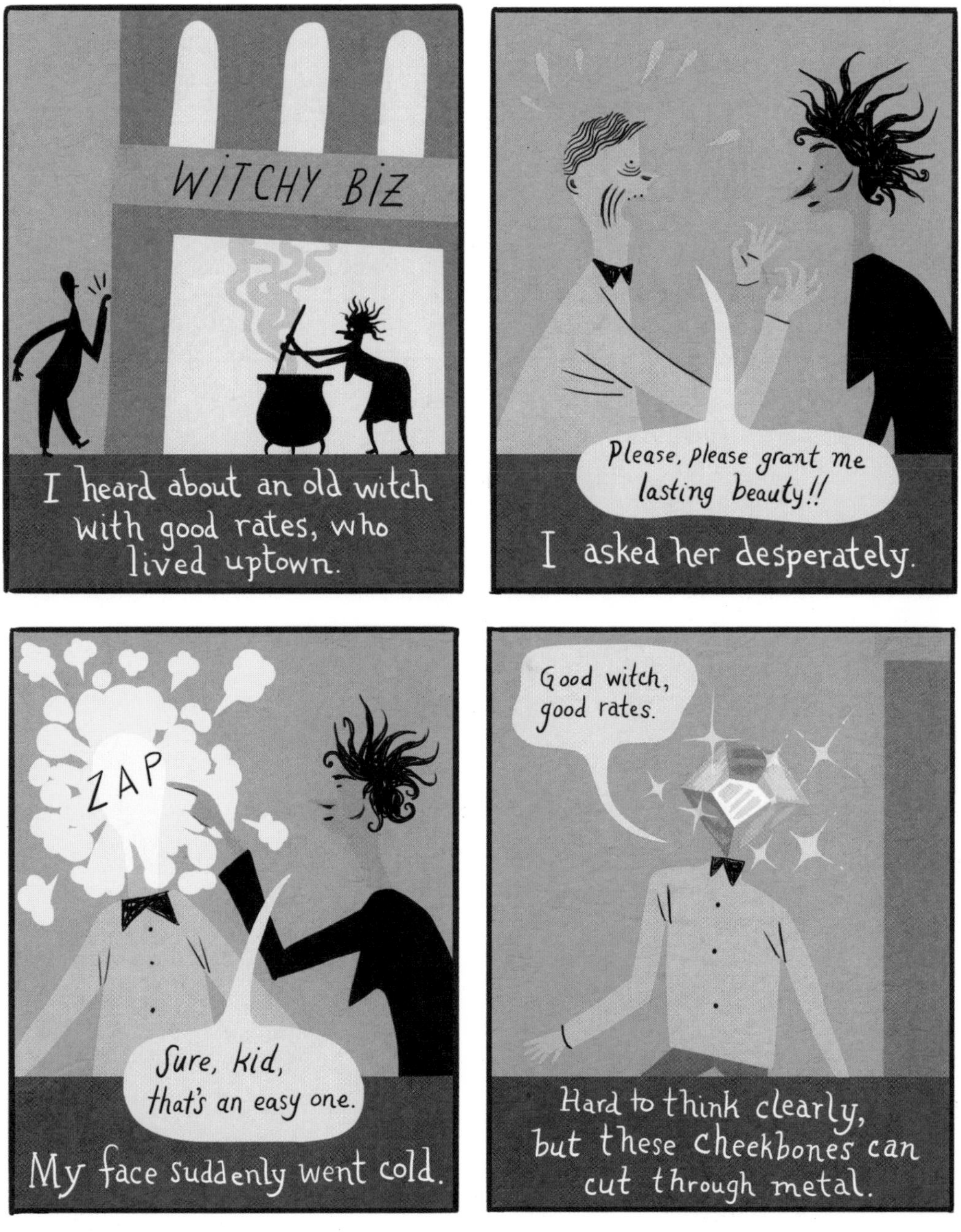
WITCHY BIZ
I heard about an old witch with good rates, who lived uptown.
Please, please grant me lasting beauty!!
I asked her desperately.
ZAP
Sure, kid, that's an easy one.
My face suddenly went cold.
Good witch, good rates.
Hard to think clearly, but these cheekbones can cut through metal.

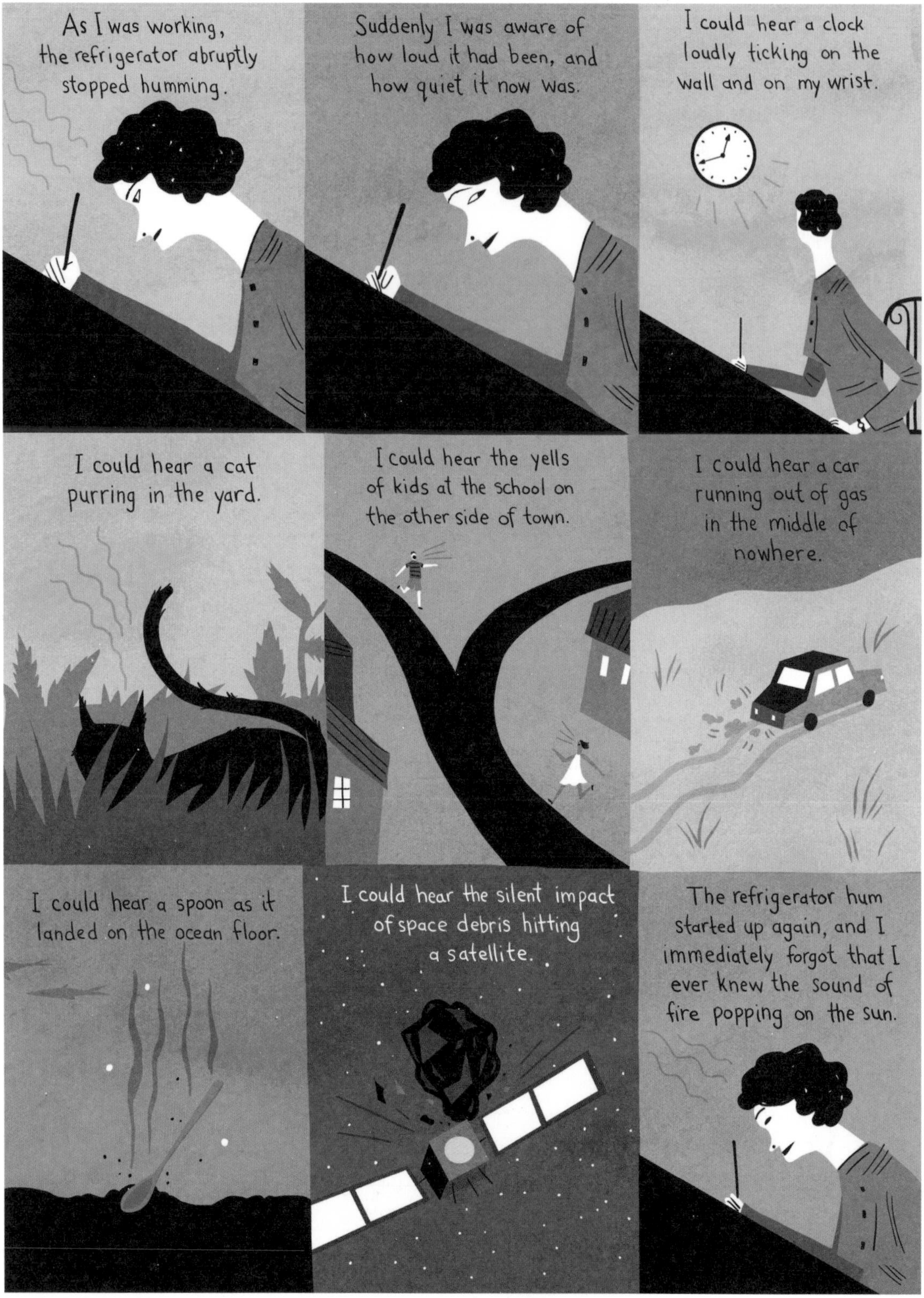
As I was working, the refrigerator abruptly stopped humming.
Suddenly I was aware of how loud it had been, and how quiet it now was.
I could hear a clock loudly ticking on the wall and on my wrist.
I could hear a cat purring in the yard.
I could hear the yells of kids at the school on the other side of town.
I could hear a car running out of gas in the middle of nowhere.
I could hear a spoon as it landed on the ocean floor.
I could hear the silent impact of space debris hitting a satellite.
The refrigerator hum started up again, and I immediately forgot that I ever knew the sound of fire popping on the sun.

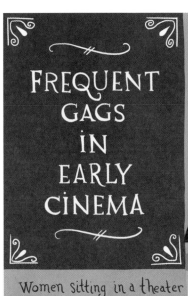

FREQUENT GAGS IN EARLY CINEMA

Strange things getting eaten.

People repeatedly knocking over Winsor McCay's large stacks of animation paper.

oop!

Women sitting in a theater with giant, fanciful hats that block the screen.

Enemies walking into each other backwards.

heh heh

heh heh

Characters unaware of extreme danger.

Switched hats.

Exaggerated sleepwalking.

The protagonist getting lost in his own pants.

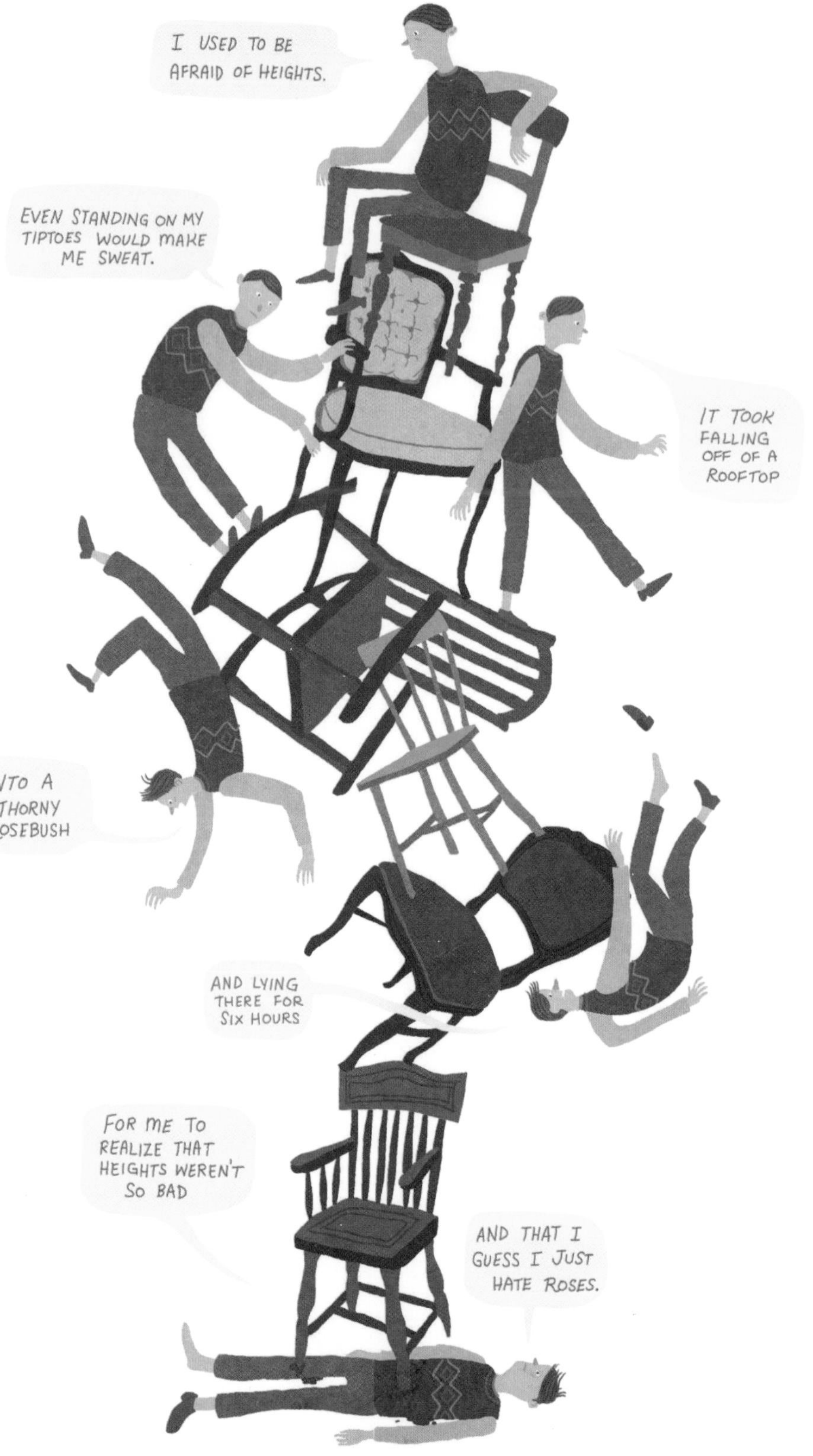
I USED TO BE AFRAID OF HEIGHTS.
EVEN STANDING ON MY TIPTOES WOULD MAKE ME SWEAT.
IT TOOK FALLING OFF OF A ROOFTOP
INTO A THORNY ROSEBUSH
AND LYING THERE FOR SIX HOURS
FOR ME TO REALIZE THAT HEIGHTS WEREN'T SO BAD
AND THAT I GUESS I JUST HATE ROSES.

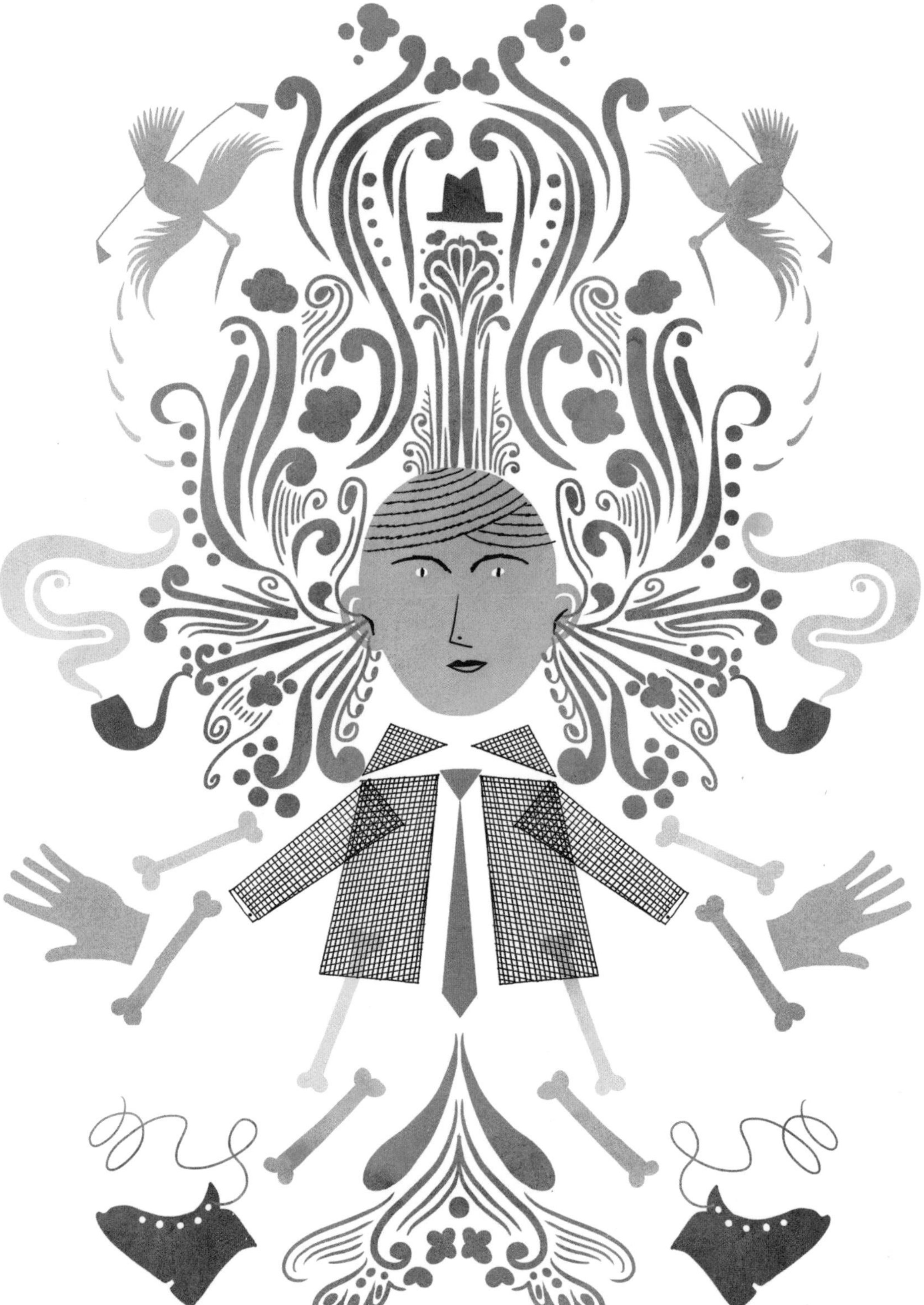

PETUNIA

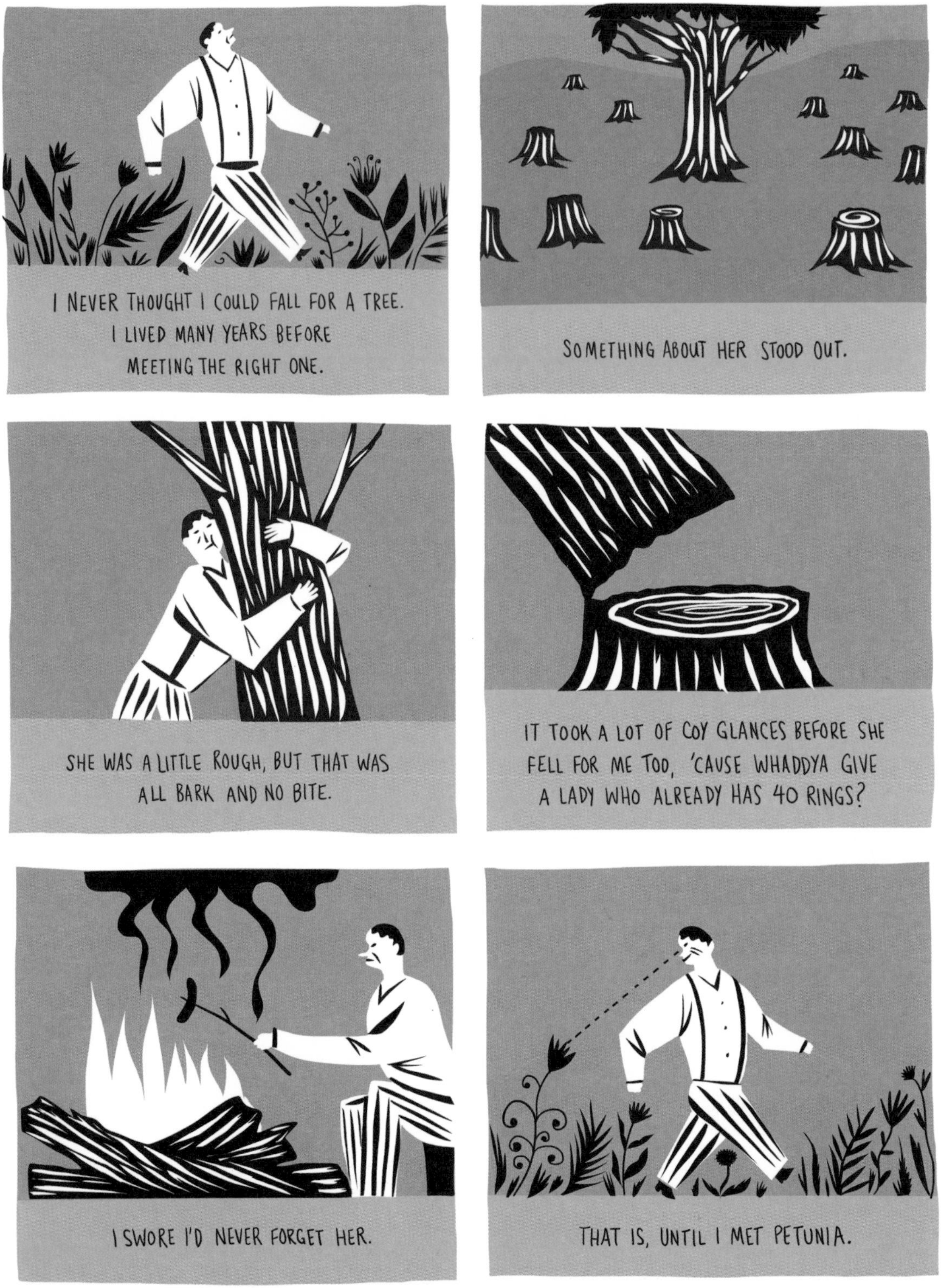
I NEVER THOUGHT I COULD FALL FOR A TREE. I LIVED MANY YEARS BEFORE MEETING THE RIGHT ONE.
SOMETHING ABOUT HER STOOD OUT.
SHE WAS A LITTLE ROUGH, BUT THAT WAS ALL BARK AND NO BITE.
IT TOOK A LOT OF COY GLANCES BEFORE SHE FELL FOR ME TOO, 'CAUSE WHADDYA GIVE A LADY WHO ALREADY HAS 40 RINGS?
I SWORE I'D NEVER FORGET HER.
THAT IS, UNTIL I MET PETUNIA.

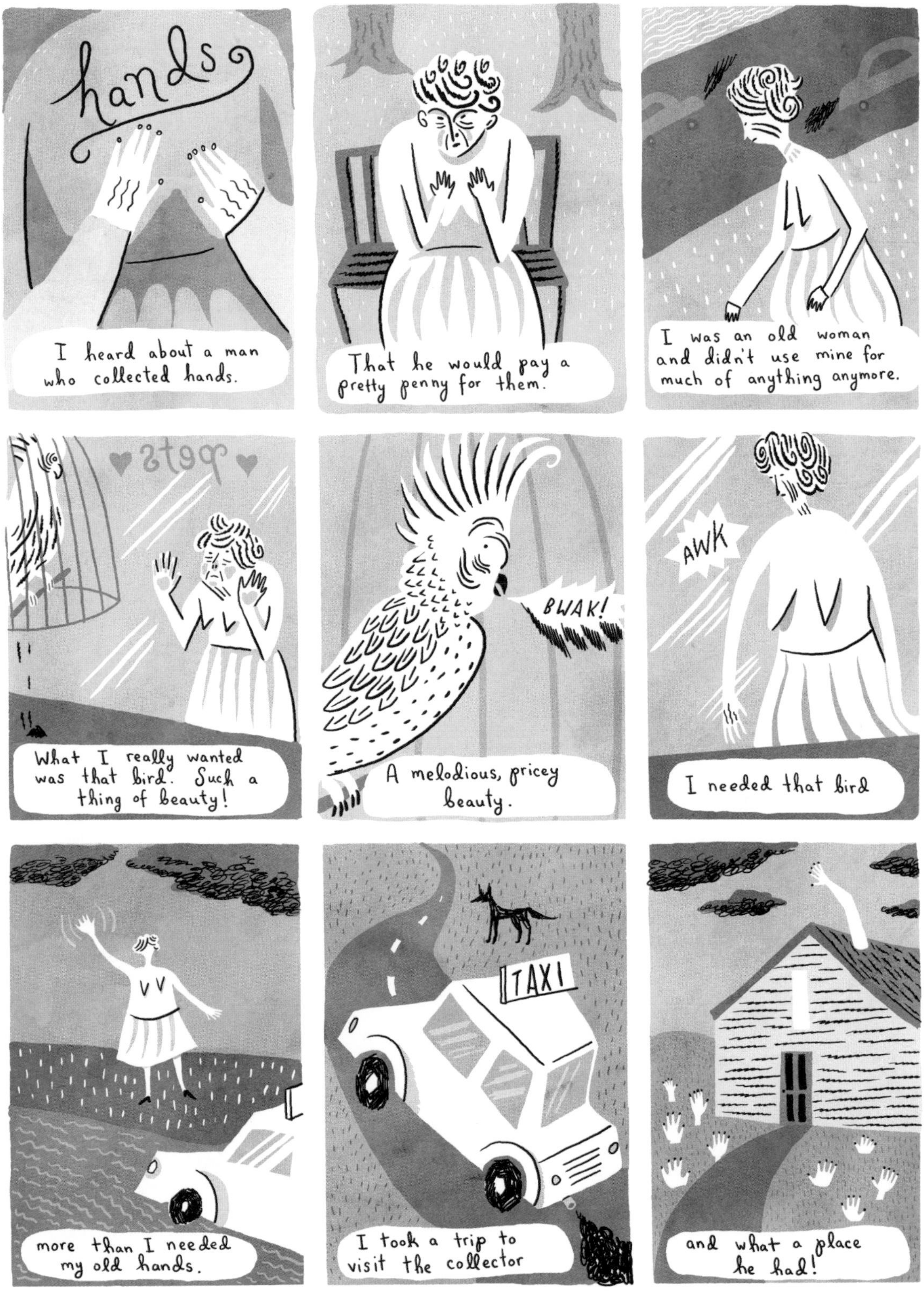
hands
I heard about a man who collected hands.
That he would pay a pretty penny for them.
I was an old woman and didn't use mine for much of anything anymore.
pets
What I really wanted was that bird. Such a thing of beauty!
BWAK!
A melodious, pricey beauty.
AWK
I needed that bird
more than I needed my old hands.
TAXI
I took a trip to visit the collector
and what a place he had!

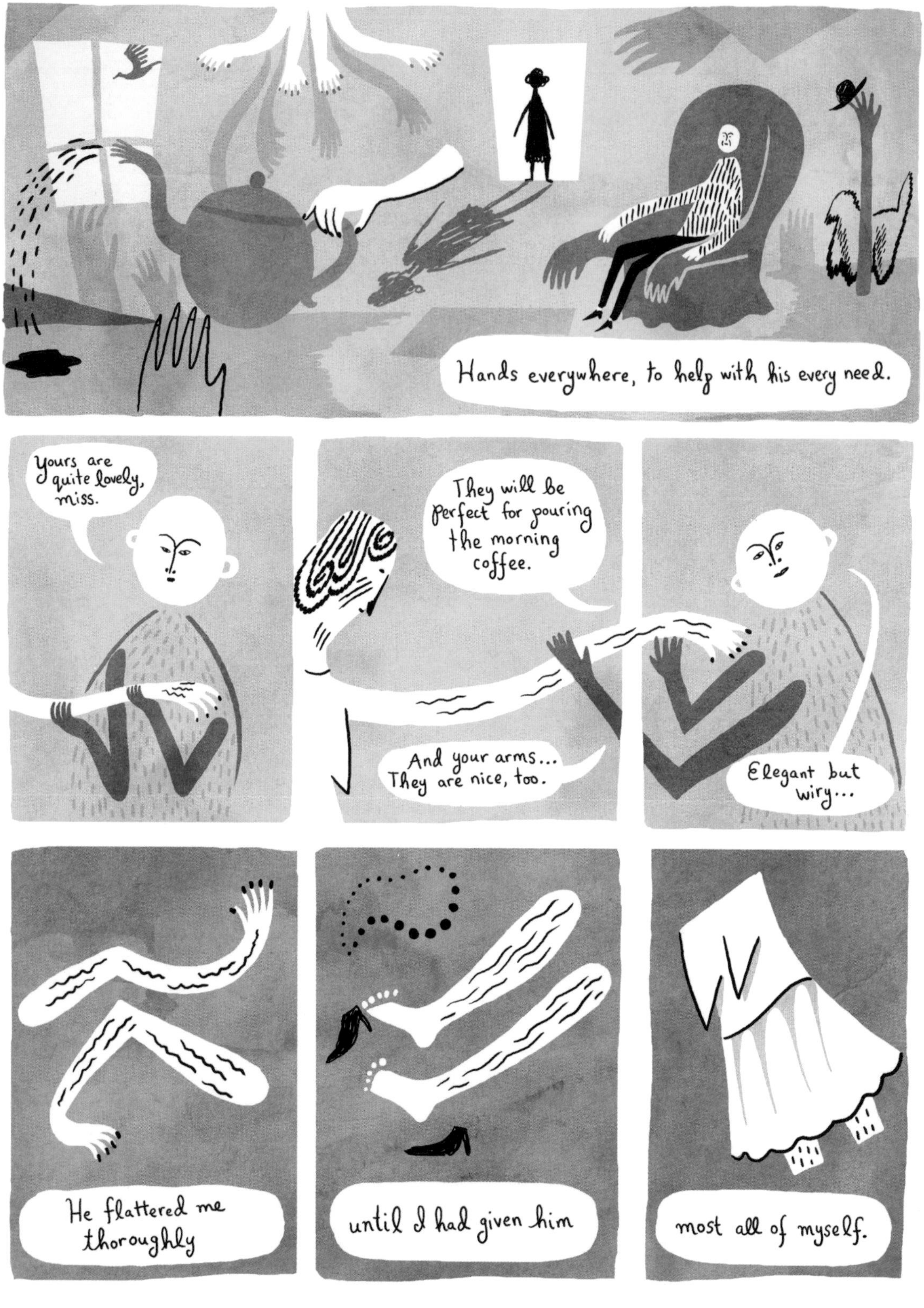
Hands everywhere, to help with his every need.
Yours are quite lovely, miss.
They will be perfect for pouring the morning coffee.
And your arms... They are nice, too.
Elegant but wiry...
He flattered me thoroughly
until I had given him
most all of myself.

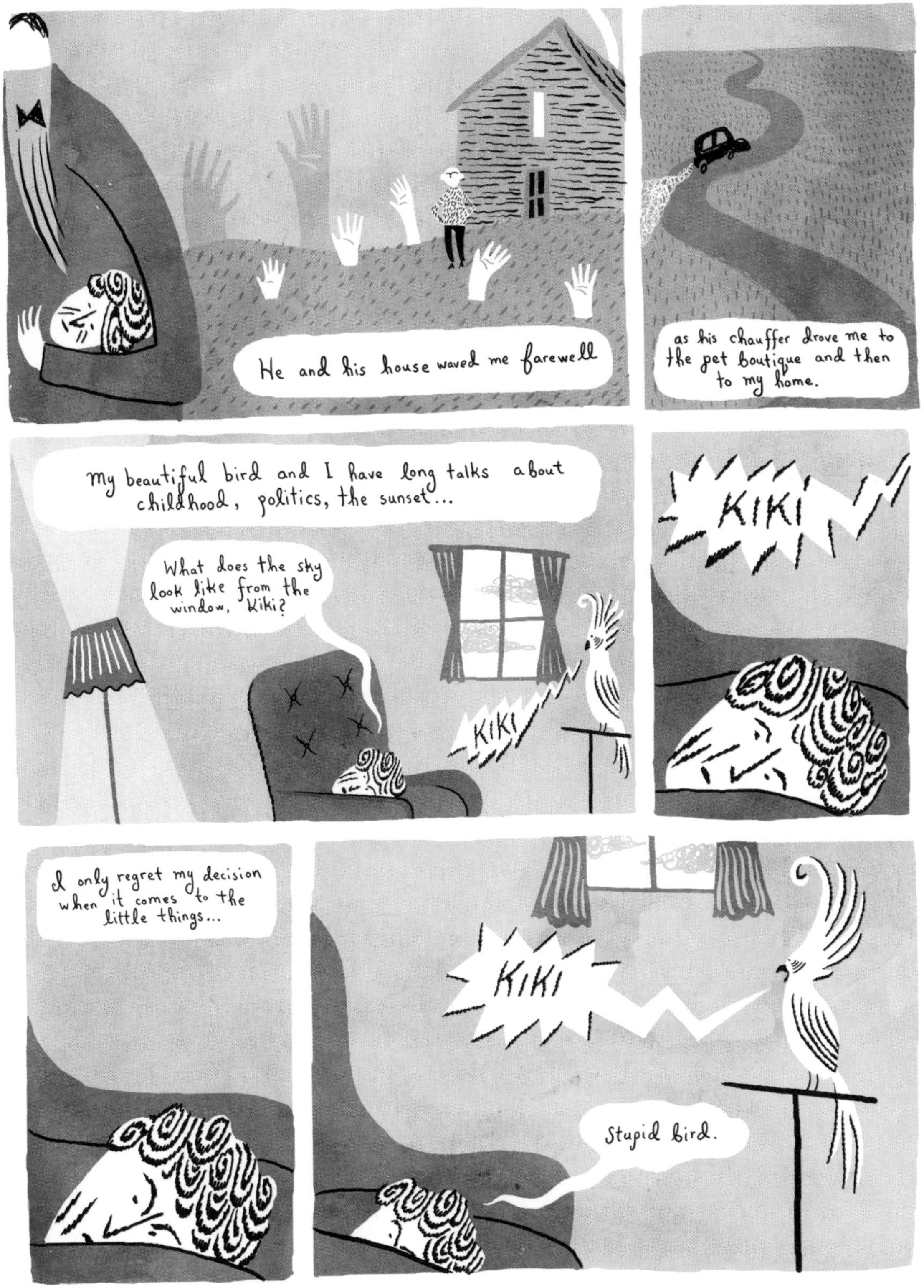
He and his house waved me farewell
as his chauffer drove me to the pet boutique and then to my home.
My beautiful bird and I have long talks about childhood, politics, the sunset...
What does the sky look like from the window, Kiki?
KIKI
KIKI
I only regret my decision when it comes to the little things...
KIKI
Stupid bird.

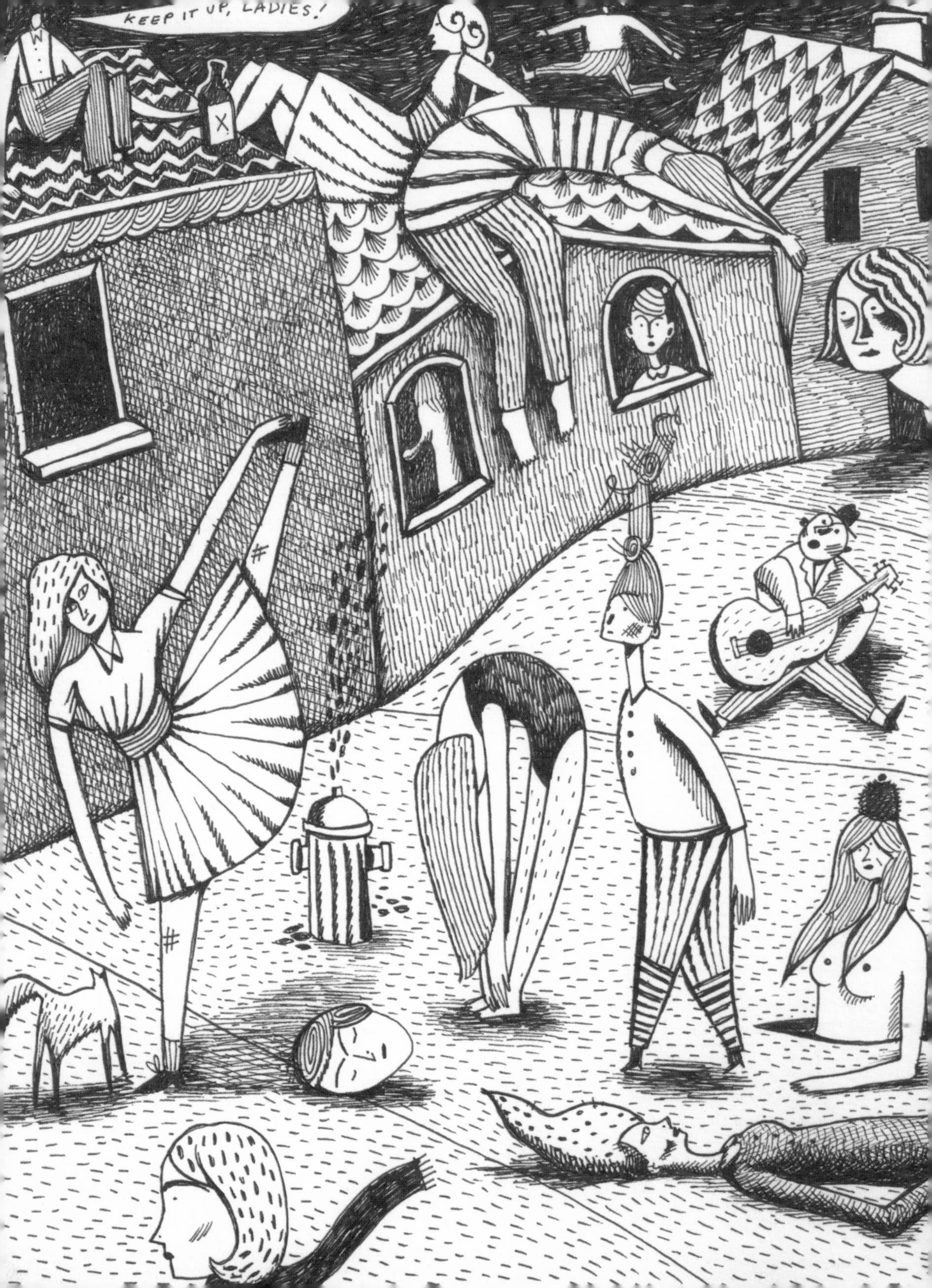
KEEP IT UP, LADIES!

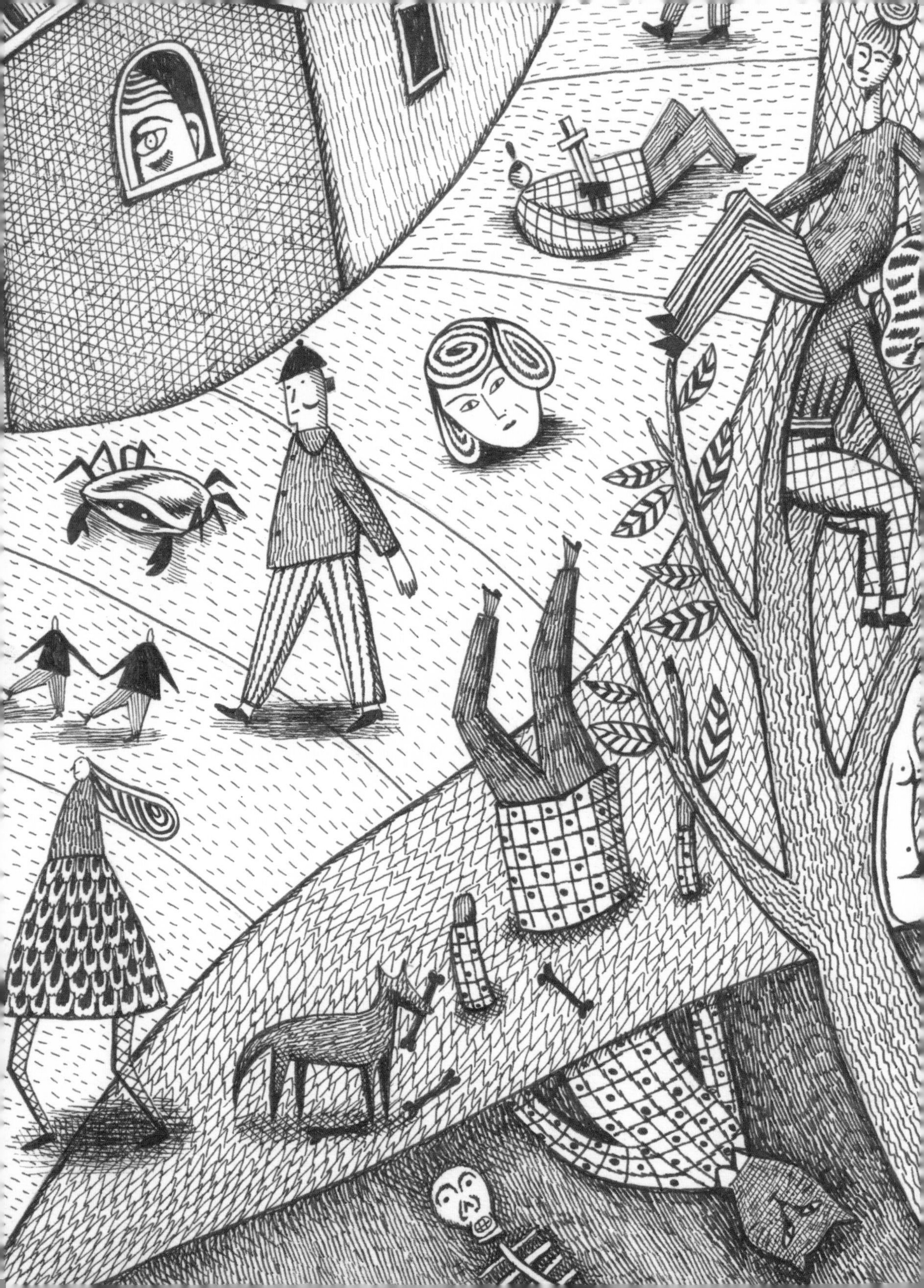

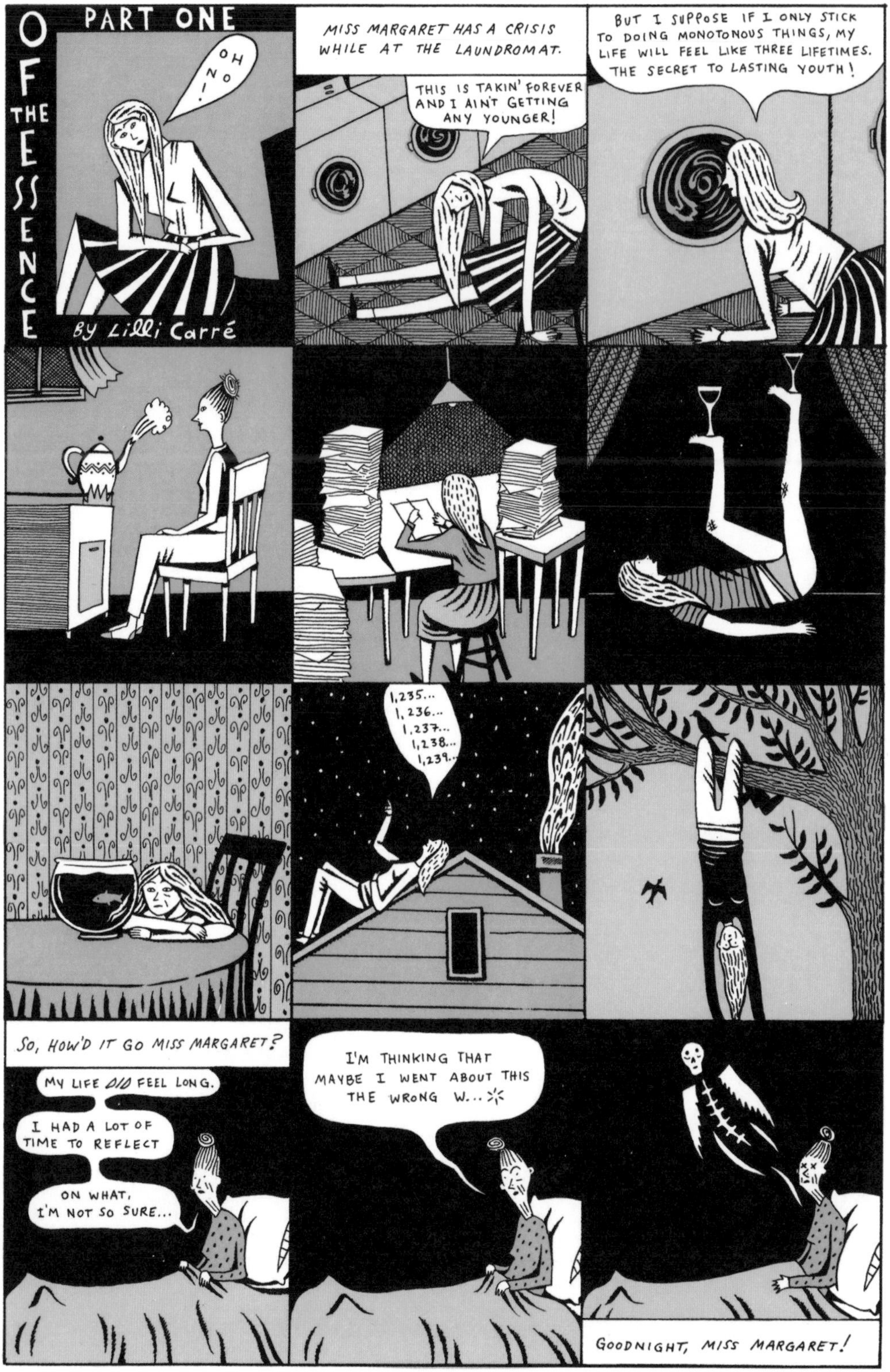
OF THE ESSENCE
PART ONE
BY Lilli Carré
OH NO!
MISS MARGARET HAS A CRISIS WHILE AT THE LAUNDROMAT.
THIS IS TAKIN' FOREVER AND I AIN'T GETTING ANY YOUNGER!
BUT I SUPPOSE IF I ONLY STICK TO DOING MONOTONOUS THINGS, MY LIFE WILL FEEL LIKE THREE LIFETIMES. THE SECRET TO LASTING YOUTH!
1,235... 1,236... 1,237... 1,238... 1,239...
SO, HOW'D IT GO MISS MARGARET?
MY LIFE DID FEEL LONG.
I HAD A LOT OF TIME TO REFLECT
ON WHAT, I'M NOT SO SURE...
I'M THINKING THAT MAYBE I WENT ABOUT THIS THE WRONG W...
GOODNIGHT, MISS MARGARET!

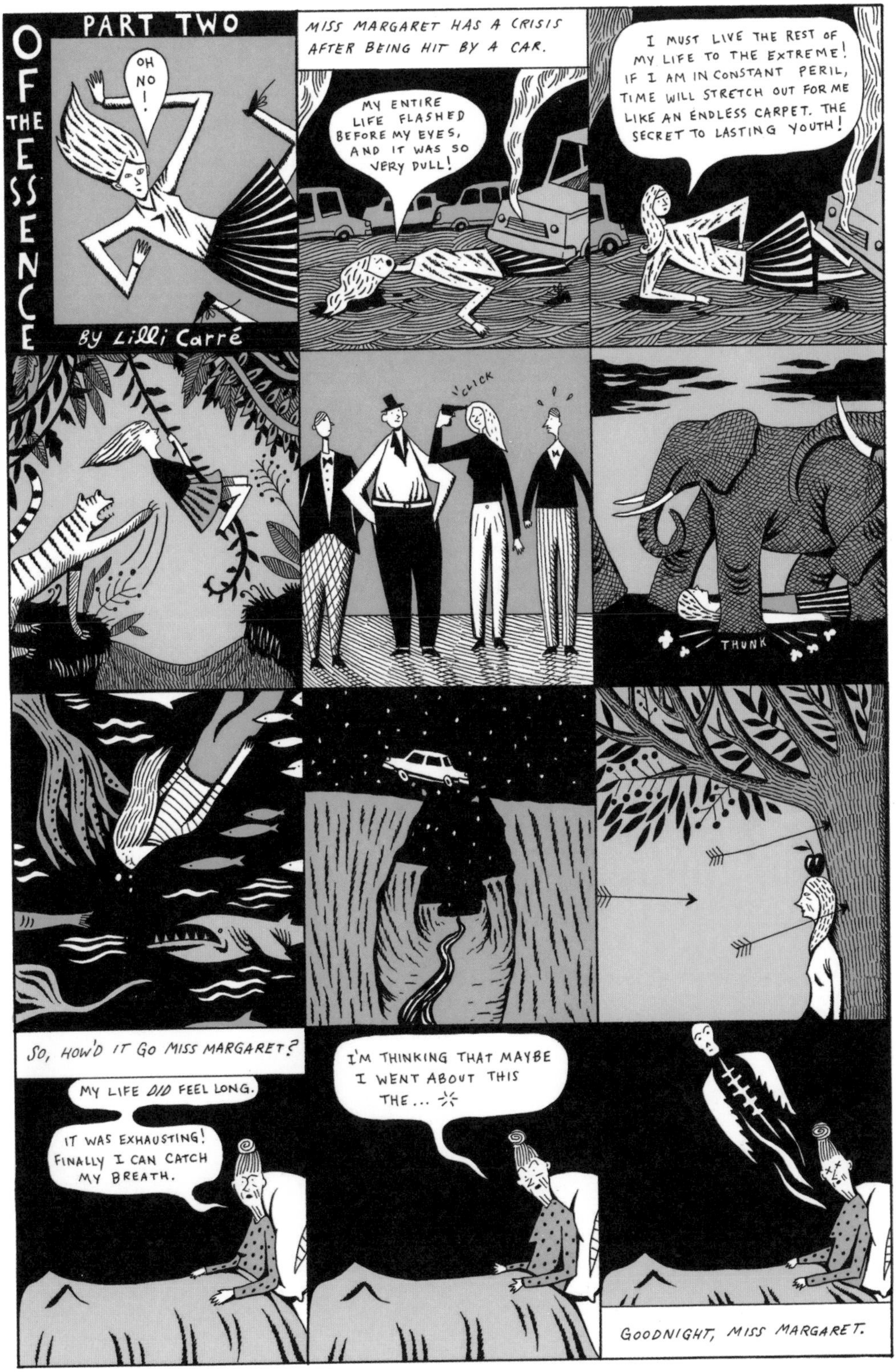
PART TWO
OF THE ESSENCE
BY Lilli Carré
OH NO!
MISS MARGARET HAS A CRISIS AFTER BEING HIT BY A CAR.
MY ENTIRE LIFE FLASHED BEFORE MY EYES, AND IT WAS SO VERY DULL!
I MUST LIVE THE REST OF MY LIFE TO THE EXTREME! IF I AM IN CONSTANT PERIL, TIME WILL STRETCH OUT FOR ME LIKE AN ENDLESS CARPET. THE SECRET TO LASTING YOUTH!
CLICK
THUNK
SO, HOW'D IT GO MISS MARGARET?
MY LIFE DID FEEL LONG.
IT WAS EXHAUSTING! FINALLY I CAN CATCH MY BREATH.
I'M THINKING THAT MAYBE I WENT ABOUT THIS THE...
GOODNIGHT, MISS MARGARET.

THE HOT STREET

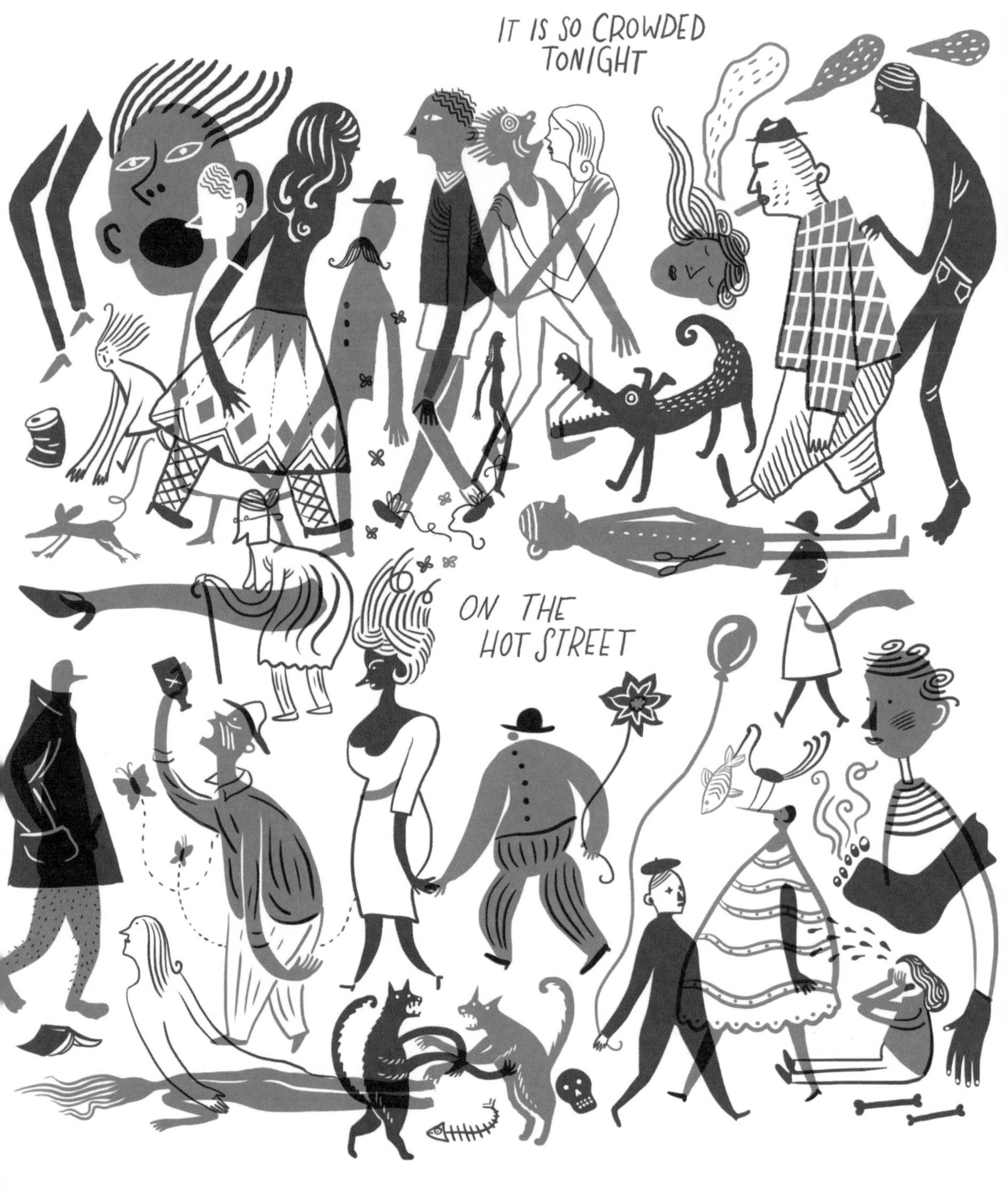
IT IS SO CROWDED TONIGHT
ON THE HOT STREET

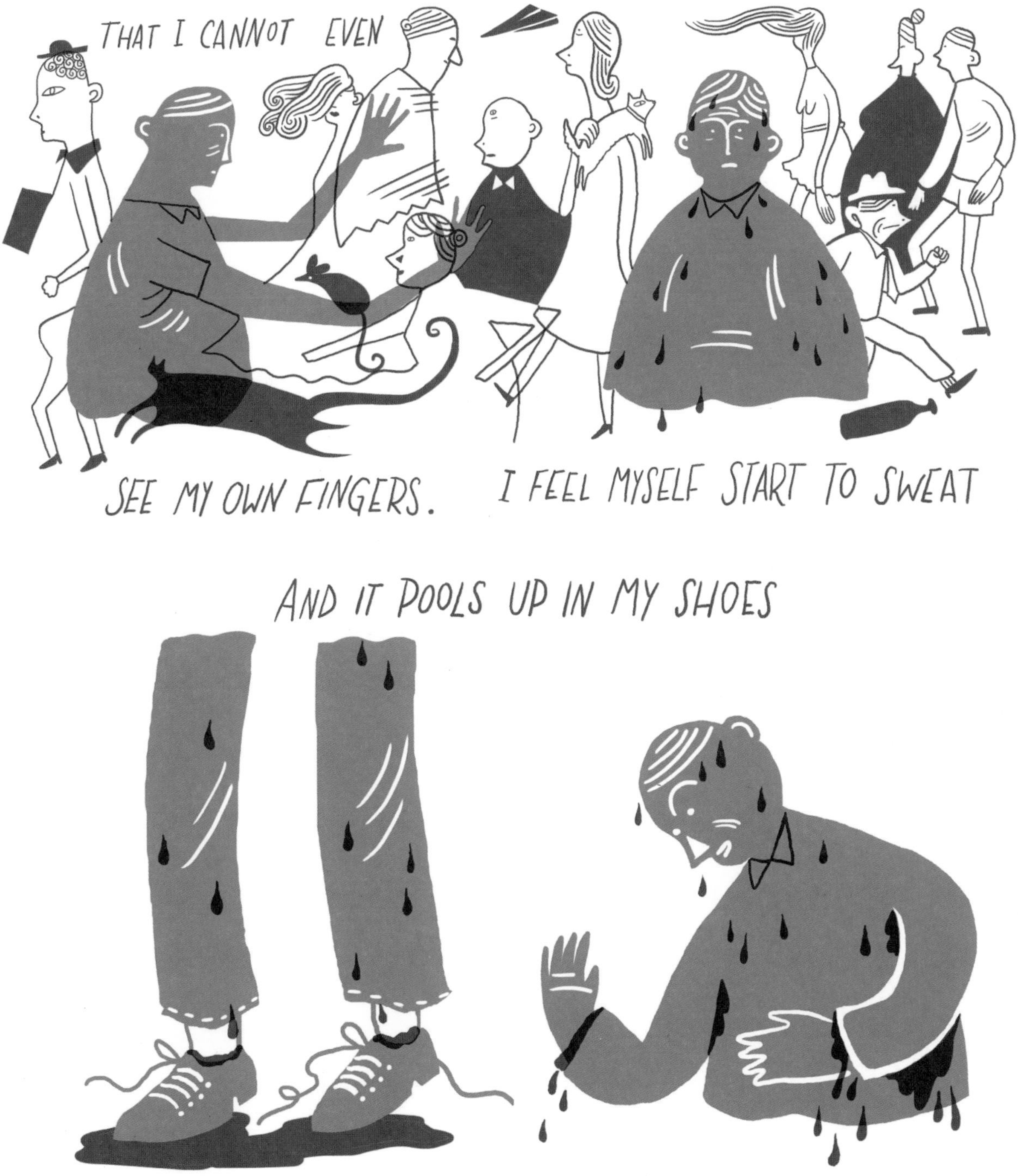
THAT I CANNOT EVEN
SEE MY OWN FINGERS.
I FEEL MYSELF START TO SWEAT
AND IT POOLS UP IN MY SHOES
AND GUSHES DOWN MY COLLAR AND SLEEVES.

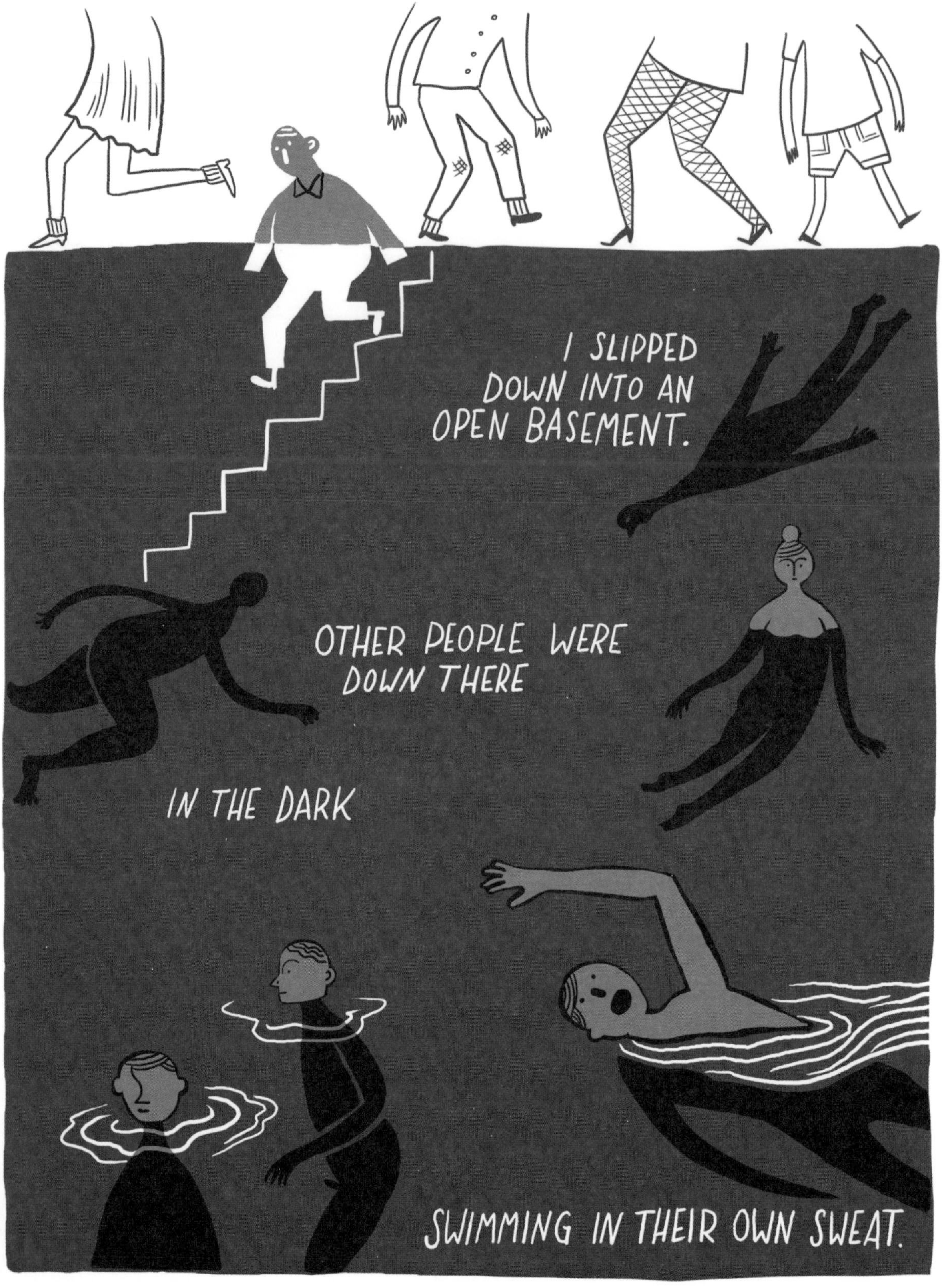
I SLIPPED DOWN INTO AN OPEN BASEMENT.
OTHER PEOPLE WERE DOWN THERE
IN THE DARK
SWIMMING IN THEIR OWN SWEAT.

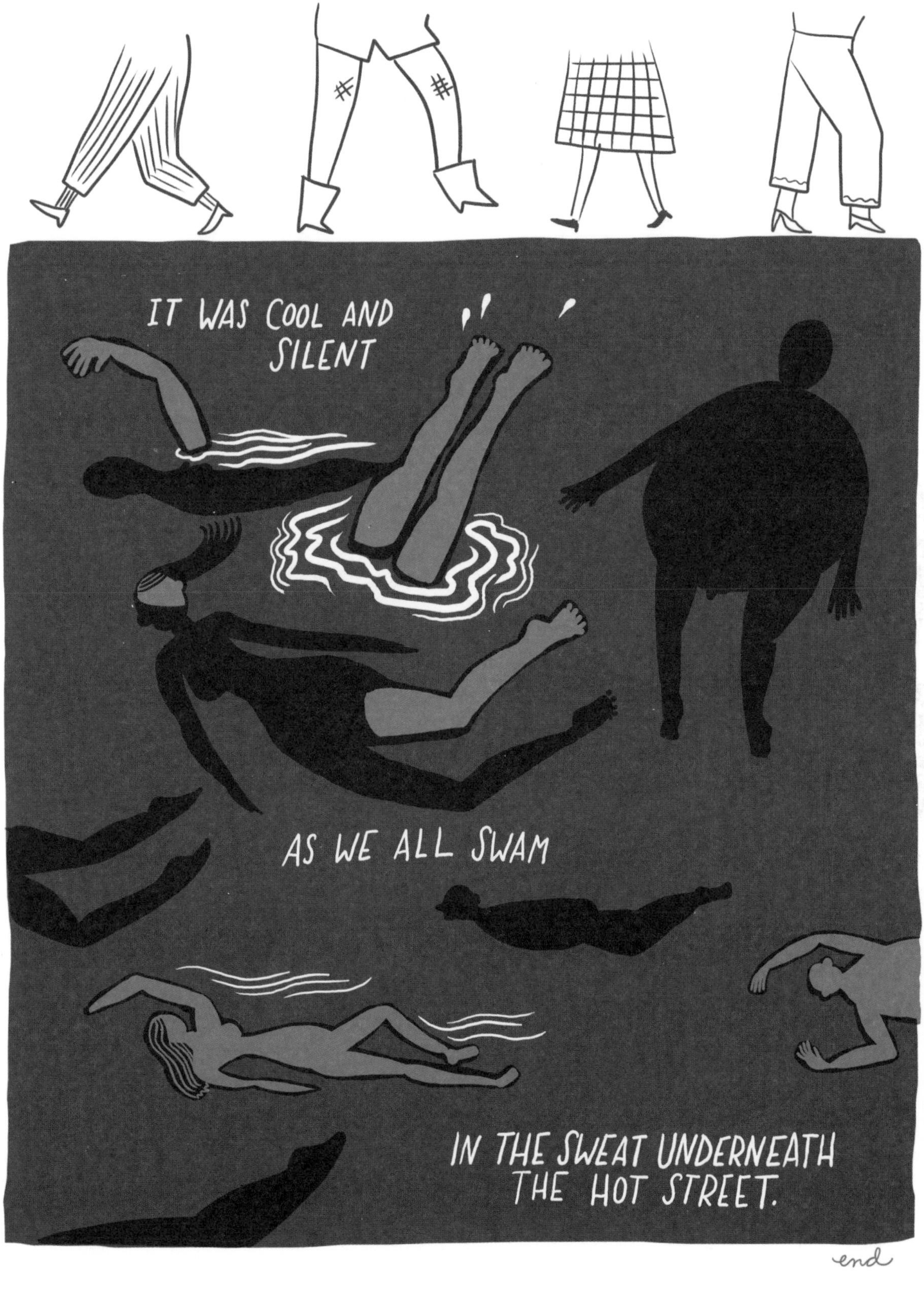
IT WAS COOL AND SILENT
AS WE ALL SWAM
IN THE SWEAT UNDERNEATH THE HOT STREET.
end

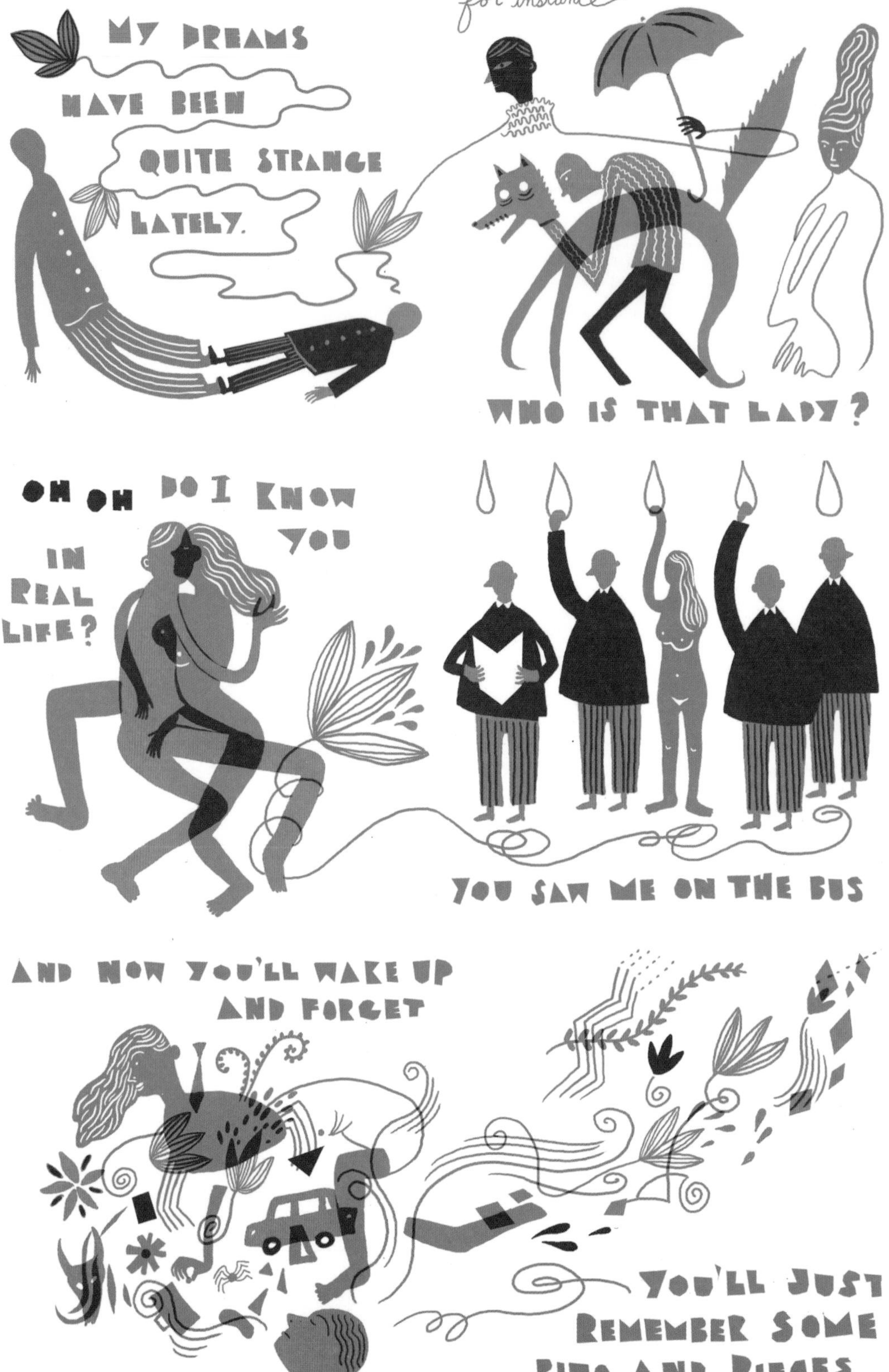
MY DREAMS
HAVE BEEN
QUITE STRANGE
LATELY.
for instance
WHO IS THAT LADY?
OH OH DO I KNOW YOU
IN REAL LIFE?
YOU SAW ME ON THE BUS
AND NOW YOU'LL WAKE UP
AND FORGET
YOU'LL JUST
REMEMBER SOME
BITS AND PIECES

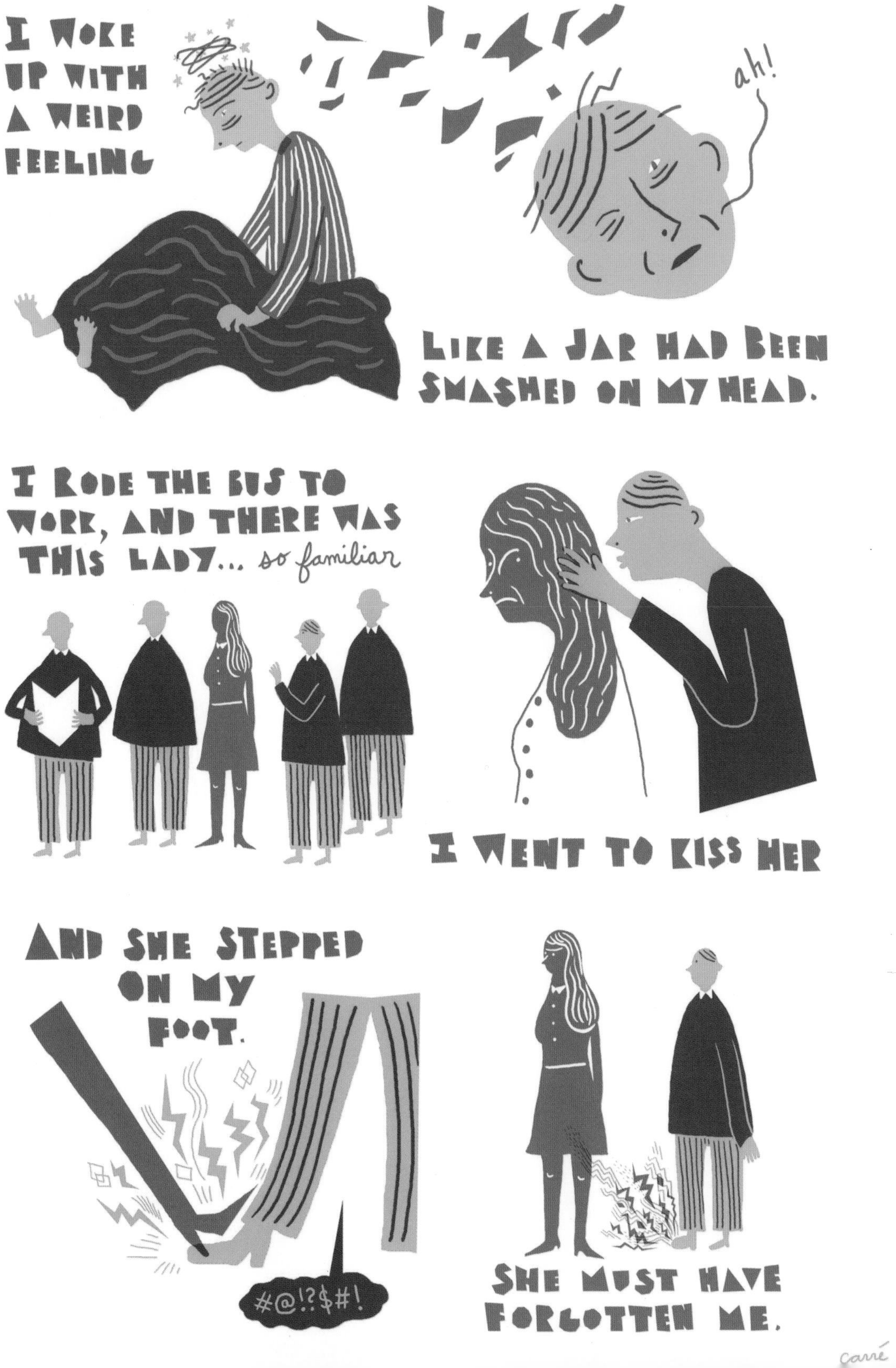
I WOKE UP WITH A WEIRD FEELING
ah!
LIKE A JAR HAD BEEN SMASHED ON MY HEAD.
I RODE THE BUS TO WORK, AND THERE WAS THIS LADY... so familiar
I WENT TO KISS HER
AND SHE STEPPED ON MY FOOT.
#@!?$#!
SHE MUST HAVE FORGOTTEN ME.
Carré

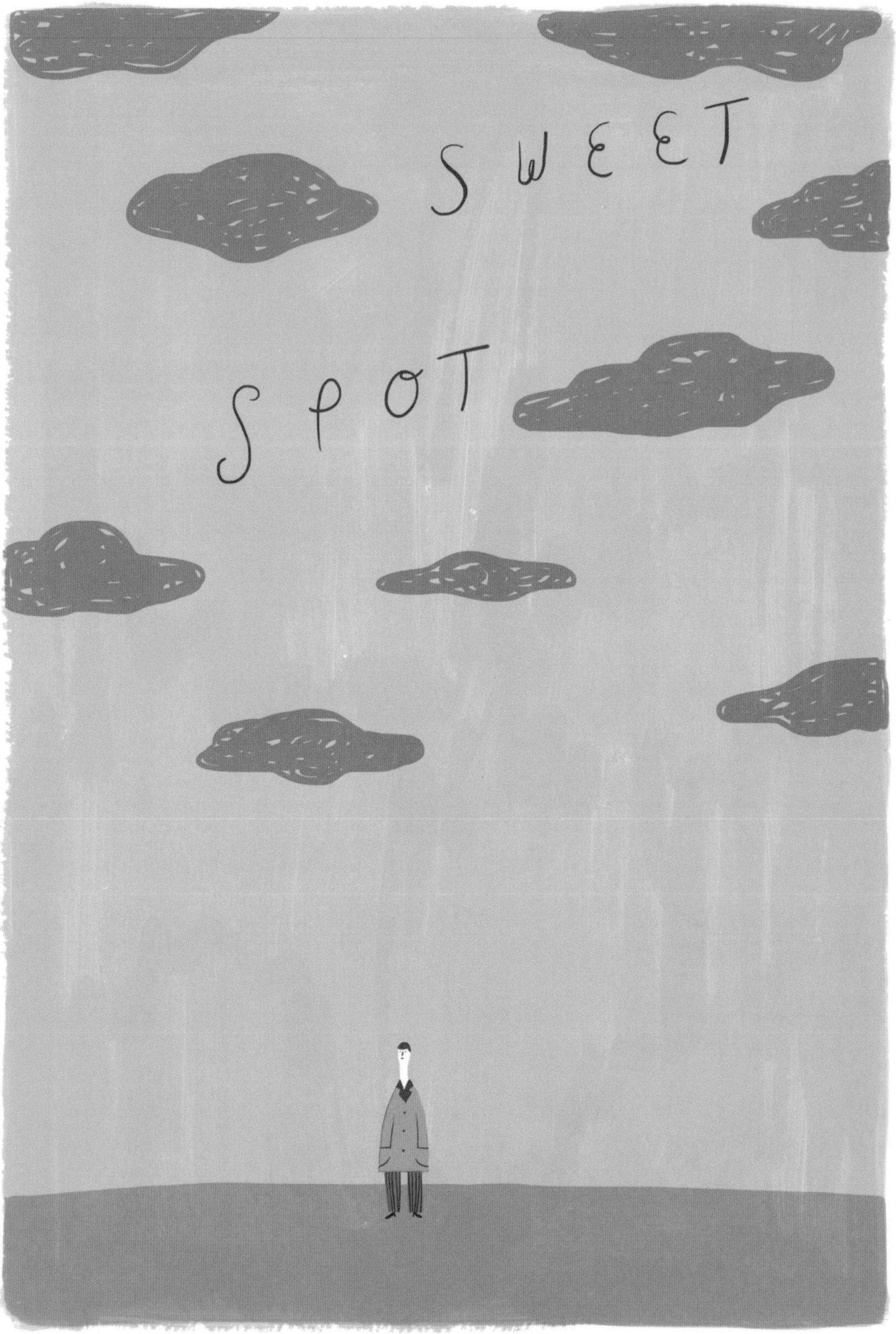
SWEET
SPOT

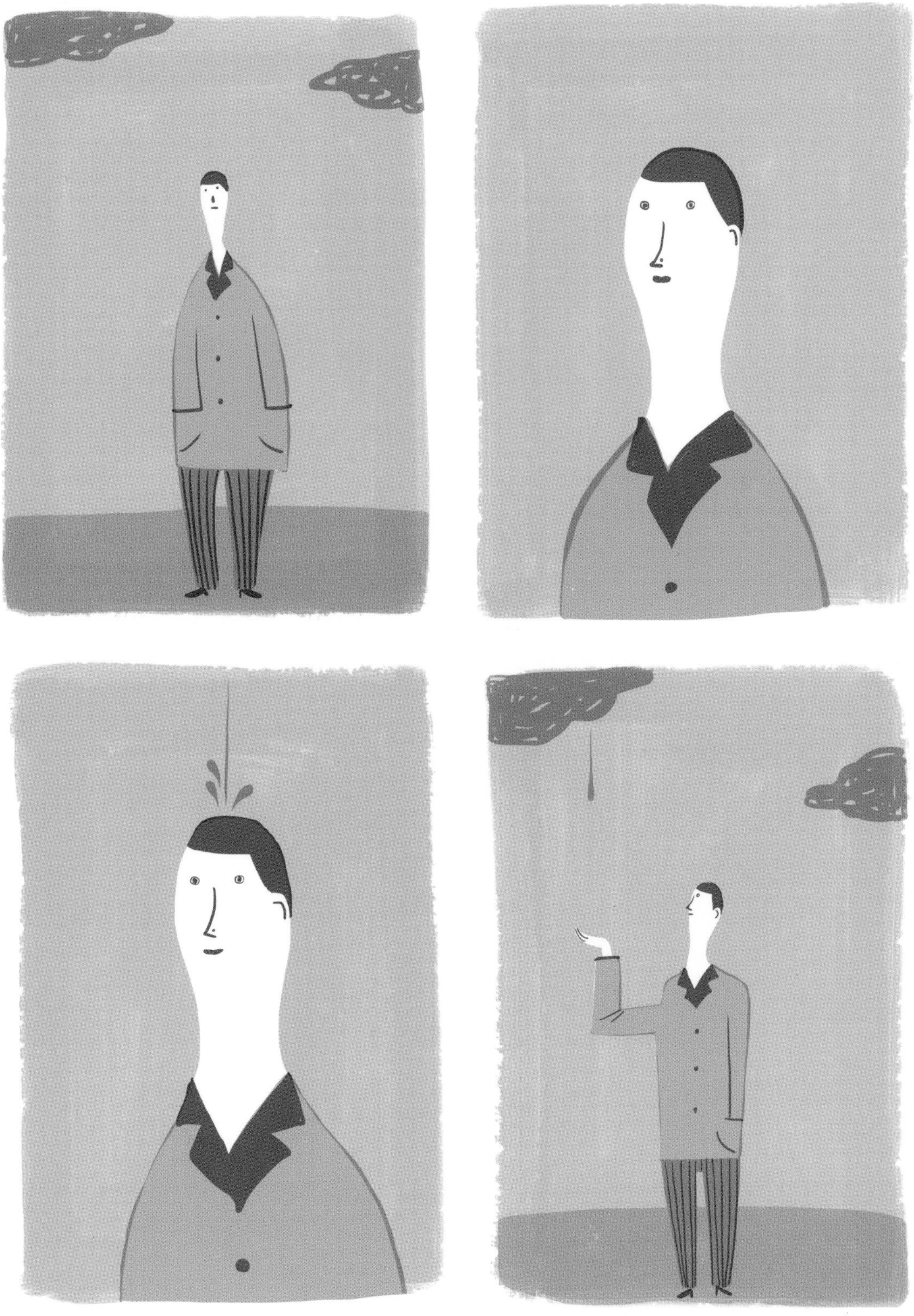

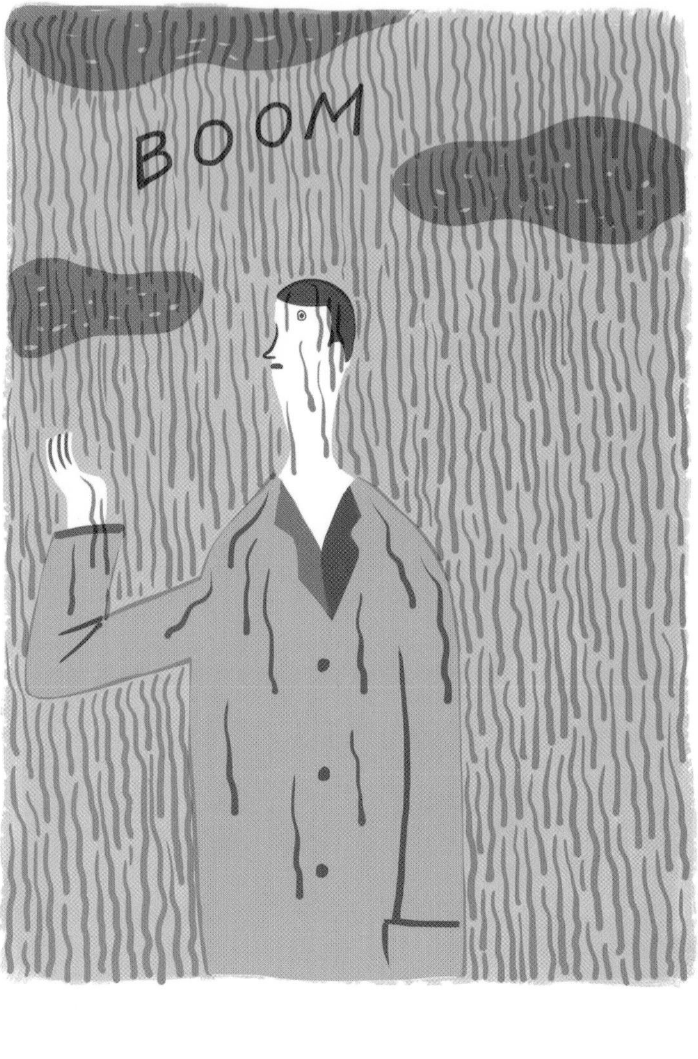
BOOM

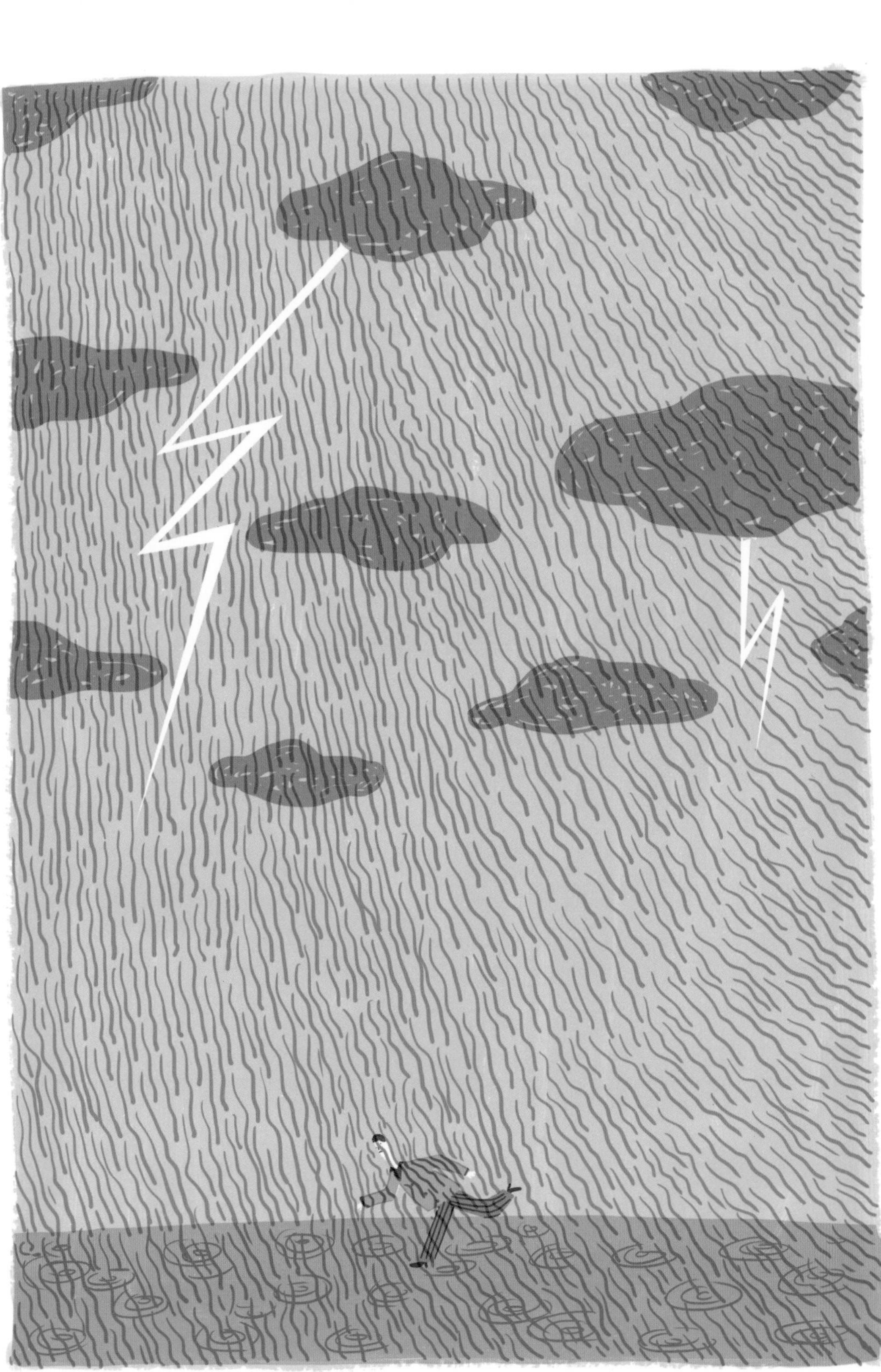

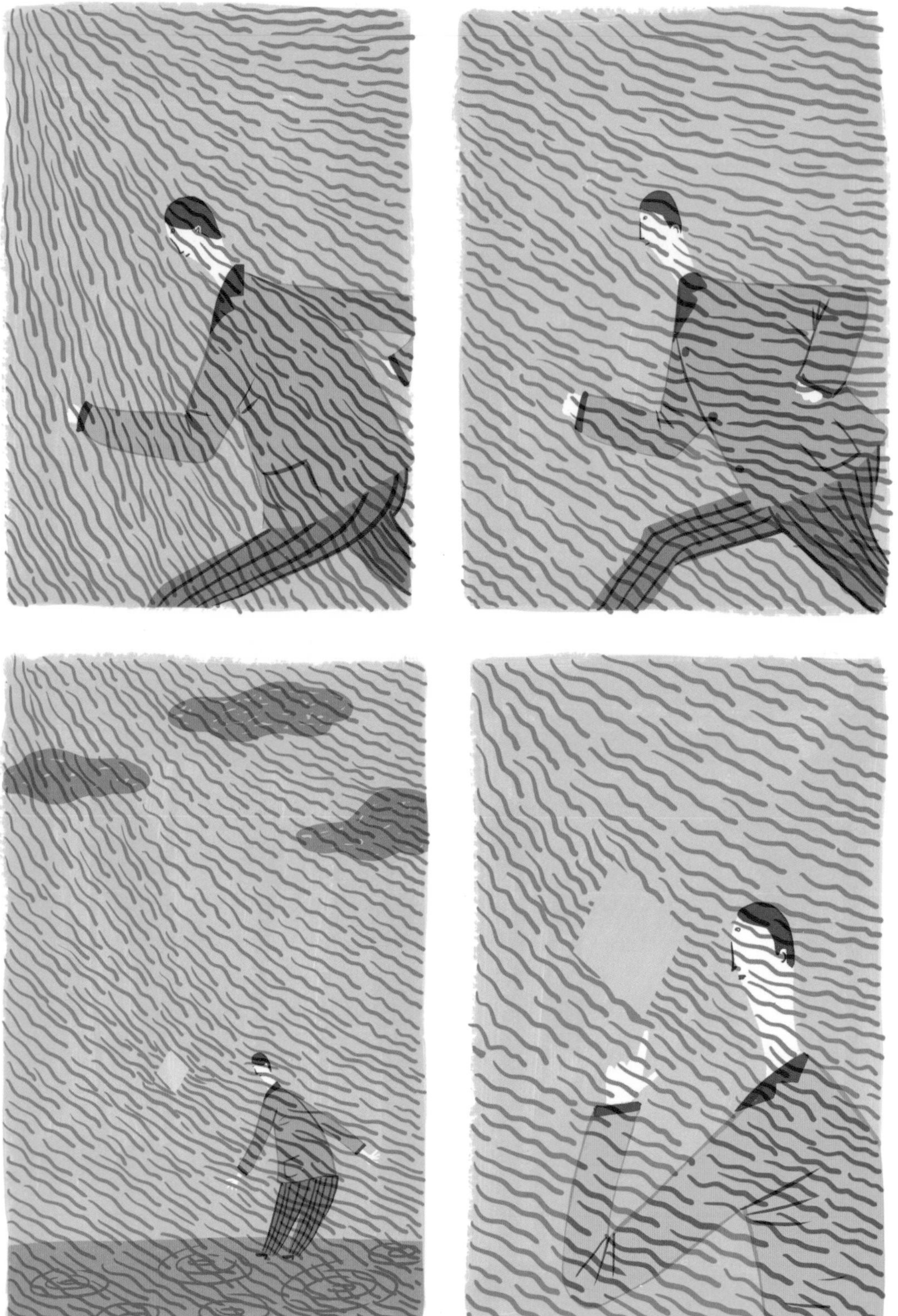

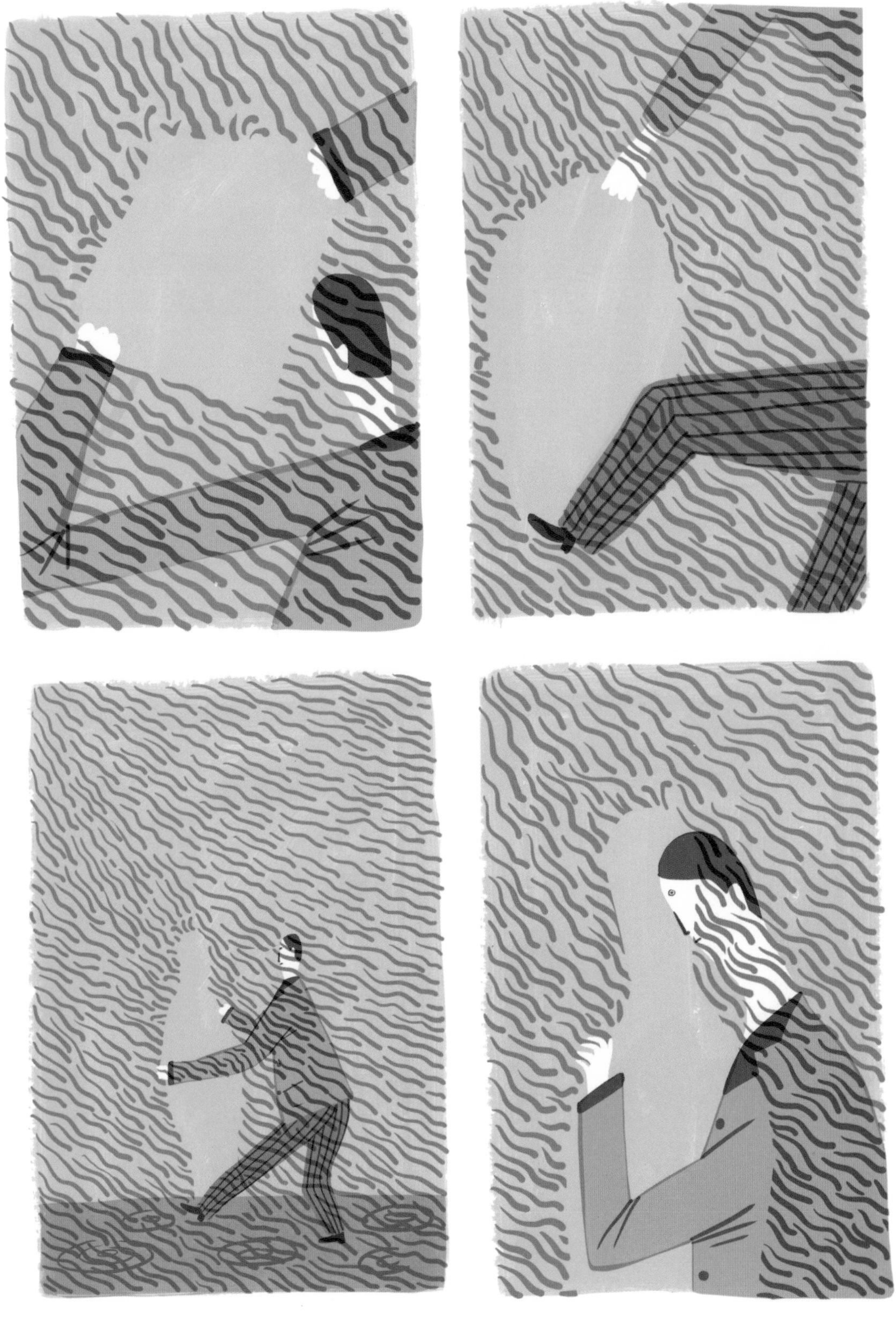

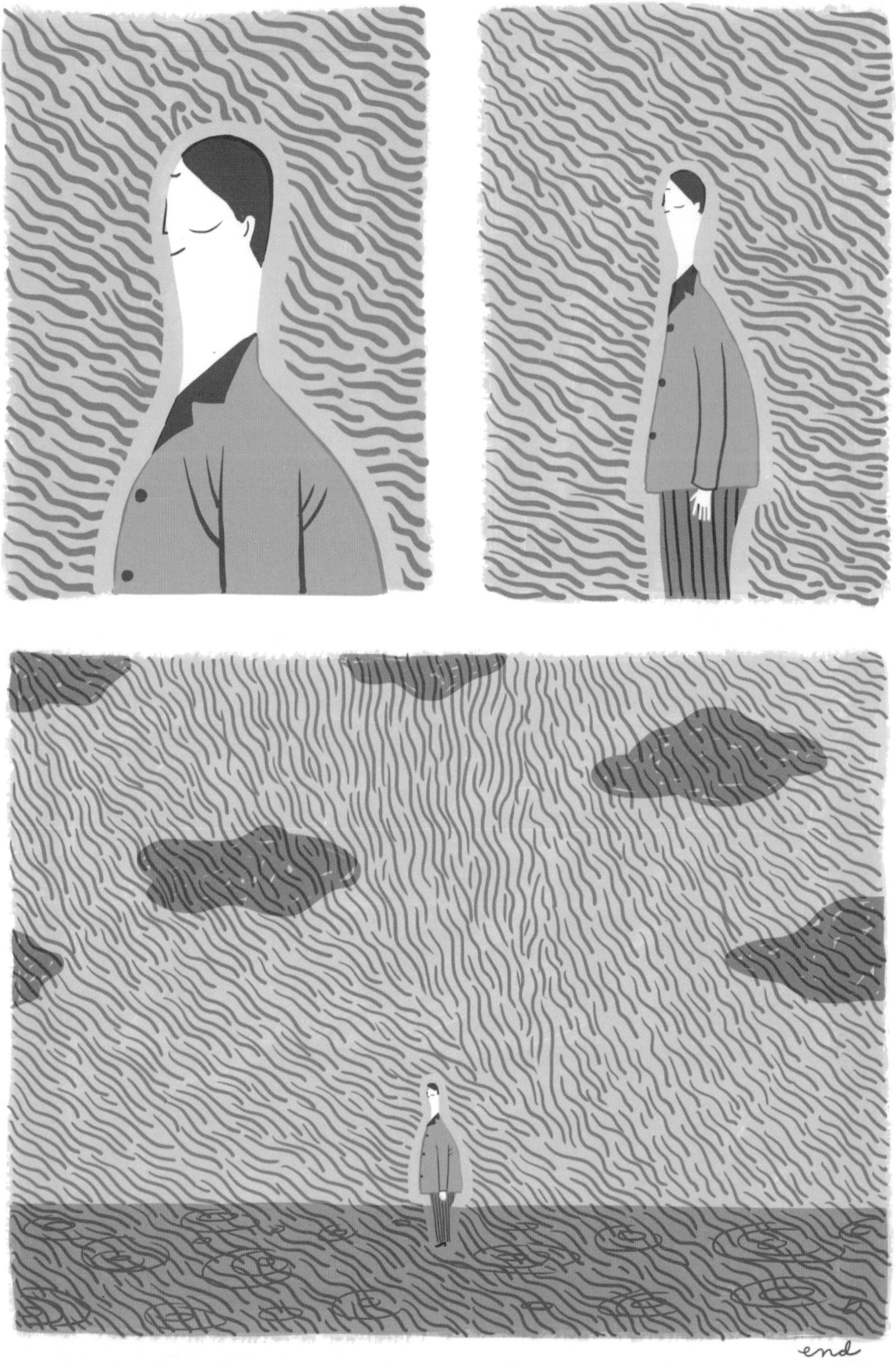
end

I've thought about you a lot... Maybe 20 times,

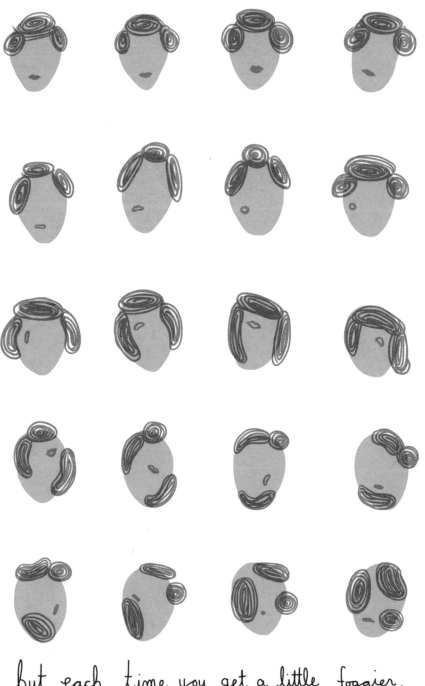

but each time you get a little foggier,

as do my memories of all the people I've ever met,

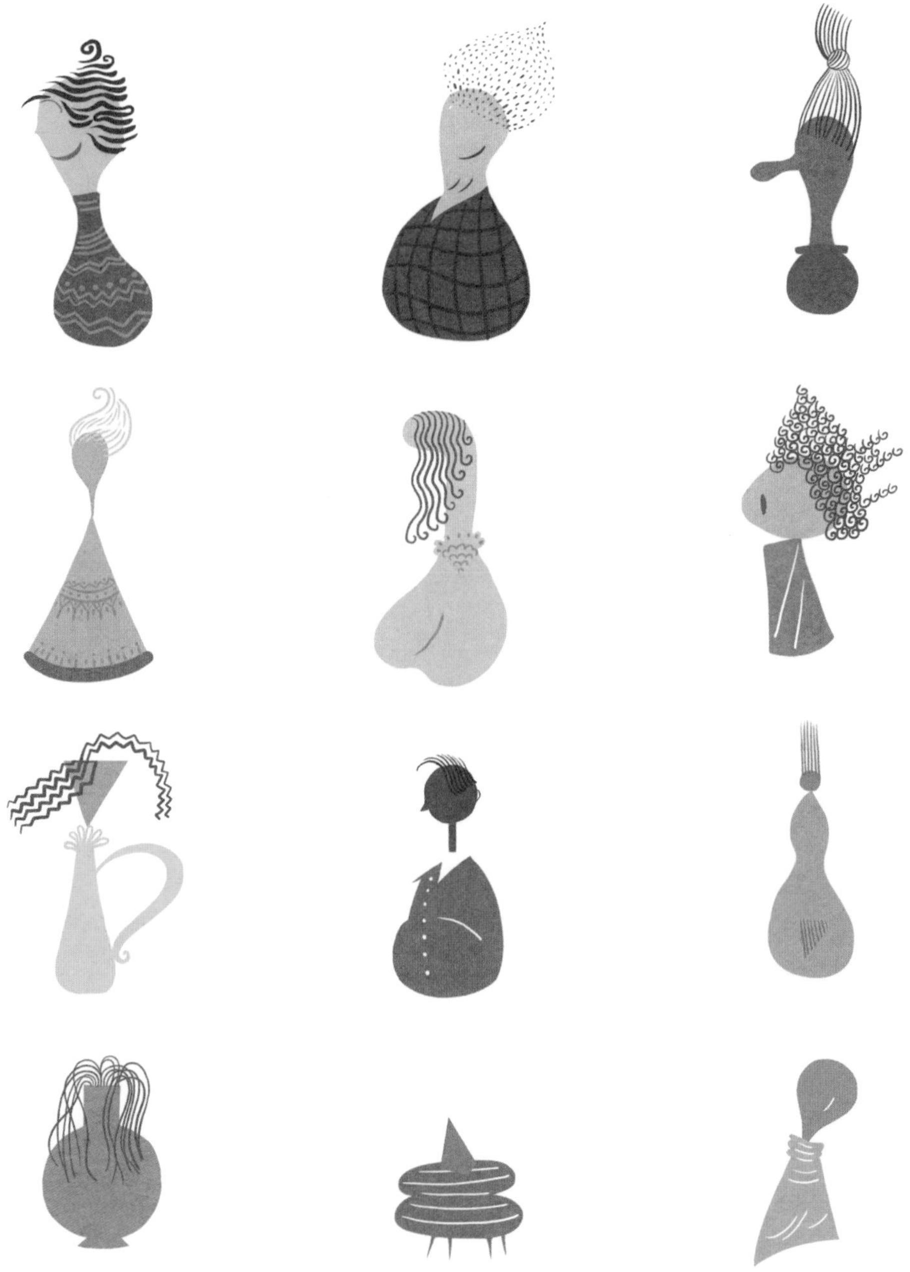

and everywhere I've ever been.

In fact, the only thing I'm quite
sure of these days

is this cup I'm drinking out of right now,
and how it feels to drink hot tea
on a boiling summer day.

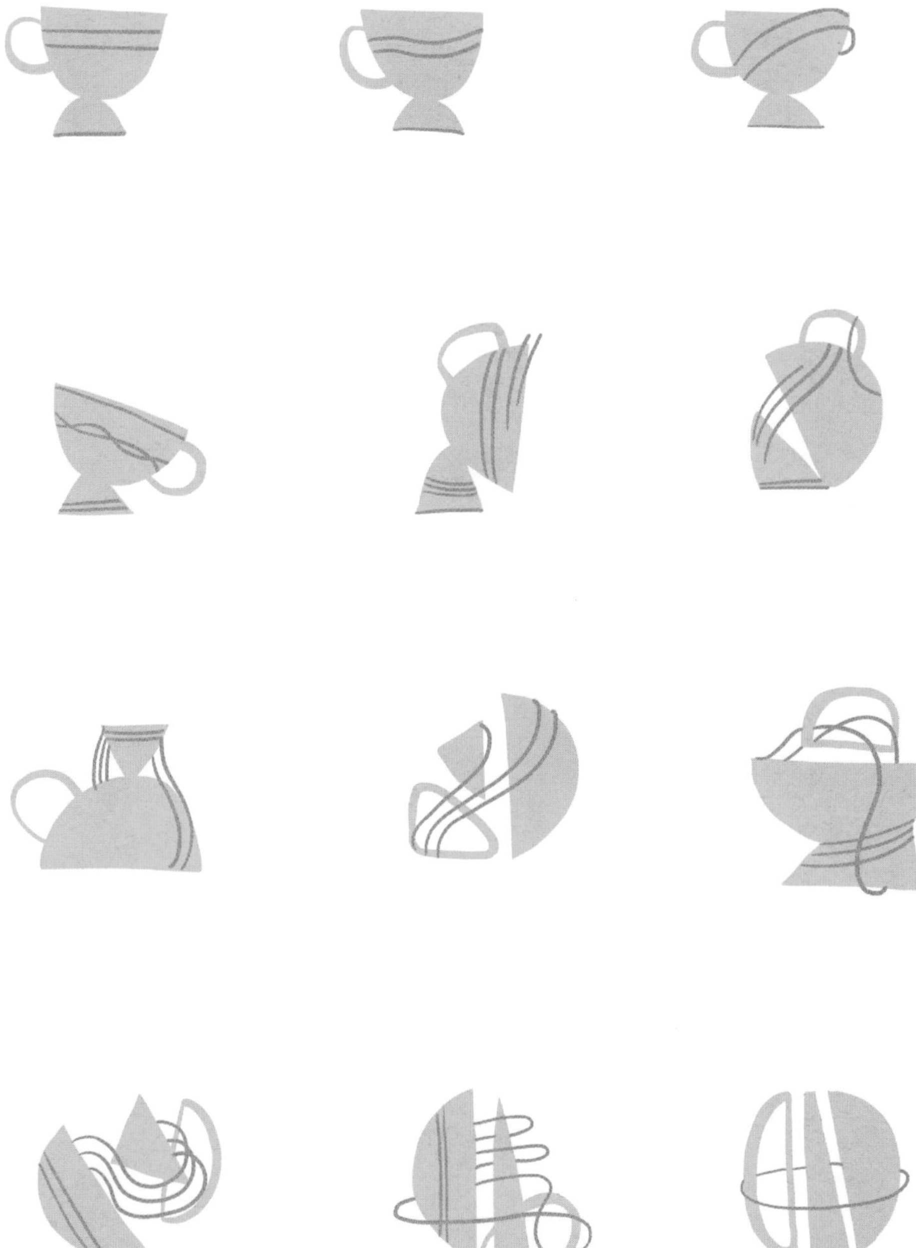

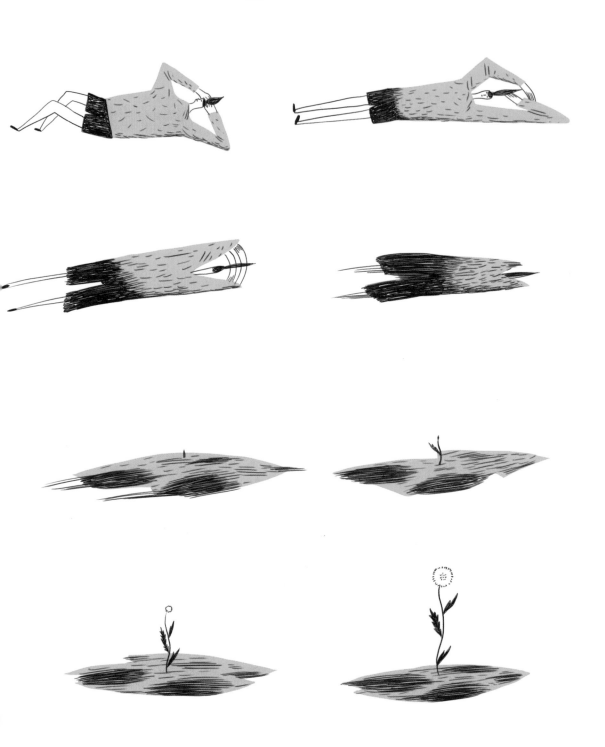

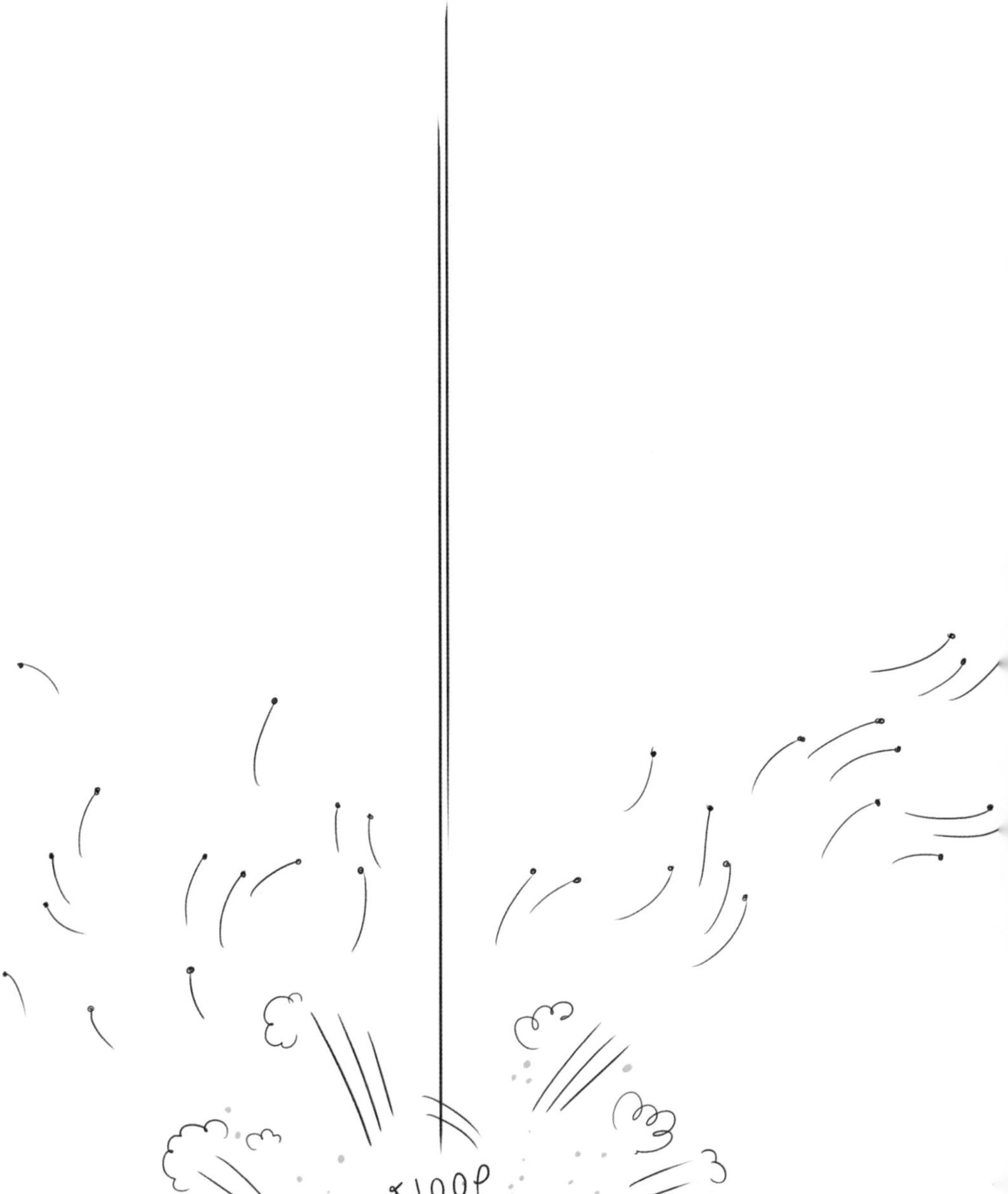
FLOOP

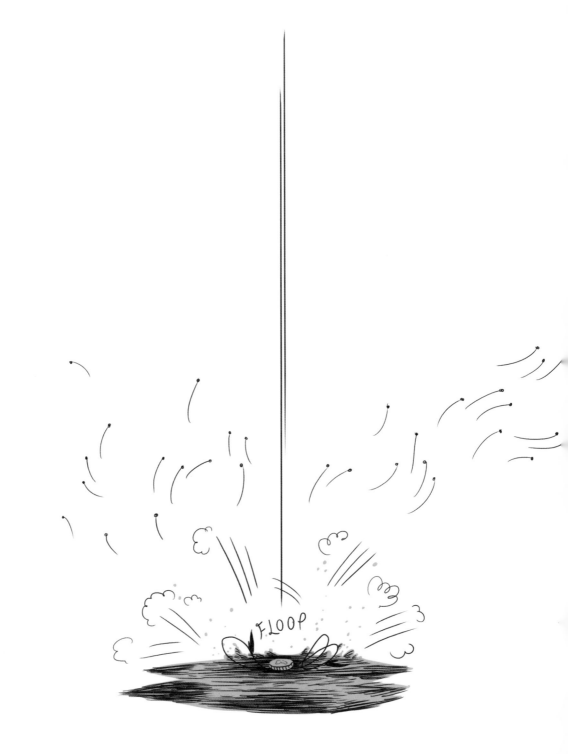

INTO THE NIGHT APPEARED IN MOME VOL. 22

THE THING ABOUT MADELINE APPEARED IN GLÖMP 9
AND THE BEST AMERICAN COMICS 2008

THE CARNIVAL APPEARED IN MOME VOL. 14
AND THE BEST AMERICAN NONREQUIRED READING 2010

TOO HOT TO SLEEP APPEARED IN MOME VOL. 16

THE IMAGE OF THE PHONE CALL EXPLOSION APPEARED
IN WINDY CORNER MAGAZINE VOL. 3

ALL IN A DAY'S WORK APPEARED IN AN ISSUE OF THE GUARDIAN

MARCHING BAND APPEARED IN MOME VOL. 21

MOSS APPEARED IN THE FIFTH ISSUE OF FOLIO CLUB

THE BATCH OF FOUR-PANEL COMICS APPEARED AS MY STRIP ANEMONE
IN ISSUES OF THE BELIEVER MAGAZINE FROM 2009-2012

THE FELLOW FALLING DOWN A STACK OF CHAIRS APPEARED AS THE
BACK COVER OF KUTI No. 14

THE FELLOW EXPLODING IN A BLAST OF STEAM APPEARED AS THE
COVER OF SMOKE SIGNAL No. 8

HANDS APPEARED IN BLACK EYE VOL. 1

OF THE ESSENCE APPEARED IN SMOKE SIGNAL No. 8

THE HOT STREET APPEARED IN A SELF-PUBLISHED SILKSCREENED BOOK
AND IN ISSUE 102 OF GALAGO MAGAZINE

SWEET SPOT APPEARED IN THE TEIERA ANTHOLOGY TEN STEPS UNTIL NOTHING

FOGGY APPEARED IN LINEWORK No. 3

THE WOMAN WITH SOMETHING STUCK BETWEEN HER TEETH IS A
VARIATION OF MY COVER ILLUSTRATION FOR THE LIFTED BROW MAGAZINE.